p2?

ord values

p 134

A FIRST COURSE
IN COMPUTER PROGRAMMING
USING PASCAL

*permutations
+
recursions.*

*factorial prog
p 35.*

McGraw-Hill Computer Science Series

McGraw-Hill Advanced Computer Science Series

A FIRST COURSE
IN COMPUTER PROGRAMMING
USING PASCAL

Arthur M. Keller
Stanford University

McGraw-Hill Book Company
New York   St. Louis   San Francisco   Auckland   Bogotá   Hamburg
Johannesburg   London   Madrid   Mexico   Montreal   New Delhi
Panama   Paris   São Paulo   Singapore   Sydney   Tokyo   Toronto

This book was typeset using the TEX document production system, and camera-ready copy was produced on a CRS Alphatype phototypesetter. Computer resources were provided by the Stanford Artificial Intelligence Laboratory and the Stanford Computer Science Department. The editors were James E. Vastyan and Joseph F. Murphy; the production supervisor was Diane Renda. The cover was designed by Steven Hoffman.
Edwards Brothers Incorporated was printer and binder.

A FIRST COURSE IN COMPUTER PROGRAMMING USING PASCAL

456789 SMSM 89876543

ISBN 0-07-033508-7

Library of Congress Cataloging in Publication Data

Keller, Arthur M.
  A first course in computer programming using
PASCAL.

  (McGraw-Hill computer science series)
  Bibliography: p.
  Includes index.
  1. PASCAL (Computer program language)
I. Title. II. Series.
  QA76.73.P2K44   001.64'24   81-23601
  ISBN 0-07-033508-7   AACR2
  ISBN 0-07-033509-5 (Instructor's manual)

To my father,
who taught me the importance of learning,

and to my mother,
who taught me the importance of not doing it all of the time.

Contents

Preface

This is a complete textbook for a first semester or two quarter course in computer programming using the PASCAL language. This book could be used at the undergraduate level or at the advanced high school level. It is compatible with the curriculum for the course **CS 1** as described in Curriculum 78.* The coverage extends beyond this curriculum to cover the entire PASCAL language.

There are several unique features of this book. Procedures are taught very early. This fits well with the technique of stepwise-refinement method of top-down decomposition style of programming. Many examples show several stages, some of which are correct and others incorrect. Examples of good programs are marked by the "thumbs-up" symbol that appears in the margin of this page. Examples of incorrect programs are marked by a "thumbs-down" symbol in the margin. In this way, the reader learns why programs are incorrect and how to debug programs. Each new topic is introduced by an example that illustrates the feature and explains the need for this new feature. In this way, the student learns to think from the point of view of solving the problem and determining what features are needed to solve a problem. After introducing a problem that motivates learning a feature, the feature is explained, and then the problem is solved in depth.

This book assumes no knowledge of higher mathematics on the part of the reader. The reader should, however, know elementary high school algebra. Although many explanations were devised for readers without mathematical backgrounds, those with mathematical sophistication should not be bored or insulted either.

There are different approaches to teaching an introductory programming course. The most common variations affect the order of covering topics. Some of the topics in this book may be covered in a different order if desired. The most important of these is the coverage of procedures and of procedure parameters.

Procedures are a very simple but important control structure. The concept of top-down programming requires the procedure abstraction. Consequently,

---

* "Curriculum '78: Recommendations for the Undergraduate Program in Computer Science" in *Comm. ACM*, **22**, 3 (March 1979), 147–166.

the first control structure covered in the text is procedure declaration and invocation. When students learn to program without being taught to decompose their programs into procedures, they often write long unstructured programs without using any procedures, even long after procedures have been covered. The main drawback with the approach of teaching procedures early is the use of references to nonlocal variables. Even when parameters are taught, students may still prefer to use nonlocal references. Introduction of procedures can be delayed until students have learned several other control structures. While this may facilitate utilization of this book with existing curricula, it only partially alleviates the objection raised. Alternatively, procedure (value) parameters may be taught earlier. Section 9.1 may be taught as early as Chapter 3. Value parameters should be taught at least a week before **VAR** parameters so that the students understand them before being introduced to the additional nuances of **VAR** parameters. Early coverage of value parameters allows such time, and it also solves the problem of nonlocal references. Value and **VAR** parameters were placed in the same chapter primarily to assist in comparing them.

Coverage of recursion may be delayed or omitted. Its placement was dictated by being a prerequisite of the merge sort. Coverage of merge sort may also be delayed or omitted. However, the merge bubble sort should be covered when the other sorting algorithms are covered, primarily because it is faster than n^2 and does not require recursion.

Chapters 16 to 21 may be covered in any order. These chapters complete the coverage of PASCAL, and their coverage may be delayed until the second course in computer programming.

An *Instructor's Manual* is available that includes brief discussions of approaches to using the text, extensive programming problems and solutions, and explanations of what is needed to solve the problems and how to go about solving them.

Acknowledgments

I have received assistance from many people while preparing this book, and for this I am extremely thankful. Rich Pattis provided many ideas and suggestions; his book* and notes were often a source of inspiration. I received much help from Dave Wall during numerous discussions. Jeff Vitter helped shape the presentation when we taught together at Stanford; he assisted further using the book in preprint form at Brown University. Brent Hailpern provided many useful suggestions for improving this book. Denny Brown gave extensive advice about pedagogy. I would also like to thank my teaching assistants who filled in the cracks in my explanations. I also thank my proofreaders for catching many of the bugs before they could confuse students. I will gladly pay a $1.00 reward to the first finder of every remaining error.

I would like to thank Stanford University, and especially the Computer Science Department, for providing an excellent learning environment and inquisitive students. The staff of the LOTS computer facility was very helpful in providing an environment where students can learn about computers and in correcting my technical misconceptions. The SAIL and SCORE computer facilities of the Computer Science Department were used to typeset this book and to test

---

* *Karel the Robot: A Gentle Introduction to the Art of Programming*, Wiley, New York, 1981.

all the programs used in the book. Much T_EX wizardry was provided by Jim Boyce. The document compiler used, T_EX, was designed by Donald E. Knuth. This book is typeset using the Computer Modern series of fonts (also designed by Knuth). Some of the graphic characters were designed by Scott Kim.

I would also like to thank the following people and organizations for their assistance in the preparation of this book: American Film Institute, Jim Arnold, Jim Celoni, S. J., Tom Dietterich, Les Earnest, Ed Feigenbaum, Robert W. Floyd, Martin Frost, David Fuchs, Richard P. Gabriel, Howard Givner, Ron Goldman, Gene Golub, Ralph Gorin, Lynn Gotelli, Susan Hill, Fran Larson, Frank Liang, Richard Manuck, John McCarthy, Jim McGrath, Mike Peeler, Jayne Pickering, Michael Plass, Stuart Reges, Betty Scott, Laurie Sinclair, Richard Southall, The Stanford University Libraries, Jorge Stolfi, Carolyn Tajnai, Chris Tucci, Jeffrey Ullman, Marilynn Walker, Gio Wiederhold, Don Woods, and Dawn Yolton. I also thank the McGraw-Hill Book Company for their extensive assistance. Finally, I would like to thank my students who made it all worthwhile.

Arthur M. Keller

Chapter 1

Introduction to Computing

In this book, we will learn how to get computers to do work for us. Even those students who will never program after reading this book will still learn what computers can do and how they work. Our problem-solving skills will be exercised and strengthened. In particular, the technique of problem decomposition will be learned.

A computer is an automatic tool. It is intended to do work for people, not to control them. It can add a column of numbers rapidly. It can make certain kinds of decisions, much like a thermostat which "knows" when to turn heat on and off.

A computer must be told how to do something. It naïvely follows instructions. We have to tell it step-by-step everything it is to do. These instructions comprise a *computer program*, which is similar to recipe in a cookbook.

Consider the following recipe for duck à l'orange:*

> This famous recipe depends for its flavor on the Seville or bitter orange,
> 135, which gives the dish its name.
> Prepare:
>
> **An unstuffed Roast Duckling, above**
>
> When it is done, remove it from the roasting pan and keep warm.
> Prepare:
>
> **Sweet-Sour Orange Sauce, 355**
>
> using Seville or bitter oranges and omitting the lemon. Degrease pan
> juices and deglaze the pan as described on 340.

---

* Irma S. Rombauer and Marion Rombauer Becker, *Joy of Cooking*, Bobbs-Merrill, New York, 1975, p. 433. Reprinted with permission of the publisher.

The first sentence tells something about the recipe. It says we can find information about the Seville orange on page 135. The first step—prepare an unstuffed roast duckling—relies on a more basic recipe shown earlier on the page. The next step is simple. After it, we reach a step described in more detail elsewhere—the preparation of the sweet-sour orange sauce. However, we prepare it differently than usual by using the Seville orange and omitting the lemon. The last step is explained on page 340.

In describing the solution to a problem, we use a layered approach. We first use a general outline of the basic steps. The outline is then elaborated with more detailed steps. Gradually, we flesh out the outline until everything is described in sufficient detail. This is also the time-honored method of writing an essay: after creating the detailed outline, we convert it into a complete paper.

Computers need to be told what to do—and how to do it—unambiguously. Unfortunately, English and other ordinary languages are too vague. Consider the sentence, "The lady made the robot fast." This brief sentence can have many meanings:

1.   The lady built the robot quickly.
2.   The lady designed the robot so that it would operate quickly.
3.   The lady took a slow robot and speeded it up.
4.   The lady tied down the robot.
5.   The lady forced the robot to stop eating.
6.   The lady attended a gathering of robots that were not eating. (Compare with "The lady made [it to] the robot *feast*.")

Rather than using English, special languages—*programming languages* or *computer languages*—have been developed. These languages are very precise, and enable the computer to interpret a program unambiguously. Just like the step in writing an essay of converting the outline form into English, there is a step in writing a program of converting the outline form into a programming language.

Once a program is written, it is not yet finished. An essay, once written, must be polished. The acid test for a computer program is to feed it to the computer. The computer takes the program and follows the instructions in it. This is called *running* or *executing* the program. The computer may have difficulty following the instructions. For example, the program may have an error in grammar. Since the computer will usually read what you tell it to do before attempting to do anything, grammatical errors are the first to be found. Once you have fixed all the grammatical errors, the computer will attempt to run your program. Your program may ask the computer to do something it cannot do. For example, you may have asked it to divide a number by zero. Such errors are usually harder to find and correct. We will learn techniques for figuring out what is wrong with one of our programs and how to correct it.

1-1 ALGORITHMS

An algorithm is a type of description of the solution of a problem. The recipe given earlier was an algorithm for making duck à l'orange. Other algorithms include knitting instructions, instructions for constructing a kit, and computer programs.

An algorithm is a vehicle for explaining how a problem can be solved. It necessarily uses a step-by-step approach. It can be formulated in a variety of ways, provided that it is unambiguous. Each field of study has developed its own specialized vocabulary for describing how things are done. Unambiguous languages, such as PASCAL, have been designed for use in describing algorithms to computers.

An algorithm must be precise. It must tell the order of steps. When putting together a kit, it is important to know whether to fit tab *a* into slot *b* before or after fitting tab *c* into slot *d*. A list of ingredients is not enough; we also have to know when to add them. An algorithm must also clearly tell when to stop doing something and to go on to something else. A recipe that just says to bake a cake until it is done is not as useful as one that also gives criteria for when the cake is done. Consider the following algorithm for making toast:*

> There's an art of knowing when.
> Never try to guess.
> Toast until it smokes and then
> twenty seconds less.

We do not know when to stop cooking the toast until it is too late! An algorithm has to describe how to choose between alternatives. When buying apples from a store, you cannot choose the tastiest apples because it is hard to know which apples are going to be the tastiest without actually tasting them. However, you could tell how tasty a bunch of grapes was by eating one (but the store might still not like it if you ate a grape before buying the bunch).

An algorithm must be definite. If you follow an algorithm twice, the same result must follow each time. Two people following the same recipe for pie should bake equally tasty pies. If this is not true, they must have used different brands of ingredients, varied the recipe slightly, or changed something else. Technically, we want an algorithm to be *deterministic*.

An algorithm must be finite. If you follow an algorithm, it must end eventually. Suppose someone else is thinking of an integer—it could be positive, zero, or negative—and we want to guess it. Consider this algorithm. Try 0. Then, try 1. Then, try 2. Continue with some more positive numbers. Then, try −1. Then, −2. Continue with some more negative numbers. This process is supposed to stop when we have guessed the number. If the other person is thinking of a negative number, we would never guess it because we would never run out of positive numbers to guess, and we guess all positive numbers before guessing any negative numbers. A better algorithm follows. Try zero. Then, try 1 and −1. Then, try 2 and −2. Continue trying positive and negative numbers until guessing the right number. The number of steps we take is about twice the magnitude (absolute value) of the right number. For example, we guess 10 in step 20 and −10 in step 21. Thus, we see that the later algorithm is finite while the former need not be.

The definition of an algorithm should describe three parts: input, process, and output. An algorithm usually involves some *input*, that is, things that exist that are used by the algorithm. The input for a recipe includes the ingredients and the utensils used. An algorithm also produces results called *output*. The output for a recipe is usually some tasty food. As we have already considered, an algorithm describes how the input is to be transformed into the output.

---

* Piet Hein, "Timing Toast" in *Grooks 2*, Doubleday, Garden City, N.Y., 1969, p. 23. Reprinted with permission of the author.

1-2 STEPS IN THE LIFE OF A PROGRAM

Only a small part of the time spent in the development of a program is actually in writing it. There are several other important steps.

The first step in writing a program is problem definition. If you do not know where you are going, you cannot know it when you get there. Often the problem we are asked to solve is ill-defined. The input or output may not be clearly stated. Consider the assignment of mailing the best customers an offer to try a new product. There are several important questions that arise. Where is the list of customers? How do we know which customers are the best customers? What should the offer look like and what should it say? These questions have to be answered before we can proceed to writing the program.

Once the problem is defined, we can outline the solution. We consider general alternative approaches to solving the problem. Our first solution may not be the best way of solving the problem. At this stage, we have not invested very much in any particular way of solving a problem. If we devise a better solution now, we will have saved more time than if we have to adopt it later. Consider the problem of finding a telephone number. Suppose we decide to look it up in the telephone book. We could search it sequentially, but on the average we would look through half of the names. Such an algorithm would be easy to describe but very slow. We could take advantage of the index entries at the top of the page by thumbing through the telephone book until we find the right page. Then, we can search the page sequentially. This algorithm is harder to describe, but will take much less time to follow. Of course, this case is clear cut, but with other problems the choice may not be as obvious.

The chosen outline is then developed into an algorithm. We will use a top-down approach to developing an algorithm. This means that we start with the outline and define each step in greater detail. This fleshing out continues until we are sure exactly how to solve the problem. To some extent, this involves using existing algorithms. For example, when a step of the outline is to do something we have done before or is in a book, we can do it the same way. As we develop more complicated programs, we will build up a repertoire of techniques that we can put together in new ways to solve new problems.

After the algorithm has been chosen, we proceed to writing it in a programming language. This step translates the abstract algorithm into PASCAL. Writing the actual statements in a programming language is called *coding*, since a sequence of such statements is called *code*. It is important not to do any coding until the algorithm is fairly well defined, lest we become committed to the code and not be willing to change our minds. Programming should not be confused with coding: coding is just one of the steps in programming.

When parts of the program are coded, they can be tested. This involves having the computer try to understand the program and then follow it. It is best to test the components of a program separately before putting it all together, especially for a large program. Otherwise, it will be hard to track down the source of the errors. Errors in a program are called *bugs* and detecting and correcting them is called *debugging*. The process of debugging involves testing the various cases the program is expected to handle. If we find any errors, such as incorrect output, we look for the cause of each error. For each error, we try to devise a change to the program that removes the problem. Such changes often remove other errors but occasionally introduce new ones, so it is necessary to retest the program to ensure that it still works for the old cases and handles the new ones properly. We continue testing the program and correcting errors until we have tested all cases and find no remaining errors. *Testing only shows the presence of bugs, not their absence.* There may be other bugs, but we have not found them, probably because we have not tested every possible case.

We have so far only considered the program, but not the explanation of the program for others. As we will find, a program can be quite complicated and confusing. Hence, it is important for the program to include explanations of what it is intended to do and how it works. These explanations are called *documentation.* In order to make programs more readable to others, several techniques are often employed. A program is formatted to reflect its structure—similar to the indentations in an outline that reflect its levels. Small discussions are sprinkled throughout the code to explain how the program works. These are elements of internal documentation, which are explained fully later in the text. A formal document—describing the input, output, function of the program, and how the program works—is written to enable the effective use of the program. Such documentation also makes modifying the program easier. Although there is some tendency to delay writing documentation until the program is fully debugged, it is best to write it during development of the program. The original specifications can become the basis for the external documentation. As the design proceeds, decisions can be incorporated into the documentation when they are made. Very little documentation should be left for the coding step or after debugging. Once the program is working, we have probably forgotten most of the design decisions. All that should be left is to polish the documentation, not to write it.

Classwork problems end there, but real programs continue to live on. A real program is written because there is some real problem to solve. Once the program is available, people may think of other useful things it could do, or cases it does not handle properly that were not clearly specified. This ushers in the *program maintenance* phase. Changes will have to be made to the program to satisfy the changed requirements for the program. Sometimes these changes will be made by the original programmer; other times they are given to someone else to do. If we are given a program to modify, we must first learn how the program works, and then figure out how it should be changed. For many programs, this process is more expensive than the original program development! Program maintenance can be facilitated by good programming habits, such as writing lucid code and providing good internal and external documentation.

1-3 COMPUTER ORGANIZATION

Learning about the organization of a computer will help us understand how a computer works and how to use it. The topology of a computer is like that of a star. The center of a computer does the work and makes the decisions, analogous to the function of the brain. Surrounding the brain are devices for communicating with the outside world. These include input devices, like sense organs, and output devices, like vocal cords. Some devices participate in both input and output, such as a computer terminal. The hands and mouth are also input and output devices.

The central part of the system is called a the *central processing unit* (CPU). This part follows the instructions of a program and directs the input and output devices. Some memory is included which contains, among other things, the parts of a program being executed and the information being manipulated by that program. This memory is often called *core memory,* originally because it was composed of tiny copper cores, but today the name continues to be used because it signifies the central or primary memory of the computer.

There are many varieties of input and output devices. A common output device is a printer. Printer speeds range from 300 lines per minute or less to more than 2000 lines per minute. Most printers print only fixed-width characters like a typewriter, and some cannot print lower case letters. Some newer printers can produce print graphics and diagrams; for example, this book was typeset on a graphics computer printer. Some computers have devices for reading and punching computer cards. The rectangular or circular holes in the cards is what the computer is interested in. The computer does not read any of the writing on the cards. The familiar warning against "folding, spindling, or mutilating" computer cards was written so that the cards can be fed into a card reader (at speeds upwards of 1000 cards per minute) and then read accurately. Customers are often instructed to write something on the card, but it is *keypunched* on the card before the computer is able to read it. An increasingly common device capable of both input and output is a computer terminal, also known as a CRT because the screen is often a cathode-ray tube. Unusual output devices include voice synthesizers and robot arms. Computers will soon be able to audibly warn a driver that a car is low on gas, or claim that it has just won a chess game. Unusual input devices include cameras and laboratory instrument sensors.

The average computer does not understand PASCAL directly. This is similar to the problem faced by the native speaker of English who also speaks French, but not fluently. That person thinks in English and translates everything heard or read from French to English and everything about to be said or written from English to French. A computer's native language is called *machine language* and consists of a binary code (numbers in base 2) containing only 0s and 1s. The first computers were programmed exclusively in machine language. A symbolic language that could be easily translated into machine language was soon developed; it was called *assembly language* because the machine instructions were assembled directly from assembly instructions using—you guessed it!—an assembler. Then, high-level languages were invented—the first was FORTRAN in the early to middle 1950s—and *compilers* were constructed to translate the programs to machine language. These languages are called high-level languages because the translation of programs written in them into machine language is complicated, and each statement in a high-level language may compile into several machine language instructions.

A compiler is a program that takes another program as input and produces machine language and messages as output. The input program is called the *source program* while the output machine language is called the *object program*. After the compiler is run, the resulting object program is run. This program does whatever is requested in the original high-level language program. It also has its own input and output.

1-4 GOOD PROGRAMMING

Good programming is an art, and opinions vary about the best way to write a program. However, three important criteria for determining whether a program is good are correctness, clarity, and efficiency.

A *correct* program does what it is supposed to. It conforms to its specifications, in that its output is correct for any acceptable input. The problem is that the program has to work for any acceptable input. It is not possible to test every single case to tell whether a program handles all input properly. A good rule of thumb is to test representative cases that exercise each possible path through the program. Boundary conditions must also be tested. A boundary condition is tested by using an input value at an extreme, so that if it were slightly smaller or larger, the program would take a different path. For example, a program that prints out all the prime numbers less than a given value should be tested for 0, 1, 2, and 3, as well as for a few prime numbers and a few composite numbers (that is, nonprimes). Depending on the algorithm used, it may be important to test other specific cases.

A *clear* program is easy for people to understand. At least ninety percent of the cost of a large program is in writing and maintenance. A clear program is easier to write, debug, and maintain, and hence cheaper in the long run than a program that is obscurely written. Developing good programming style is helpful for writing clear programs. It is useful to read other people's programs to get an idea of different styles. Style is often rather subjective and personal, but some businesses have attempted to get a uniform style by promulgating programming standards. While programming standards may be annoying to experienced programmers, they do facilitate program modification and they help educate novice programmers.

An important consideration for a program is the resources it consumes when running. An *efficient* program consumes few resources considering the job it performs. The most common resources considered are *space* (how large the program is and how much information it needs to keep track of), *time* (how long it takes to run), and *input-output operations* (how many times does it ask the same information). Often, there are tradeoffs involved. For example, input-output operations can often be reduced by increasing the amount of information retained or the program's space requirements.

Good programming is considered to some extent in this book. There are other books that treat the topic more thoroughly.*

---

* See Henry F. Ledgard, *Programming Proverbs*, Hayden, Rochelle Park, N. J., 1975. For an interesting book about the social aspects of programming, see Gerald M. Weinberg, *The Psychology of Computer Programming*, Van Nostrand Reinhold, New York, 1971.

Chapter 2

Introduction
to PASCAL

We are going to learn how to *program the computer*, that is, to tell it to do something for us. To do this, we must speak to it in a *programming language*. In this book, we have chosen the programming language PASCAL. For historical reasons, FORTRAN and COBOL are more widely used than PASCAL. FORTRAN, designed in the early 1950s, was the first widely used high-level computer language. Quite a remarkable development for its day and age, FORTRAN is very useful for numerical applications. COBOL, designed in the late 1950s, was intended for business data processing applications. PASCAL, designed in the late 1960s, is just coming into wide use. Although most of the concepts are the same among the three languages, certain concepts in PASCAL are not found in either FORTRAN or COBOL; therefore, it is easier to learn FORTRAN or COBOL after learning PASCAL than the other way around. Also, PASCAL was "intended" to be simple to understand and use.

Let us now describe PASCAL. There is a recurring theme in our discussion: the distinction between *names* and *objects*. An analogy is the distinction between a word and its definition in a dictionary. In the computer, we will often create objects to which we assign names so that we can refer to them. We will talk more about this point when we get to *variables*.

In PASCAL, there are four classes of things we will talk about. The first class is *declarations*, which are associations of names with objects. Then, we have *statements*, which are instructions for the computer to do something. Next we have *input*, which is the information the computer works with. Lastly, we have *output* or the actual results. The first two classes make up a program. Input and output are separate from a program. The format of a program is:

```
PROGRAM name (output);
     declarations
BEGIN
     statements
END (* name *).
```

How a program looks is as important as how it works. Considerations of the format of a program are called *syntax issues*. Let us mention a few syntax issues related to the program above. Our language contains words (such as `PROGRAM`, `output`), numbers (such as 50), and special symbols [such as "(", ")", ";", "(*", "*)", "."]. Words start with a letter* and consist of letters and digits. Spaces are needed to separate words and numbers. Special symbols, however, do not need spaces around them, but spaces may be inserted preceding or following them for readability. Extra spaces are irrelevant; that is, if we can put in one space, we can put in several. In general, we can also go to the next line wherever we can put in a space. There are *keywords* that mean special things, such as `PROGRAM`, `BEGIN`, and `END`. We will write them in capitals or boldface. Statements are separated by semicolons. Notice that the program ends with a period.

2-1 OUTPUT

The computer program tells us what it has done is by producing *output*. *Output statements* are statements *inside* the program that produce text that appears *outside* the program. Output appears in lines that are separated by a *carriage return*, which we have symbolized by ⌐.

There are several statements that we will use to produce output. The first is the `Write` statement. It signifies that something is to be written without any carriage returns. For example, we can say

```
Write ('TEXT');
```

Notice that what is written appears in single quotes inside the parentheses. A series of characters inside quotes is called a *character string*. We can have several `Write` statements in a row:

```
Write ('FOO');
Write ('BAR');
Write ('BAZ');
```

And they will all write on the same line:

```
FOOBARBAZ
```

Notice that the text is written without any intervening blanks. Also notice that we have put a semicolon following each statement.† These statements are called a *program fragment* and are also known as *code*.

What if we wanted to have our output appear on several lines? We cannot start a character string on one line and continue it on another; a character string must fit entirely on one line. There is a statement that causes the computer to go to the next line of the output:

---

* On some systems, the characters #, @, and $ are considered to be like letters for historical reasons.

† It is only necessary to put semicolons between each pair of statements. The subtle difference will be explained later when we learn about `ELSE`.

```
Writeln;
```

Now, anything else that is to be written will appear on the next line. For example, consider these statements:

```
Write ('FOO');
Writeln;
Write ('BAR');
Write ('BAZ');
```

These four statements will write the following:

```
FOO
BARBAZ
```

As a shorthand notation, we can say, "Go to the next line *after* writing this text," by including the text in the **Writeln** statement. For example,

```
Writeln ('End of the line');
```

will put a carriage return after the output text. What will the following set of statements do?

```
Write ('My name is ');
Writeln ('Arthur Keller.');
Write ('What''s yours? ');
```

It will write

```
My name is Arthur Keller.
What's yours?
```

There is a space between **is** and **Arthur** because there is a space between the **s** and the closing quote (') in the first statement. Also, to write one quote, you put two consecutive quotes in the text. The symbol ✎ indicates where the cursor is, that is, where the next output will go.

Exercises

Determine what the following instructions will print. Answers are found in Appendix A.

```
1.   Writeln ('HI');
     Write ('HO');
     Writeln ('HI');
     Write ('HO');
```

2.
```
Write ('ABC');
Write ('DEF');
Writeln ('GHI');
Writeln ('JKL');
Write ('MNO');
Writeln ('PQR');
```

3.
```
Write ('Aren''t computers wonderful?');
Write ('Notice how we printed the quote!');
```

4. Write a statement that prints a single quote.

5. Write a statement that prints the following, including the quote:

```
'Twas the night before Christmas
```

2-2 COMMENTS

Comments make a program more readable for people. There are several reasons why your program should be readable. You might want to show it to other people, especially if you need help getting it to work. Someone else might want to use the program or modify it. Comments are helpful for improving the readability of programs for people. They can go anywhere a space can, and are enclosed between "(*" and "*)". Using comments will allow you to explain why you did something. Similarly, the layout of the program can improve readability. The program is indented to reflect its structure.* Since extra spaces are irrelevant, this indentation is ignored by the computer, but is a big help to people when they read the program. Remember that comments and indentation are for people— the computer doesn't care about them.

2-3 PROCEDURES

We will use a style of designing programs known as *stepwise refinement*. It is also known as *functional decomposition* or *top-down design*. This is one of the techniques known as *structured programming*. We will describe this process by an example. Suppose we want to draw 2 four-by-four open boxes, one above the other. We can decompose this problem into several subproblems:

draw a four-by-four open box
write a blank line
draw a four-by-four open box

Drawing a four-by-four open box can be refined to:

---

* The *structure* of a program is the way the components of the program fit together. So far, we have seen declarations and statements. Soon we will encounter procedures and variables.

draw top line
draw side lines
draw bottom line

We know how to write code (a piece of a computer program) for this last part.
It is:

```
Writeln ('****');
Writeln ('*  *');
Writeln ('*  *');
Writeln ('****');
```

This program fragment can be used for both commands that say, "Draw a four-
by-four open box." We could copy these four lines in both places, but this seems
unnatural. We would like to be able to say, "Here is how to draw a box," and
then command, "Draw a box; Write a blank line; Draw a box." We will soon
learn how to do this.

   In PASCAL we can take a group of statements and give them a name. This
is done with a declaration that links the statements together into a unit called
a *procedure*. This procedure is given a name by which we may invoke it. An
analogy is the distinction between a word and its definition in a dictionary. For
example, our program to write two boxes now becomes:

```
PROGRAM TwoBoxes (output);

    PROCEDURE DrawBox;                    (**************)
        (* draw one four-by-four open box *) (*            *)
    BEGIN                                 (*  Procedure  *)
       Writeln ('****');                  (*            *)
       Writeln ('*  *');                  (* Declaration *)
       Writeln ('*  *');                  (*            *)
       Writeln ('****');                  (*            *)
    END; (* DrawBox *)                    (**************)

BEGIN      (* Main procedure follows *)
    (* now for the real instructions *)
    DrawBox;         (* procedure call *)
    Writeln;
    DrawBox;         (* procedure call *)
END (* TwoBoxes *).
```

Let us first consider the structure of the program. The first line is the *program
header*. The word output in parentheses indicates that the program is expected
to produce output. We then have a declaration for the procedure DrawBox. A
declaration is a definition. Here we define what we mean by DrawBox; we do not
do anything yet. The four Writeln statements tell what is to be done when we
want to do DrawBox. They are called the *procedure body* or, alternatively, the
code for the procedure DrawBox. We now reach the *main procedure*, where the
computer is actually told what to do and in what order. The statements that
say DrawBox are called *procedure calls*. These are statements, just as Write or

`Writeln`, that perform the statements associated with the procedure name; the effect is like substituting the *procedure body* for the procedure named. But it is better in that you only have to list the code for the procedure once, and it is easier to understand.

Notice that the declaration for the procedure precedes the use of the procedure. In PASCAL, we must generally declare things before we use them.

The output of the previous program follows.

```
****
*  *
*  *
****

****
*  *
*  *
****
```

Remember that there is a distinction between a name and an object. The procedure declaration associates a group of statements with a procedure name. When we write this name in a statement, we are telling the computer to do the instructions associated with that name.

2-4 IDENTIFIERS

An *identifier* is the name we assign to an object. For example, `DrawBox` was an identifier used in the previous section. We now use identifiers for the names of procedures. (We will soon employ identifiers for other uses.)

Identifiers must start with a letter and consist only of letters and numbers. Only the first 8 characters of the identifier are significant.* If your identifiers are longer, make sure they differ in the first 8 characters.

Identifiers should be informative. Names like `I` and `J` are easy to type but are rather uninformative. The time invested in typing longer names will be more than made up by the savings in understanding the program later.

2-5 REPETITION: THE FOR STATEMENT

Consider the following procedure for drawing triangles:

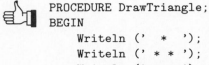

```
PROCEDURE DrawTriangle;
BEGIN
    Writeln ('  *  ');
    Writeln (' * * ');
    Writeln ('*****');
END; (* DrawTriangle *)
```

---

* According to Jensen and Wirth (in *Pascal User Manual and Report*), the number of significant characters is at least 8. On IBM machines, 8 characters are generally used. On DEC computers, 10 characters are generally used.

In order to draw a triangle, we use

```
DrawTriangle;
```

But suppose we want to draw 6 triangles. We would then say

```
DrawTriangle;
DrawTriangle;
DrawTriangle;
DrawTriangle;
DrawTriangle;
DrawTriangle;
```

It would be more useful to say "draw 6 identical triangles" than to say "draw a triangle" 6 times. In PASCAL, we can do this by:

```
FOR index := 1 TO 6 DO
    DrawTriangle;
```

If we wanted a different number of triangles, we could change the number 6 to specify how may triangles we actually wanted to print. Doing exactly the same thing several times is called *repetition*. The statement that calls **DrawTriangle** in the above example is done repeatedly. This statement is referred to as the *body* of the FOR loop. In general, the body of the FOR loop is the very next statement following the keyword DO. If we put the above statements into a complete program, the output would be the following:

```
  *
 * *
*****
  *
 * *
*****
  *
 * *
*****
  *
 * *
*****
  *
 * *
*****
  *
 * *
*****
```

Noting that the triangles touch, we decide to put a blank line after each triangle. We wish to say something like

```
FOR index := 1 TO 6 DO
        ⎰DrawTriangle;
        ⎱Writeln;
```

We need some way to enter the multiline brace ({) into the terminal! In PASCAL, we group these statements by enclosing them in a BEGIN-END pair. Therefore, we write

```
FOR index := 1 TO 6 DO
    BEGIN
        DrawTriangle;
        Writeln;
    END; (* FOR index *)
```

Then the whole thing from BEGIN to END is the body of the FOR loop. What would happen if we did the following?

```
FOR index := 1 TO 6 DO
    DrawTriangle;
    Writeln;
```

In this case, DrawTriangle would be done 6 times, while Writeln would be done only once. Do not be fooled by the indentation. To the computer, these statements have the same effect as

```
FOR index := 1 TO 6 DO
    DrawTriangle;
Writeln;
```

The computer does not care about indentation. But indentation does make the program easier to read. It conveys some information about the structure of the program, and can be misleading if it does not match the logic of the program.

The FOR statement consists of a prefix and a statement to be repeated. The prefix (FOR index := 1 TO 6 DO) may be inserted in front of any statement to be repeated. Usually, the repeated statement is the single statement following DO. If we want more than one statement repeated, we enclose the statements in BEGIN-END brackets, as we have seen. Then the statements from BEGIN to END are treated as a single statement, so the whole thing is repeated by the FOR statement.

Let us talk a little about the variable, index, which we mentioned earlier. The computer is an idiot—it will do exactly what it is told. The computer even counts on its fingers! It needs a piece of workspace—called an *index variable*—to keep track of how many times it has done the body of the FOR loop.

Remember that we had to declare procedures before we used them. We also have to declare variables before we use them. We do that in the VAR section of the program. After the PROGRAM header, we write the keyword VAR and then the variable declarations. Each variable declaration is a list of variables separated by commas, and followed by a colon and the type of variable, which is integer.* The following complete program illustrates the use of variable declarations.

---

* We consider other types of variables in Chapter 4.

```
PROGRAM WriteTriangles (output);
    VAR index: integer;


    PROCEDURE PrintTriangle;
    BEGIN
        Writeln ('  *  ');
        Writeln (' * * ');
        Writeln ('*****');
    END; (* PrintTriangle *)

BEGIN
   FOR index := 1 TO 6 DO
        BEGIN
            PrintTriangle;
            Writeln;
        END (* FOR index *);
END (* WriteTriangle *).
```

This program produces the following output.

```
  *
 * *
*****

  *
 * *
*****

  *
 * *
*****

  *
 * *
*****

  *
 * *
*****

  *
 * *
*****
```

We can also have **VAR** sections in procedures.

```
PROCEDURE DoIt10Times;
    VAR j: integer;
BEGIN
    FOR j := 1 TO 10 DO
        It;
END; (* DoIt10Times *)
```

Notice that we have used the name j as the index variable; we can use any identifier as long as we declare it in the procedure. Later in this book, we will talk about why we declare variables in the main procedure or in an inner procedure. A rule of thumb for now is to declare variables in the procedure that uses them.

Exercises

Determine what the following instructions will print.

1.  ```
    FOR count := 1 TO 5 DO
        Writeln ('HI');
    ```

2.  ```
    FOR count := 1 TO 5 DO
        Write ('HI');
    ```

3.  ```
    FOR index := 1 TO 5 DO
        BEGIN
            Write ('HI');
            Writeln (' ARTHUR');
        END (* FOR index *);
    ```

4. Do not be fooled by the indenting on this one!

    ```
    FOR foo := 1 TO 5 DO
        Write ('HI');
        Writeln (' AMY');
    ```

5.  ```
    PROGRAM SolveIt;
        VAR vert: integer;

    (* And now, some procedures *)
        PROCEDURE Flat;
            VAR length: integer;
        BEGIN
            FOR length := 1 TO 10 DO
                Write ('*');
            Writeln;
        END (* Flat *);
    ```

```
      PROCEDURE Side;
          VAR space: integer;
      BEGIN
          Write ('*');
          FOR space := 1 TO 8 DO
              Write (' ');
          Writeln ('*');
      END (* Side *);

  (* The main event *)
  BEGIN
      Flat;
      FOR vert := 1 TO 6 DO
          Side;
      Flat;
  END (* SolveIt *).
```

2-6 EXPRESSIONS

We now know how to print strings of characters and to repeat statements; however, these are things that we can do with a typewriter. The computer can also deal with numbers. For example, we can ask the computer to print the number 5 by using the statement **Write (5)**. This statement will simply print

    5

We can also ask the computer to do addition. For example, we know that $5 + 7 = 12$; so when we ask the computer to do **Write (5 + 7)**, it will print

    12

The computer can also subtract, multiply, and divide. The following list gives some operations that the computer can do.

+	Add two integers, resulting in the sum.
−	Subtract the second integer from the first, resulting in the difference.
*	Multiply two integers, resulting in the product.
DIV	Divide the second integer into the first, resulting in the integer quotient; for example, 11 DIV 4 is 2, while −11 DIV 4 is −2.
MOD	Divide the second integer into the first, resulting in the integer remainder; for example, 11 MOD 4 is 3, while −11 MOD 4 is −3.

The subtraction symbol (−) can also be used as a unary operator to take the negation of the integer value to its right. For example, **Write (-(3+5))** will print **-8**. Note that we must use the asterisk (*) for multiplication. We cannot use familiar mathematical notations for multiplication: the multiplication sign (×) would be confused with the variable name X; the centered dot (·) would also cause confusion; omission of the centered dot would run numbers together—instead of 3 · 4, we would have 34.*

For example, let us consider the following statements.

```
Writeln (75);
Writeln (75 + 43);
Writeln (64 - 18);
Writeln (15 * 7);
Writeln (23 DIV 7);
Writeln (17 MOD 4);
```

These statements produce the following output.

```
 75
118
 46
105
  3
  1
```

Notice that the numbers line up. Numbers are preceded by blanks when they are printed to make them line up. Just like character strings, they are not followed by a blank. For example, the statement

```
Writeln (5 + 9, 'is the sum.');
```

will print

```
14is the sum.
```

To get a blank between **14** and **is**, we would have to put a blank between the quote and **is**.

We can also have multiple operations in an expression. For example, we can say `Writeln (5+6+7)` to get 18. Or we can say `Writeln (5+6-7)` to get 4. An ambiguity results from having several different operations in an expression. For example we could have

3 + 4 * 5   evaluates to   23 (if multiplication is done first)
                                  35 (if addition is done first)

One way to resolve this ambiguity is to insert parentheses, just as we do in mathematics. In the above example, if we want multiplication to be done first, we can say `Writeln (3 + (4 * 5))`; if we want addition to be done first, we

---

* There is no exponentiation operator in PASCAL.

can say `Writeln ((3 + 4) * 5)`. Extra parentheses are useful for improving readability; when in doubt, put parentheses in an expression.

However, in mathematics, we can often avoid using parentheses by appealing to the convention that multiplication is done before addition if there are no parentheses. Similarly, PASCAL associates a precedence level with each operator. The high precedence level is occupied by the `*`, `DIV`, and `MOD` operators, so they are done first. The low precedence level is occupied by the `+` and `-` operators. When two operators of equal precedence occur in an expression, they are evaluated in a left-to-right order. Thus, the interpretation of

$$3 + 4 * 5 \qquad \text{is} \qquad 3 + (4 * 5)$$
$$6 - 7 + 8 \qquad \text{is} \qquad (6 - 7) + 8$$

But this default precedence sometimes gets in our way—assume we wish to subtract 6 + 7 from 4. PASCAL allows us to add parentheses wherever it is necessary to override the default precedence. Thus, the interpretation of

$$4 - (6 + 7)$$

is first to add 6 and 7 and then subtract the sum from 4. A reasonable way to think about this is that the subtraction operator cannot be evaluated until the subexpressions on its left and right have been evaluated.

Thus, to evaluate an expression, we use the following rules: We evaluate parenthesized expressions from the innermost out. We then evaluate operations of high precedence from left to right. Lastly, we evaluate operations of low precedence from left to right.

One last point involves the difference between an expression and a character string. When we put something in quotes, we are talking about that exact sequence of characters. If we have an expression without quotes, we are asking for evaluation. For example, consider the following statement:

```
Writeln ('5 is', 5, 'while 5 + 7 is', 5 + 7);
```

It will write the following:

```
5 is        5while 5 + 7 is        12
```

Exercises

Determine what the following instructions will print.

```
1.    Write (10 - 3);
      Writeln ('was for subtraction');
      Writeln ('ABC', 1, 2, 3, 'DEF');

2.    Writeln (10 + 3 * 4);
      Writeln ( (10 + 3) * 4);
      Writeln (10 + (3 * 4) );
```

3.  ```
    Writeln (23 DIV 4);
    Writeln (4 DIV 23);
    Writeln (23 MOD 4);
    Writeln (4 MOD 23);
    ```

4.  ```
    Writeln (13 - 4 + 5);
    Writeln ( (13 - 4) + 5);
    Writeln (13 - (4 + 5) );
    ```

5. Write statements that print the values of the following formulas. Do *not* do the arithmetic yourself; your statements should describe how to do the arithmetic.

    (a) $$6 \times \frac{2+3}{4+5}$$

    (b) $$\frac{42}{7} \times 5^2 + 6 \times 3 + 4$$

2-7 ITERATION

Thus far, we have been able to do the same operation many times. Often, we would like to do something several times, but each time vary it slightly. This is called *iteration*. Suppose we wanted to print the numbers from 1 to 10, each on a separate line. This involves the following iteration:

Do 10 times
 Print next number

This translates to the following program fragment:

```
FOR number := 1 TO 10 DO
    Writeln (something);
```

What goes in place of *something*? In order to answer this question, we need to learn more about the way the FOR statement works.

When we first considered the FOR statement, we learned that there is an index variable—called **number** in the above example—that the computer uses to remember how many times it has done the repeated statement. This index variable is given values ranging between the bounds given in the FOR statement. In the above example, **number** ranges from 1 to 10. That is, the first time we go through the loop, **number** has the value 1; the second time it is 2; the third time 3; and the tenth time, 10. We can use the variable **number** the same way we use actual numbers in expressions. Let us now complete the program in the above example.

```
PROGRAM Sequence (output);
(* Prints the numbers from 1 to 10 *)
    VAR number: integer;    (* index variable *)

BEGIN
    FOR number := 1 TO 10 DO
        Writeln (number);
END (* Sequence *).
```

The output from the program would be

```
        1
        2
        3
        4
        5
        6
        7
        8
        9
        10
```

Let us print the first 10 even numbers. That is, we want to print 2, 4, 6, . . . , 20. One way to do this is to consider that each time we go through the FOR loop, the index variable has a value that we can use to compute the number we want to print. The FOR loop index variable has values ranging from 1 to 10, and the numbers we want are precisely twice those numbers. Adapting the program above, we get

```
PROGRAM EvenNumbers (output);
    (* Prints the first 10 even numbers *)
    VAR number: integer;    (* index variable *)

BEGIN
    FOR number := 1 TO 10 DO
        Writeln (2 * number);
END (* EvenNumbers *).
```

The output from the program would be

```
        2
        4
        6
        8
        10
        12
        14
        16
        18
        20
```

Let's print the first 10 odd numbers. That is, we want to print 1, 3, 5, 7, . . . , 19. This is similar to the example of printing even numbers. We could simply subtract 1 from each number we just printed. Students with mathematical backgrounds may notice the following generalization. Converting from the number in the index variable to the number we want to print is similar to getting an equation for a line given points known to lie on it. If y is the number we want to print, and x is the index variable, then $y = mx + b$; so, $y = 2x - 1$. Adapting the program above, we get

```
PROGRAM OddNumbers (output);
    (* Prints the first 10 odd numbers *)
    VAR number: integer;    (* index variable *)

BEGIN
    FOR number := 1 TO 10 DO
        Writeln (2 * number - 1);
END (* OddNumbers *).
```

The output from the program would be

```
        1
        3
        5
        7
        9
       11
       13
       15
       17
       19
```

Exercises

1.   What does the following program do?

```
PROGRAM Mystery (output);
    VAR number: integer;    (* index variable *)

BEGIN
    FOR number := 1 TO 10 DO
        Writeln (number * number);
END (* Mystery *).
```

2.   Write a program that prints the first 10 cubes.

3.   Write programs that print the following series:
    (a)   3, 8, 13, 18, 23, ..., 48.
    (b)   −2, 3, 8, 13, 18, ..., 43.
    (c)   48, 43, 38, 33, 28, ..., 3.

2-8 NESTING LOOPS

Suppose that we wanted to draw a 10 × 10 filled square of plus signs. We could write this as

Do 10 times
    Write a line with 10 +'s

Similarly, we can refine *Write a line with 10 +'s* to

Do 10 times
    Write a +
Writeln

Code for this might look like

```
FOR index := 1 TO 10 DO
    BEGIN
        FOR index := 1 TO 10 DO
            Write ('+');
        Writeln;
    END (* FOR index *)
```

There is a problem with this! The computer has only one workspace allocated for keeping track of the row and column numbers, so it cannot do both. We need different workspaces for the row number and the column number.

```
FOR row := 1 TO 10 DO
    BEGIN
        FOR column := 1 TO 10 DO
            Write ('+');
        Writeln;
    END (* FOR row *);
```

But if we have two disjoint loops we can use the same index variable.

```
PROGRAM TwoSquares (output);
    (* Illustration of nested loops *)

    VAR row, column: integer;
            (* note two variables in one declaration *)
```

```
BEGIN
    FOR row := 1 TO 10 DO
            (* outer loop uses different index variable *)
        BEGIN
            FOR column := 1 TO 10 DO  (* first disjoint loop *)
                Write ('+');
            Write (' ');
            FOR column := 1 TO 10 DO (* second disjoint loop *)
                (* uses same index variable as first *)
                Write ('+');
            Writeln;
        END (* FOR row *);
END (* TwoSquares *).
```

What will that last program do? It will print two 10×10 boxes:

```
++++++++++ ++++++++++
++++++++++ ++++++++++
++++++++++ ++++++++++
++++++++++ ++++++++++
++++++++++ ++++++++++
++++++++++ ++++++++++
++++++++++ ++++++++++
++++++++++ ++++++++++
++++++++++ ++++++++++
++++++++++ ++++++++++
```

The body of a FOR loop may be any statement. The BEGIN-END brackets are a way of converting a series of statements so that they are treated as one statement for the purpose of being the body of a FOR loop. The line FOR ··· DO is a prefix; when it is followed by a statement, the prefix and the loop body are called the FOR statement, and this combination is also considered a single statement.

Exercises

1.   Determine what the following instructions will print.

```
FOR foo := 1 TO 5 DO
    BEGIN
        FOR bar := 1 TO 3 DO
            Write ('MUMBLE-');
        Writeln ('MUMBLE');
    END (* FOR foo *);
```

2.   Write a program that prints a 5×10 rectangle of stars. Note that we use the convention *row-by-column*, so that the rectangle should have 5 rows and 10 columns.

3.   Write a program that prints 6 such rectangles in a 3×2 configuration. Put a blank row or column between rectangles. Try to use procedures in your program.

2-9 NESTED ITERATION

Suppose that we want to print a right triangle. The number of columns printed in a row depends on which row it is. So, to print a 10×10 triangle, we would do something like

```
Do 10 times
    Do ? times
        Print character
    Writeln
```

The question mark above depends on which row we are in. A program to print out a 10×10 triangle of plus signs is

```
PROGRAM PrintTriangle (output);
    VAR row: integer;    (* note use of two declarations *)
        column: integer;

BEGIN
    FOR row := 1 TO 10 DO
        BEGIN
            FOR column := 1 TO row DO
                Write ('+');
            Writeln;
        END (* FOR row *);
END (* PrintTriangle *).
```

Let us now write a square where the lower left triangle is one character and the upper right triangle is another character.

```
PROGRAM TwoToneSquare (output);
    VAR row, column: integer;

BEGIN
    FOR row := 1 TO 10 DO
        BEGIN
            FOR column := 1 TO row DO
                    (* print row of lower triangle *)
                Write ('+');
            FOR column := row + 1 TO 10 DO
                    (* print row of upper triangle *)
                Write ('*');
            Writeln;
        END (* FOR row *);
END (* TwoToneSquare *).
```

We can make a few interesting observations about the second `FOR column` loop. First, it does not start at 1, but at a different place each time. This is an instance of a more general rule: the starting and ending places of a `FOR` loop may be any integer expression. Second, the loop does not get executed for `row = 10`. That is, if the ending expression is greater than the starting expression, the loop is not executed. The resulting output shows that this is exactly what is wanted:

```
+*********
++********
+++*******
++++******
+++++*****
++++++****
+++++++***
++++++++**
+++++++++*
++++++++++
```

Exercises

1. What does the following program fragment print?

    ```
    FOR lcount := 1 TO 4 DO
        BEGIN
            Writeln (lcount);
            FOR j :=  lcount + 1 TO 2 * lcount DO
                Write (j);
            Writeln ('')
        END (* FOR lcount *);
    ```

2. Write a program that prints a figure similar to the following except expanded to 10 rows and 19 columns

    ```
       *
      ***
     *****
    *******
    ```

3. Write a program that prints a figure similar to the following except expanded to 10 rows and 19 columns

    ```
    ...*...
    ..***..
    .*****.
    *******
    ```

4. Write a program that prints a figure similar to the following except expanded to 10 rows and 38 columns

```
...*.......*...
..***....***..
.*****..*****.
*************
```

2-10 DOWNTO CLAUSE

What if we want to print some numbers in descending order? As we have just seen, we cannot simply make the ending expression less than the starting expression. We could do:

```
FOR index := 1 TO 3 DO
    Write (4 - index);
```

This writes

```
      3       2       1
```

However, there is a way to count downward.

```
FOR index := 3 DOWNTO 1 DO
    Write (index);
```

This also writes

```
      3       2       1
```

Exercises

1. Write a program that prints

```
*
**
***
****

****
***
**
*
```

2.   What does the following code fragment do?

```
FOR index1 := 1 TO 5 DO
    BEGIN
        FOR index2 := index1 DOWNTO 1 DO
            Write (index2);
        Writeln;
    END (* FOR index1 *);
```

Chapter 3

Variables and Assignment

In this chapter, we will generalize the concept of variables that we learned with index variables. We will greatly increase our ability to write interesting and useful programs on the computer.

3-1 FACTORIALS

Suppose we want to write a table of the first 11 factorials. "What are factorials?" you ask. Factorials are the product of consecutive positive integers starting from 1, so that the factorial of 3 (written 3!) is $1 \times 2 \times 3$, and the factorial of 5 is $1 \times 2 \times 3 \times 4 \times 5$. The factorial of 0 is defined as 1. We notice that $n! = n \times (n-1)!$. So when we have computed a factorial, say $(n-1)!$, to get the next one $n!$, we need to multiply by n. Also, since there is a special rule for 0 (the initial case), we probably need to handle it specially. Our first attempt at this program could be

print 0!
FOR base := *1 TO 10 DO*
    print **base** *times previous factorial printed*

A program to do this would be similar to

```
PROGRAM FactorialTable (output);

    VAR base: integer;          (* factorial number *)

BEGIN
    Writeln (0, ' factorial is', 1);
    FOR base := 1 TO 10 DO
        Writeln (base, ' factorial is',
            base * last factorial printed)
END (* FactorialTable *).
```

31

First, we notice a space between the quote and `factorial is`, but not between that and the closing quote. PASCAL prints some spaces before numbers, but does not insert a space after them. But more importantly, we need some way of keeping track of the *last factorial printed*. In the next section, we will learn how to do this, and then we will return to finish our problem.

3-2 VARIABLES

Thus far we have seen index variables that keep track of how often we have gone through a `FOR` loop. We often want to hold onto other values as well. We can do this through the use of *variables*.

A variable is a workspace into which we put values and from which we retrieve them. We have encountered index variables, which are simply a special case of ordinary variables. We have used the `FOR` statement to put values into index variables. To put values in ordinary variables, we use a new statement—the *assignment statement*.

Variable declarations can be considered the environment for the procedure that contains them. They describe what workspaces are available to the procedure, what their names are, and what kind they are.

3-3 ASSIGNMENT STATEMENT

The assignment statement is used to put values into variables. The form of the assignment statement is

variable := *expression*;

The variable on the left is the name of the variable into which we want to put the value. The expression on the right is an expression, as in `Write` statements, that gets evaluated. Its value gets placed into the variable on the left. The `:=` is a nonalphabetic keyword that identifies this as an assignment statement. For example, the following are valid assignment statements:

```
count := 3;
count := count + 1;
length := width - 2;
chapter := 3;
```

The first statement sets the value of `count` to 3. The second statement sets the value of `count` to 1 greater than the current value, or 4. The third statement sets the value of `length` to 2 less than the value of `width`. The last statement sets the value of `chapter` to 3.

Let us compare the statement `x := y` with `y := x`. The first one sets the value of `x` to the current value of `y`. The second sets the value of `y` to the value of `x`. They do *different* things. The first one leaves the value of `y` unchanged, while the second one alters the value of `y`. Also note that `:=` must appear in that order, that is, colon preceding equals.

The following instruction is understood by PASCAL.

```
x := x
```

The net result of executing this instruction is that nothing has been changed. Can you justify this by explaining exactly what the instruction does? It takes the value of the variable **x** and stores it back into **x**.

We can use ordinary variables in expressions similar to numbers or index variables. We also need to declare ordinary variables just as we need to declare index variables.

Note that statements are done sequentially. We do each one completely before doing the next. Let us look at the following statements:

```
number := 5;
double := number * 2;
number := 6;
Writeln (double);
```

What will be printed? Let us go through the program fragment step-by-step. We first assign the value 5 to **number**. We next give **double** the value of twice **number** or 10. We then give **number** the value 6. Changing **number** to 6 does not change **double**. The **Writeln** statement will then print 10. Assignment statements are *not* definitions but instructions to do something.

The following instructions might look like they could be correct, but PASCAL will not understand them.

```
13 := x;        (* wrong *)
13 =: x;        (* wrong *)
```

The assignment instruction is not symmetric. The left side of := must be a variable; the right side can be an expression. We cannot reverse := (that is, =:) and then interchange the left and right sides.

A variable can only have one value at a time. When we store a new value into a variable, the old value is forgotten. Before we have given a variable a value, it is said to be undefined. A variable should not be used in an expression, such as on the right side of an assignment statement, before it is defined.

Remember that there is a distinction between a name and an object. When we write down a variable name, we are referring to a place in the computer where the value is stored. When we use the name of a variable in an expression, we are asking the computer to use the current value of the variable. When the name of a variable appears on the left-hand side of an assignment statement, we are asking the computer to associate a new value with that variable.

Exercises

Determine what the following instructions will print. Answers are found in Appendix A. Assume that all variables are declared.

```
1.   a := 3;
     b := 5;
     Writeln ('THE NUMBERS ARE', a, b);
```

2.   Be methodical on this problem.

```
a := 28;
b := 96;
a := b;
b := a;
Writeln (a, b);
```

3.     ```
a := 3;
b := 5;
c := 8;
d := a * (b + c * 3) - 7;
e := a - b - c;
Writeln (a, b, c, d, e);
a := a + 1;
b := (4 * a + 1) DIV 10;
c := (4 * a + 1) MOD 10;
Writeln (a, b, c, d, e);
```

## 3-4 FACTORIALS CONTINUED

Now we have the necessary machinery to continue programming factorials.  It might be worthwhile to review the earlier section on factorials before proceeding with this section.

We need a variable to hold the most recently computed factorial.  Let us create a variable **lastfact** to do this.

```
PROGRAM FactorialTable (output);

    VAR base: integer;          (* factorial number *)
        lastfact: integer;      (* last factorial printed *)

BEGIN
    Writeln (0, ' factorial is', 1);
    lastfact := 1;
    FOR base := 1 TO 10 DO
        Writeln (base, ' factorial is',
            base * lastfact);
END (* FactorialTable *).
```

We will use the following symbol to indicate that the output from running the program follows.
```

```
 0 factorial is          1
 1 factorial is          1
 2 factorial is          2
 3 factorial is          3
 4 factorial is          4
 5 factorial is          5
 6 factorial is          6
 7 factorial is          7
 8 factorial is          8
 9 factorial is          9
10 factorial is         10
```

Notice that it works for 0, 1, and 2, but it does not work for any of the higher numbers—the result of not updating `lastfact`.

```
PROGRAM FactorialTable (output);

    VAR base: integer;          (* factorial number *)
        lastfact: integer;      (* last factorial printed *)

BEGIN
    Writeln (0, ' factorial is', 1);
    lastfact := 1;
    FOR base := 1 TO 10 DO
        BEGIN
            Writeln (base, ' factorial is',
                base * lastfact);
            lastfact := base * lastfact;
        END (* FOR base *)
END (* FactorialTable *).
```

```
 0 factorial is          1
 1 factorial is          1
 2 factorial is          2
 3 factorial is          6
 4 factorial is         24
 5 factorial is        120
 6 factorial is        720
 7 factorial is       5040
 8 factorial is      40320
 9 factorial is     362880
10 factorial is    3628800
```

This program would be better written as the following program, which has *better style* and is simpler. It is generally better to do computations once. The above program computes `base * lastfact` twice. Therefore, it is a good idea, when computing a value that is needed later, to assign it to a variable, rather than including an expression in a `Write` statement.

```
PROGRAM FactorialTable (output);

    VAR base: integer;           (* factorial number *)
        factorial: integer;      (* value of the factorial *)

BEGIN
    Writeln (0, ' factorial is', 1);
    factorial := 1;
    FOR base := 1 TO 10 DO
        BEGIN
            factorial := base * factorial;
            Writeln (base, ' factorial is', factorial);
        END (* FOR base *)
END (* FactorialTable *).
```

3-5 FIBONACCI NUMBERS

Let us consider another problem—Fibonacci numbers. Fibonacci numbers were discovered by a 13th century mathematician who liked to think about one property of rabbits. Suppose that each month a mature pair of rabbits breeds another pair of rabbits. It takes 1 month for rabbits to mature. (Oh, by the way, these mathematical rabbits are immortal.) Fibonacci observed that the number of pairs of rabbits in any month is the sum of the number of pairs of rabbits in the two preceding months. The sequence of Fibonacci numbers starts with 1, 1, 2, 3, 5, 8, 13, 21, etc., as the number of pairs of rabbits there are each month. So, let us define $f_1 = 1$ and $f_2 = 1$ and, for $n \geq 3$, $f_n = f_{n-1} + f_{n-2}$. We cannot translate this immediately into a loop because f_1 and f_2 are different from the rest. So, we break it down into

```
calculate f1 and print it
calculate f2 and print it
FOR count := 3 TO 20 DO
    calculate fi from the rule
        fn = fn-1 + fn-2
```

We need a way to keep around the two previous values, say `lastFibonacci` and `nextFibonacci`.

```
lastFibonacci := 1;  Writeln (lastFibonacci);
nextFibonacci := 1;  Writeln (nextFibonacci);
FOR count := 3 TO 20 DO
    Writeln (lastFibonacci + nextFibonacci)
```

But this does not work since after computing f_3, the variables `lastFibonacci` and `nextFibonacci` still contain f_1 and f_2 and not, as we want, f_2 and f_3, respectively. We need to add something to our loop to change them. How about the following?

```
lastFibonacci := 1;  Writeln (lastFibonacci);
nextFibonacci := 1;  Writeln (nextFibonacci);
FOR count := 3 TO 20 DO
    BEGIN
        lastFibonacci := nextFibonacci;
        nextFibonacci := lastFibonacci + nextFibonacci;
        Writeln (nextFibonacci);
    END (* FOR count *);
```

The result will be

```
        1
        1
        2
        4
        8
        16
        32
        64
        etc.
```

However, the statement that gives a new value to `lastFibonacci` changes its value to that of `nextFibonacci`. The next statement uses the new value of `lastFibonacci`, so that it effectively doubles it. But we can compute the sum of `lastFibonacci` and `nextFibonacci` and save it somewhere, say `temporary`. We can then update `lastFibonacci`, since we no longer need it. Lastly, we can put the sum into `nextFibonacci`.

```
PROGRAM FibonacciNumbers (output);

    VAR lastFibonacci, nextFibonacci, temporary: integer;
                    (* recent Fibonacci numbers *)
        count: integer; (* count of Fibonacci numbers *)

BEGIN
    Writeln ('The first 20 Fibonacci numbers follow:');
    lastFibonacci := 1;  Writeln (lastFibonacci);
    nextFibonacci := 1;  Writeln (nextFibonacci);
    FOR count := 3 TO 20 DO
        BEGIN
            temporary := lastFibonacci + nextFibonacci;
            lastFibonacci := nextFibonacci;
            nextFibonacci := temporary;
            Writeln (nextFibonacci)
        END (* FOR count *)
END (* FibonacciNumbers *).
```

What if we want to print only the 20th Fibonacci number? We would use

```
PROGRAM FibonacciNumbers (output);

    VAR lastFibonacci, nextFibonacci, temporary: integer;
                            (* recent Fibonacci numbers *)
        count: integer; (* count of Fibonacci numbers *)

BEGIN
    lastFibonacci := 1;
    nextFibonacci := 1;
    FOR count := 3 TO 20 DO
        BEGIN
            temporary := lastFibonacci + nextFibonacci;
            lastFibonacci := nextFibonacci;
            nextFibonacci := temporary;
        END; (* FOR count *)
    Writeln ('The 20th Fibonacci number is', nextFibonacci);
END (* FibonacciNumbers *).
```

Notice that this program does much computation in the loop before producing output. This makes it harder to detect errors, because the program does not print intermediate results. For example, if you first wrote the program to print out the 20th Fibonacci number, you would have to decide whether to print out **lastFibonacci**, **nextFibonacci**, or **temporary** after the loop. You might have a *fencepost error.** The way to debug such an error is to print out intermediate values or try to test small numbers by hand. For example, you could calculate the fifth Fibonacci number.

Exercise

Determine what the following instructions will print. Assume that all variables are declared.

```
1.    sum := 0;
      FOR k := 4 TO 9 DO
          sum := sum + k;
      Writeln (sum);
```

3-6 CONSTANTS

Not only can we associate names with procedures and with variables that change, but we can also associate names with values, such as constants. We declare

---

* A fencepost error—or boundary error—is illustrated by answering this problem: How many fenceposts are needed for a 100-foot-long straight fence if posts are placed 10 feet apart? The obvious answer of 10 is *wrong* because you need fenceposts either at both ends or at neither end of the fence. Therefore, the correct answer is 9 or 11.

constants in much the same way we declare variables. We say CONST followed by a list of constant declarations, each of which is a constant name, an equals sign (=), and the value, all followed by a semicolon. For example,

```
CONST
    rowcount = 6;
    perfectScore = 100;
```

Why use constants instead of variables? Constants improve program readability. Using a constant ensures that the value does not change. It also defines the name at the same time it supplies the value, so that there is no need to have a separate assignment statement to supply the value. This makes it easy to change the value of the constant, since it appears in only one place.

Why use a constant instead of using its value all over? We define the constant once and use it all over. If we want to rerun the program with a different value for the constant, we only need to change one thing. A constant also provides useful self-documentation; it gives an informative name to the value.

We can use a constant much like a value; that is, a constant can appear in expressions. An example using a constant appears in the following section.

3-7 FLOYD'S TRIANGLE

Suppose we want to print a right triangle of consecutive numbers so that there is one number on the first line, two on the second, three on the third, etc. This problem is due to R. W. Floyd. This program is similar to the program for printing a right triangle in Section 2-9, except that we write consecutive numbers instead of a plus. We could write the following program.

```
PROGRAM Floyd (output);
    CONST
        rowcount = 6;
    VAR row, column: integer;
        number: integer;

BEGIN
    number := 0;
    FOR row := 1 TO rowcount DO
        BEGIN
            FOR column := 1 TO row DO
                BEGIN
                    number := number + 1;
                    Write (number);
                END; (* FOR column *)
            Writeln;
        END (* FOR row *);
END (* Floyd *).
```

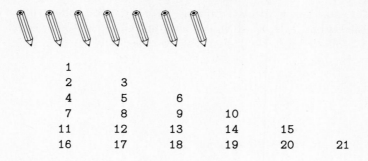

```
1
2       3
4       5       6
7       8       9       10
11      12      13      14      15
16      17      18      19      20      21
```

Note that the CONST section of the program must follow the PROGRAM section and precede the VAR section.

Input and Conditional Execution

Thus far, we have written programs that do exactly the same thing each time we run them. In order to get them to do something else, we have had to resort to changing the program. In this chapter, we will learn other ways to get values into our variables. We will also learn how to do different things depending on the values of variables.

4-1 READING INPUT

Until now, we have had only one way of getting information into our programs—supplying it as constants. However, each time we want to run the program with different values, we have had to alter the program and recompile it. There is another method of getting values into our program: to read them as *input*. First, we put the input values into a file. We create and edit the input file the same way we create and edit a file containing a program.

The statement to read values from the input file into program variables is the **Read** statement. We say **Read**, followed by an open parenthesis [(], list the variables to be read separated by commas, and then a close parenthesis [)]. If we do input in a program, we must also alter the **PROGRAM** header to include **input** as shown below.

Let us write a program that reads in 5 numbers and prints them and their sum. Our first version might appear as

Do 5 times
    Read and print a number
    Add it to the sum
Print the sum

This translates into

```
PROGRAM Summation (input, output);
    (* read and sum five numbers *)

CONST amountOfInput = 5;

VAR sum: integer;         (* sum so far *)
    number: integer;      (* number just read *)
    index: integer;       (* count of numbers *)

BEGIN
    sum := 0;             (* no numbers read yet *)
    Write ('Input: ');
    FOR index := 1 TO amountOfInput DO
        BEGIN
            Read (number);
            Write (number);
            sum := sum + number;
        END (* FOR index *);
    Writeln;
    Write ('The sum is', sum);
END (* Summation *).
```

Assume that the input is the following:

```
1 9 6 5 3
```

The program above will then produce the following output:

```
Input:          1       9       6       5       3
The sum is      24
```

Let us consider how this program reads its input. The first time we go through the FOR loop, we read the first number, 1. This has the same effect as the statement number := 1. We also remember that we have already read the 1 and are now up to the 9. We proceed to write the 1 and add it to the sum, which is now 1. We go through the loop again and read 9 into number. We print the 9 and go on to adding 9 to the sum. The Read statement is similar to an assignment statement that gets its value from the next value to be read in.

Let us make a few observations about how this program works. First, we have remembered to set sum to 0 before reading any numbers, because it is not correct to use an uninitialized variable in an expression. Many compilers do not check for this, so it is possible to get unexpected results by forgetting to initialize variables. Second, we have copied the input into the output file before doing anything else to the data. This is called *echoing* and is accomplished by following the Read statements in the program by Write statements. This is a good practice to follow as it will allow people looking at the program output to figure out what is going on. It is also a good idea to intersperse some other information when printing the input so that it is clear which value is which.

Exercises

1.   Write a program that averages 5 numbers read from input.

2.   What happens if there are not enough numbers in the input file to satisfy
a read request? That is, assume that all numbers in the input have already
been read.

3.   Determine what the following program fragment prints. Assume that all
variables used are declared.

```
Read (value);
Writeln ('The value is', value);
value := value + 5;
Writeln ('The value is now', value);
FOR index := 4 TO 6 DO
    BEGIN
        Write (index);
        Read (next);
        Write (next);
        value := value + next MOD index;
        Writeln (value);
    END (* FOR index *);
```

Assume the input file contains the following

3 17 36 2 10

4-2 VARIABLE-LENGTH INPUT

Let us suppose that we want to write a program that gives the sum of a list
of numbers. This program would not be very different from the program in
Section 4-1 that took the sum of 5 numbers. That program only accepted 5
numbers. If we wanted to sum more or fewer numbers, we would have to change
the program. We can make our program take the sum of an arbitrary amount
of numbers by first reading in how many numbers there are. That is, instead
of defining `amountOfInput` as a constant, we read it in. This program might
appear as

```
PROGRAM Summation (input, output);
    (* read and sum a variable quantity of numbers *)
```

```
VAR sum: integer;        (* sum so far *)
    number: integer;     (* number just read *)
    index: integer;      (* count of numbers *)
    amountOfInput: integer; (* number of input values *)
```

```
BEGIN
    Read (amountOfInput);
    Writeln ('There are ', amountOfInput, ' input values.');
    sum := 0;            (* no numbers read yet *)
    Write ('Input: ');
    FOR index := 1 TO amountOfInput DO
        BEGIN
            Read (number);
            Write (number);
            sum := sum + number;
        END (* FOR index *);
    Writeln;
    Write ('The sum is', sum);
END (* Summation *).
```

Assume that the input is the following:

```
7 1 9 6 5 3 8 2
```

The program above will then produce the following output:

```
There are        7 input values.
Input:       1      9      6      5      3      8      2
The sum is      34
```

Exercise

1. What is the difference between using a constant definition and reading the value from input?

4-3 IF STATEMENTS

Suppose that we want to read in each person's favorite number, but if the favorite number matches 14, a special message is printed. To do this, we need a new statement that allows us to do something if the number is equal to 14. This statement is the IF statement.

```
IF number = 14
    THEN Write (' is my favorite number too');
```

The preceding statement will print out the phrase "is my favorite number too" if number has the value 14. The part IF number = 14 THEN is a prefix that says that the statement following it is to be done when the condition number = 14 is true. If number is not 14, nothing is done. Let us see the complete program now.

```
PROGRAM FavoriteNumber (input, output);
    (* read favorite numbers and see if they match 14 *)

CONST
    myFavoriteNumber = 14;

VAR
    number: integer;     (* number just read *)
    index: integer;      (* count of numbers *)
    amountOfInput: integer; (* number of input values *)

BEGIN
    Read (amountOfInput);
    Writeln ('There are ', amountOfInput, ' input values.');
    FOR index := 1 TO amountOfInput DO
        BEGIN
            Read (number);
            Write (number);
            IF number = myFavoriteNumber
                THEN Write (' is my favorite number too');
            Writeln;
        END (* FOR index *);
END (* FavoriteNumber *).
```

Assume that the input is the following:

6 10 14 57 69 16 14

The program above will then produce the following output:

```
There are        6 input values.
     10
     14 is my favorite number too
     57
     69
     16
     14 is my favorite number too
```

4-3-1 Conditions

We have seen that we can do something special if 2 numbers are equal. Now we will see that we can do other comparisons. Also, we can compare the values of expressions as well as the values of variables and constants. We will generalize the IF statement to the following form.

```
IF condition
    THEN statement;
```

The following can be conditions:

<u>Example</u>

$expression_1$ = $expression_2$	means equals	5 = 6 is false
$expression_1$ < $expression_2$	means less than	5 < 6 is true
$expression_1$ <= $expression_2$	means less than or equal to	5 <= 6 is true
$expression_1$ > $expression_2$	means greater than	5 > 6 is false
$expression_1$ >= $expression_2$	means greater than or equal to	5 >= 6 is false
$expression_1$ <> $expression_2$	means not equal to	5 <> 6 is true

Note that the compound symbols, such as <>, must be written without internal spaces. As usual, spaces can lie outside these symbols.

For an example, let us read in a series of numbers. The first number will tell how many values to test. The second number is the number for comparison. We will coin the word "comparand" to refer to the objects of a comparison. Let us find the quantity of subsequent values in the input that are greater than the number for comparison. This means that we want to have a counter, and we want to add 1 to the counter each time the value we read is greater than the comparand. Our first version might appear as

Read number of values
Read comparand
Set count to zero
Do number of values times
      Read value
      IF *value > comparand*
             THEN *add 1 to count*
Write count

Let us convert this to PASCAL.

```
PROGRAM Compare (input, output);
(* Count input that's greater than selected value *)
    VAR amountOfInput: integer;    (* first input value *)
        comparand: integer;        (* second input value *)
        value: integer;            (* ordinary input value *)
        count: integer;            (* count of values read *)
        greater: integer;          (* count of values greater *)

BEGIN
    Read (amountOfInput);
    Writeln ('There are ', amountOfInput, ' input values.');

    Read (comparand);
    Writeln ('We will check for values greater than ',
        comparand, '.');
    greater := 0;
```

```
    FOR count := 1 TO amountOfInput DO
        BEGIN
            Read (value);
            Write (value);
            IF value > comparand
                THEN BEGIN
                    Write (' is greater.');
                    greater := greater + 1;
                    END (* IF value > comparand *);
            Writeln;
        END (* FOR count *);
    Writeln ('There were ', greater, ' values greater.');
END (* Compare *).
```

Assume that the input contains the following:

5 10 15 10 6 20 11

```
There are                5 input values.
We will check for values greater than              10.
        15 is greater.
        10
         6
        20 is greater.
        11 is greater.
There were               3 values greater.
```

Exercises

Determine what the following program fragments will print.

```
1.  IF 5 < 5
        THEN Write ('yes');
     Writeln (' was the answer');
```

```
2.  var1 := 3;
    var2 := 6;
    IF var1 + 2 < var2
        THEN Write ('foo');
    IF var1 + 4 < var2
        THEN Write ('bar');
    IF var1 + 4 > var2
        THEN Write ('baz');
    Writeln ('ola');
```

4-3-2 ELSE

Suppose that when **value** is not greater than **comparand**, we want to print the message "is not greater." Instead of executing one statement based on a condition, we want to execute one of two statements based on a condition. The way to do that is:

```
IF condition
     THEN statement₁
     ELSE statement₂;
```

Note that there is no semicolon before the **ELSE**, because **IF-THEN-ELSE** is one statement that contains two statements as part of it. Although we have put a semicolon at the end of each statement, the rule actually is that semicolons *separate* statements. That is, you need to insert a semicolon after a statement only if there is a another statement following it. In practice, however, there is an **END**, **ELSE**, or another statement following each statement. Although unnecessary, inserting a semicolon before **END**, as we have always done, does not cause errors. Inserting a semicolon before **ELSE**, though, is an error that will be detected by the compiler. A good rule of thumb is "Insert a semicolon after each statement, but *never* before an **ELSE**."

Revising the program in the previous section, we obtain the following:

```
PROGRAM Compare (input, output);
(* Count input that are greater that selected value *)
(* and also those not greater than selected value *)

     VAR amountOfInput: integer;     (* first input value *)
         comparand: integer;         (* second input value *)
         value: integer;             (* ordinary input value *)
         count: integer;             (* count of values read *)
         greater: integer;           (* count of values greater *)
         smaller: integer;           (* count of values smaller *)

BEGIN
     Read (amountOfInput);
     Writeln ('There are ', amountOfInput, ' input values.');

     Read (comparand);
     Writeln ('We will check for values greater than ',
         comparand, '.');

     greater := 0;
     smaller := 0;
```

```
    FOR count := 1 TO amountOfInput DO
        BEGIN
            Read (value);
            Write (value);
            IF value > comparand
                THEN BEGIN
                    Write (' is greater.');
                    greater := greater + 1;
                    END (* IF value > comparand *)
                ELSE BEGIN
                    Write (' is not greater.');
                    smaller := smaller + 1;
                    END (* IF value > comparand *);
            Writeln;
        END (* FOR count *);
    Writeln ('There were ', greater, ' values greater.');
    Writeln ('There were ', smaller, ' values not greater.');
END (* Compare *).
```

Assume that the input contains the following:

5 10 15 10 6 20 11

```
There are              5 input values.
We will check for values greater than        10.
        15 is greater.
        10 is not greater.
         6 is not greater.
        20 is greater.
        11 is greater.
There were             3 values greater.
There were             2 values not greater.
```

An ambiguity results from having nested IFs and ELSEs. Consider the following program fragment.

```
IF condition₁
    THEN IF condition₂
        THEN statement₁
        ELSE statement₂
```

When do we execute $statement_2$? Does the **ELSE** match the first **IF**, so it is done when the first **IF** condition is **false**? Or does the **ELSE** match the second **IF**, so it is done when the second **IF** condition is **false** (and the first one **true**)? In general, an **ELSE** matches the most recent **IF** that has not been matched (or closed off by an **END**).

Let us consider the possibilities for the preceding program fragment. If $condition_1$ is **false**, nothing is done. On the other hand, if $condition_1$ is **true** but $condition_2$ **false**, $statement_2$ is executed. Note that $statement_1$ is executed only when both $condition_1$ and $condition_2$ are **true**.

How would we change the preceding fragment so that $statement_2$ is executed when $condition_1$ is **false**, and nothing is executed when $condition_2$ is tested **false**? One way is to put the second **IF** inside a compound statement.

```
IF  condition₁
    THEN BEGIN
        IF  condition₂
            THEN  statement₁
        END (* THEN of  condition₁ *)
    ELSE  statement₂
```

Note that there is *no* semicolon after **END**, because it is before **ELSE**. Furthermore, the following could be used if something is to be done when $condition_2$ is **false**.

```
IF  condition₁
    THEN IF  condition₂
            THEN  statement₁
            ELSE  statement₂
    ELSE  statement₃
```

Let us consider the cases for this program fragment. If $condition_1$ is **false**, $statement_3$ is executed. If $condition_1$ is **true** but $condition_2$ is **false**, $statement_2$ is executed. Note that $statement_1$ is executed only when both $condition_1$ and $condition_2$ are **true**.

Indentation should be used as a guide to the intended meaning of the program. The discussion of ambiguous **ELSE**s above demonstrates how good indentation improves readability.

Exercises

1.   What does the following program print?

```
a := 10;
b := 20;
IF a < b
    THEN c := a
    ELSE c := b;
Writeln (a, b, c)
```

2.   Describe in general terms what the instruction

```
IF a < b
    THEN c := a
    ELSE c := b
```

does to **c** for an arbitrary **a** and **b**. What if **a** and **b** are equal?

4-4 CHESS

We will now do a series of examples of using conditionals in playing chess. Many people have heard that computers play chess, but few people know how they do it. While determining strategy is very difficult for a computer, the movement of the pieces is rather straightforward.

Our first problem is to read in a chess board position and print out the chess board with that position marked. This problem is somewhat different from the problem of simply printing a chess board, but it might be useful to try to solve this simpler problem first. The first version of this simpler problem follows:

Do 4 times
> *Write the line "*`WBWBWBWB`*"*
> *Write the line "*`BWBWBWBW`*"*

However, in our original problem, we needed to print a star in the appropriate position. Since that position could be anywhere on the board, we need to test for printing the star before printing each **B** or **W**. We could change the above solution to do that directly, but there would be a lot of duplicate code for each "test for printing a star." For example, it might appear as

Do 4 times
> *Write star or* W
> *Write star or* B
> *Write star or* W
> *Write star or* B
> *Write star or* W
> *Write star or* B
> *Write star or* W
> *Write star or* B
> *Do a* `Writeln`
>
> *Write star or* B
> *Write star or* W
> *Write star or* B
> *Write star or* W
> *Write star or* B
> *Write star or* W
> *Write star or* B
> *Write star or* W
> *Do a* `Writeln`

This seems rather repetitive. Let us try again.

Do 8 times
> *Do 8 times*
>> *Write a star or* W *or* B
> *Do a* `Writeln`

This seems shorter and easier to understand, but we have deferred much to the line "Write...." Let us expand that to

IF *we are at the desired position*
      THEN *Write a star*
      ELSE *Write a* W *or* B

Therefore, we have reduced this problem to deciding whether to write a W or B. Perhaps a look at a numbered chess board would help.

(1,1) W	(1,2) B	(1,3) W	(1,4) B	(1,5) W	(1,6) B	(1,7) W	(1,8) B
(2,1) B	(2,2) W	(2,3) B	(2,4) W	(2,5) B	(2,6) W	(2,7) B	(2,8) W
(3,1) W	(3,2) B	(3,3) W	(3,4) B	(3,5) W	(3,6) B	(3,7) W	(3,8) B
(4,1) B	(4,2) W	(4,3) B	(4,4) W	(4,5) B	(4,6) W	(4,7) B	(4,8) W
(5,1) W	(5,2) B	(5,3) W	(5,4) B	(5,5) W	(5,6) B	(5,7) W	(5,8) B
(6,1) B	(6,2) W	(6,3) B	(6,4) W	(6,5) B	(6,6) W	(6,7) B	(6,8) W
(7,1) W	(7,2) B	(7,3) W	(7,4) B	(7,5) W	(7,6) B	(7,7) W	(7,8) B
(8,1) B	(8,2) W	(8,3) B	(8,4) W	(8,5) B	(8,6) W	(8,7) B	(8,8) W

We now need a way to determine whether to print W or B given the row and column. After trying several possibilities, we discover that when the sum of the row and column is even [for example, (1,1) or (7,5)], W is printed; otherwise B is printed.

    Let us proceed to writing the program.

```
PROGRAM Chess (input, output);
(* print out a chess board *)

    VAR atRow, atColumn: integer;
            (* position of star *)
        row, column: integer;
            (* position we are at *)

BEGIN
    Read (atRow, atColumn);
    Writeln ('Position is (', atRow, ',', atColumn, ').');
```

```
    FOR row := 1 TO 8 DO
        BEGIN
            FOR column := 1 TO 8 DO
                IF we are at atRow and atColumn
                    THEN Write ('*')
                    ELSE IF (row + column) MOD 2 = 0
                        (* row + column is even *)
                        THEN Write ('W')
                        ELSE Write ('B');
            Writeln;
        END (* FOR row *);
END (* Chess *).
```

Let us go back to the question of deciding whether we are at the position where the star is to be printed. We know how to decide whether we are at the right row or the right column, but we do not yet know how to combine those decisions. We will learn how in the next section.

4-5 AND

We want to print a star if both atRow = row and atColumn = column. To do this, we say

```
IF (atRow = row) AND (atColumn = column)
    THEN Write ('*');
```

Notice that we have taken two conditions and have combined them with an AND. The statement following THEN is now executed only when both conditions are true. Also notice that there are parentheses around the conditions. Since there are only inconvenient precedence rules for AND, all parentheses must be stated explicitly. Failure to insert parentheses needed because of an AND will result in an error message. The text of the error message will probably be rather obscure; therefore, if you get an error message in an IF statement involving an AND, check your parentheses.

Let us complete our program from the last section.

```
PROGRAM Chess (input, output);
(* print out a chess board *)

    VAR atRow, atColumn: integer;
            (* position of star *)
        row, column: integer;
            (* position we are at *)
```

```
BEGIN
    Read (atRow, atColumn);
    Writeln ('Position is (', atRow, ',', atColumn, ').');
    FOR row := 1 TO 8 DO
        BEGIN
            FOR column := 1 TO 8 DO
                IF (atRow = row) AND (atColumn = column)
                    THEN Write ('*')
                    ELSE IF (row + column) MOD 2 = 0
                        (* row + column is even *)
                        THEN Write ('W')
                        ELSE Write ('B');
            Writeln;
        END (* FOR row *);
END (* Chess *).
```

Suppose we give the program the following input.

5 3

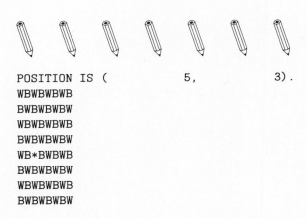

```
POSITION IS (         5,          3).
WBWBWBWB
BWBWBWBW
WBWBWBWB
BWBWBWBW
WB*BWBWB
BWBWBWBW
WBWBWBWB
BWBWBWBW
```

Exercise

1. Write an **IF** instruction that sets **c** to 0 when **a** is strictly greater that
    0 and strictly less than **b**. If this is not the case, do not change **c**. The
    mathematical way to write the condition is: $0 < a < b$. Be very careful,
    since a subtle point is being made. *Hint:* Say this condition aloud slowly.

4-6 CHESS: BISHOP MOVES

Let us now modify our program for printing a chess board to print out the
squares to which a bishop can move. The bishop will start out on the position
we read. It is possible for the bishop to remain in the same place during the
move. Remember that a bishop only moves diagonally. It might help to look at
a numbered chess board again. Assume that the bishop starts at (5,3).

(1,1) W	(1,2) B	(1,3) W	(1,4) B	(1,5) W	(1,6) B	(1,7) *	(1,8) B
(2,1) B	(2,2) W	(2,3) B	(2,4) W	(2,5) B	(2,6) *	(2,7) B	(2,8) W
(3,1) *	(3,2) B	(3,3) W	(3,4) B	(3,5) *	(3,6) B	(3,7) W	(3,8) B
(4,1) B	(4,2) *	(4,3) B	(4,4) *	(4,5) B	(4,6) W	(4,7) B	(4,8) W
(5,1) W	(5,2) B	(5,3) *	(5,4) B	(5,5) W	(5,6) B	(5,7) W	(5,8) B
(6,1) B	(6,2) *	(6,3) B	(6,4) *	(6,5) B	(6,6) W	(6,7) B	(6,8) W
(7,1) *	(7,2) B	(7,3) W	(7,4) B	(7,5) *	(7,6) B	(7,7) W	(7,8) B
(8,1) B	(8,2) W	(8,3) B	(8,4) W	(8,5) B	(8,6) *	(8,7) B	(8,8) W

Consider the upper left to lower right diagonal. After short observation, we realize that the common characteristic of these squares is that the difference between the row and the column is constant. That is, `row - column = 2`. Now, consider the lower left to upper right diagonal. Notice that the sum of the row and column are constant. That is, `row + column = 8`. Let us modify our last program to include these formulas.

```
PROGRAM Chess (input, output);
(* print out a chess board and bishop moves *)

    VAR atRow, atColumn: integer;
            (* position of star *)
        row, column: integer;
            (* position we are at *)

BEGIN
    Read (atRow, atColumn);
    Writeln ('Position is (', atRow, ',', atColumn, ').');
    FOR row := 1 TO 8 DO
        BEGIN
            FOR column := 1 TO 8 DO
                IF we are on a diagonal
                    THEN Write ('*')
                    ELSE IF (row + column) MOD 2 = 0
                        (* row + column is even *)
                        THEN Write ('W')
                        ELSE Write ('B');
            Writeln;
        END (* FOR row *);
END (* Chess *).
```

Now we need a way to combine two conditions where only one of them need be true. We will learn how to do this in the Section 4-7.

4-7 OR

We want to print a star if either **row - column = 2** or **row + column = 8** is true, or if both are true. To do this, we say

```
IF (row - column = 2) OR (row + column = 8)
    THEN Write ('*');
```

Notice that we have once again used parentheses around the conditions. We execute the **THEN** clause if either or both of the conditions are true.

Let us now consider how we can use this new feature in our program. Notice that 2 and 8 were chosen because they are the difference and sum of the desired row and column, respectively. Our program now becomes

```
PROGRAM Chess (input, output);
(* print out a chess board and bishop moves *)

    VAR atRow, atColumn: integer;
                (* position of star *)
        row, column: integer;
                (* position we are at *)

BEGIN
    Read (atRow, atColumn);
    Writeln ('Position is (', atRow, ',', atColumn, ').');
    FOR row := 1 TO 8 DO
        BEGIN
            FOR column := 1 TO 8 DO
                IF  (row - column = atRow - atColumn) OR
                    (row + column = atRow + atColumn)
                    THEN Write ('*')
                    ELSE IF (row + column) MOD 2 = 0
                        (* row + column is even *)
                        THEN Write ('W')
                        ELSE Write ('B');
            Writeln;
        END (* FOR row *);
END (* Chess *).
```

Suppose we give the program the following input.

```
POSITION IS (          5,          3).
WBWBWB*B
BWBWB*BW
*BWB*BWB
B*B*BWBW
WB*BWBWB
B*B*BWBW
*BWB*BWB
BWBWB*BW
```

We will learn more about using conditionals in Chapter 5.

Exercise

1. Write a statement that prints "outside" when **int** is less than 4 or greater than 10.

Types

In this chapter, we will learn more about the kinds of data the computer can handle. We have already learned about integers. We will now learn about a generalization of conditionals, and then about characters and real numbers.

5-1 TYPE BOOLEAN

We already know that integer expressions can be assigned to integer variables. We will now learn about assigning conditions.

When we said `row = atRow`, we were evaluating that expression and obtaining a value, either `true` or `false`. Values from conditions are called *boolean* values. They can be stored in boolean variables. The operations `AND` and `OR` work on boolean values and give boolean results. Such operations as = and < also give boolean results. One boolean operation that we have not encountered is `NOT`. The operation `NOT` takes the negation of its single operand. For example, `NOT (row = column)` is the same as `row <> column`.

To review, here are the boolean operators:

AND	Compute the logical AND of two boolean values
OR	Compute the logical OR of two boolean values
NOT	Negate a single boolean value

The truth tables for the AND, OR, and NOT operators are:

AND	true	false
true	true	false
false	false	false

OR	true	false
true	true	true
false	true	false

NOT	
true	false
false	true

Suppose that we want to read in a list of values and print out one of two messages depending on whether a particular number appears later in the list. The first number is the length of the list (not including the first or second numbers). The second number is that particular number, or comparand. Our first version might appear as

Read length of list
Read comparand

Set no match found
Do length times
   Read number
   IF *number = comparand*
      THEN *set match found*

IF *match found*
   THEN *print match found message*
   ELSE *print match not found message*

Let us consider the kind of variable used for keeping track of whether a match has been found. It has two states: match found and match not found. That is, we could use a boolean variable, say **matchFound**, and give it values of **true** and **false**. Notice that we have used a new programming technique in using **matchFound**, a *flag*. We have initialized a flag, and then set it inside a loop. We then test the flag outside the loop. If the desired condition has occurred, we have set the flag and it will have this new value outside the loop. If the desired condition does not occur, we have not set the flag, and so it will have the initialized value outside the loop. Note that we do not change the value of the flag when the condition does not occur. If it has not yet occurred, the flag will have the initialized value; if it has occurred, we want to preserve our record of that fact.

Let's now proceed to writing the program.

```
PROGRAM Search (input, output);
(* search for occurrences of a desired value in a list *)

    VAR matchFound: boolean;     (* true if match found *)
        numberOfValues: integer; (* amount of input *)
        comparand: integer;      (* value to search for *)
        value: integer;          (* value in list *)
        count: integer;          (* count of values in list *)

BEGIN
    Read (numberOfValues);
    Writeln ('There are', numberOfValues, ' values.');
    Read (comparand);
    Writeln ('Searching for', comparand, '.');
```

```
    matchFound := false;           (* no match found yet *)
    FOR count := 1 TO numberOfValues DO
        BEGIN
            Read (value);
            Writeln (value);
            IF value = comparand
                THEN matchFound := true;
                        (* we've found a match *)
        END (* FOR count *);
    IF matchFound
        THEN Writeln ('There was a match found.')
        ELSE Writeln ('There were no matches found.');
END (* Search *).
```

Note that the last **IF** statement in the above program uses a boolean variable directly, because the **IF** wants a boolean, which can be a variable or an expression. It does not have to be **matchFound = true**!

Exercises

1. Determine what the above program does with the following sets of input.

    (a) 5 10 15 20 25 30 35
    (b) 5 10 5 10 15 20 25
    (c) 5 10 5 5 5 5 5
    (d) 5 10 10 10 10 10 10

2. Determine what the following program fragment prints:

    ```
    a := 3;
    b := 4;
    stillgo := true AND (a + b < 2 * a);
    IF stillgo
        THEN Writeln ('HI')
        ELSE Writeln ('LOW')
    ```

    Justify the answer by telling how (in English) you derived it.

5-2 TYPE COMPATIBILITY

We now understand two types of values: integer and boolean. Integer values are ordinary numbers; boolean values are **true** and **false**. It makes sense to add two integer values, but it does not make sense to add two boolean values. We will formalize this concept in the notion of type compatibility. Also, we will use the analogy of a pegboard to visualize it.

Variables have these attributes: a name, a location, a type, and a value. The *name* is used in the declaration and in all statements that refer to the variable. The *location* is the area in the computer's memory that keeps track of the value of the variable; this is analogous to a hole in a pegboard. This analogy is due to Rich Pattis. Variables and values also have types associated with them. The *type* of a variable describes the kinds of values it can take on. A *datum* is a value and its type. We can visualize a datum as a peg with writing on it. The type of a datum is analogous to the shape of the peg; the value of a datum is analogous to the information written on the peg. The simple data types available in PASCAL are *integers*, *reals*, *booleans*, and *characters*.

Let us consider how variables take on values. Variables start out without a value. We say that the value is *undefined*. This is analogous to a hole that does not contain a peg. Each peg can have only one piece of information written on it. When we assign a value to the variable, the old value is first discarded, and then the new one is stored in the hole. Note that this is done *after* we decide the value to be stored in the variable. Consider the statement `x := x + 1`. We first take the existing value of `x`, and then take 1 greater than that value. We now wish to store the new value, so we do that after discarding the old value. The old value is no longer accessible.

The type *integer* refers to numerical values without decimal points. We will use prism-shaped pegs for integers. Both positive and negative numbers can be integers. Some numbers that can be written on integer prisms are 10 , 15 , 0 , −123 , and 10000 . If we want to write the number 1 million, we write it as 1000000; we are not allowed to use commas in an integer.

The second type is called *boolean*. It could be represented by a cylinder-shaped peg on which we can write the words `true` or `false`. This data type has been used in PASCAL's `IF` instruction, when the computer has to know whether some condition it tested was `true` or `false`.

The type *real* consists of numerical values with decimal points. Block-shaped pegs will be used for real datums. Again, positive and negative numbers can be reals. Some sample numbers that can be written on real blocks are 10.0 , −142.34 , 0.75 , and −0.00334 . PASCAL requires every real number to have at least one digit before the decimal point (that is, we must write .75 as 0.75) and at least one digit after the decimal point (that is, we must write 10. as 10.0).

Let us clear up a possible misunderstanding quickly. The problem concerns the integer 10 and the real 10.0. The integer 10 can be written on a prism but not on a block. The real 10.0 can be written on a block but not on a prism. Although the integer 10 and the real 10.0 do not seem much different to us, they are very different to the computer; they have different types. This difference will become more apparent when we learn which operations can be performed on which data types. Thus, when programming in PASCAL, we must be very careful to distinguish integers from reals.

The final simple type is called a *character*, and it is represented by a hexagon. The information that can be written on this type of peg will be discussed in a subsequent chapter.

There are several key facts about variables that the pegboard analogy is intended to illustrate.

1. PASCAL can store a value into a variable only if the two are *type-compatible*. This can be paraphrased as, "We cannot put a round peg in a square hole."
2. There can be only one piece of data in a variable at a time. Before putting a new value into a variable hole, we must first remove and discard the value currently there.
3. The computer can find out the value of any variable without changing the value of that variable. It can just look at the peg in the required hole and read its value.

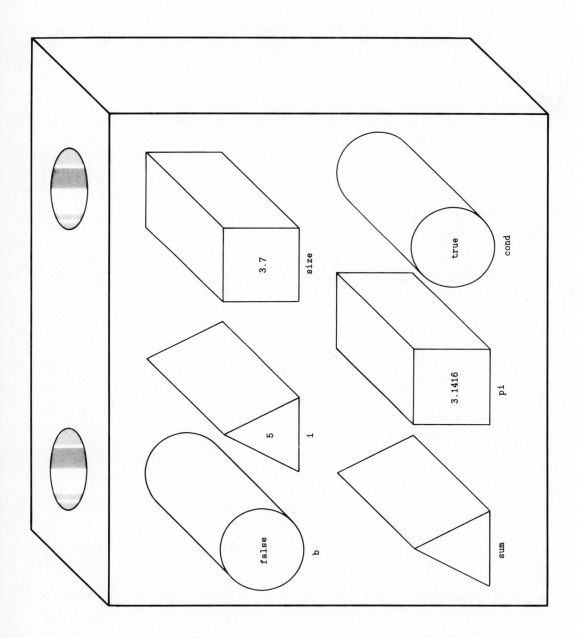

The variable sum has not been given a value.

Figure 5-1 A pegboard.

5-3 TYPE REAL

There are several real operators similar to the integer operators. These operators work on reals and give a real result:

> \+   Add two reals, resulting in the real sum.
> \-   Subtract the second real from the first,
>   resulting in the real difference.
> *   Multiply two reals, resulting in the real product.
> /   Divide the second real from the first,
>   resulting in the real quotient; for example,
>   10.0 / 5.0 is 2.0, while 15.0 / 2.0 is 7.5.

There is also a unary minus for real arithmetic. The same rules for expression formation apply to reals as well as to integers, so that all of the following are expressions (assuming the variables involved are reals):

```
rate * time * amount
(acc * time * time) / 2.0 + v0 * time + d0
total - sales
```

Evaluation of real expressions follows the same methods used for integer expressions. The * and / operators have precedence over the + and - operators.

We can read in real numbers into real variables and print the values of real variables or expressions.

Suppose we want to compute the area of triangles given their bases and heights. Recall that the formula for the area of a triangle is one-half of the product of base and height. Our first version of the program follows.

Read amount of input
Do amount of input times
      Read base and height
      Print area = 1/2 * base * height

We can now convert this into a PASCAL program.

```
PROGRAM TriangleArea (input, output);
(* Computes area of triangles *)

    VAR base, height, area: real;
                    (* values associated with a triangle *)
        amountOfInput: integer;
                    (* total number of triangles *)
        count: integer;
                    (* count of triangles read so far *)
```

```
BEGIN
    Read (amountOfInput);
    Writeln ('There are', amountOfInput,
        ' sets of input values.');

    FOR count := 1 TO amountOfInput DO
        BEGIN
            Read (base, height);
            Writeln ('A triangle with base ', base,
                ' and height ', height);
            area := 0.5 * base * height;
            Writeln ('will have area ', area);
        END (* FOR count *);
END (* TriangleArea *).
```

Assume that the input contains the following:

3 1.0 1.0 2.0 5.0 5.0 2.0

```
There are                3 sets of input values.
A triangle with base 1.000000000E+00 and height 1.000000000E+00
will have area 5.000000000E-01
A triangle with base 2.000000000E+00 and height 5.000000000E+00
will have area 5.000000000E+00
A triangle with base 5.000000000E+00 and height 2.000000000E+00
will have area 5.000000000E+00
```

Notice that the real numbers are printing in *scientific notation*. We will explore this further after the next example.

Suppose we want to write a program that reads in amounts of time and computes how far a body will fall in that amount of time. It seems that time and distance are real quantities, as opposed to integer quantities. Recall that the formula for distance traveled by a body starting at rest to which a force has been applied is

$$d = \frac{1}{2}at^2$$

Also, the acceleration a of gravity is about 32 feet per second per second. Our first version of the program is

Read amount of input
Do amount of input times
        Read time
        *Print distance = 1/2 * gravity * time * time*

Let us convert this to a PASCAL program.

```
PROGRAM FallDistance (input, output);
(* Computes fall distance given time *)
    CONST acceleration = 32.0;
        (* acceleration due to gravity *)
        (* notice that it is a real constant *)
    VAR time, distance: real;
        amountOfInput: integer;
        count: integer;

BEGIN
    Read (amountOfInput);
    Writeln ('There are', amountOfInput, ' input values.');
    FOR count := 1 TO amountOfInput DO
        BEGIN
            Read (time);
            Writeln ('In', time, ' seconds,');
            distance := 0.5 * acceleration * time * time;
            Writeln ('the body will fall', distance,
                ' feet.');
        END (* FOR count *);
END (* FallDistance *).
```

Assume that the input contains the following:

5 1.0 2.0 3.0 0.5 0.25

```
There are              5 input values.
In 1.000000000E+00 seconds,
the body will fall 1.599999994E+01 feet.
In 2.000000000E+00 seconds,
the body will fall 6.399999976E+01 feet.
In 3.000000000E+00 seconds,
the body will fall 1.439999997E+02 feet.
In 5.000000000E-01 seconds,
the body will fall 4.000000000E+00 feet.
In 2.500000000E-01 seconds,
the body will fall 1.000000000E+00 feet.
```

Notice that real numbers are printed in *scientific notation*. The E signifies "times 10 to the"; therefore, 1.599999994E+01 means 15.99999994. One might think that the answer should be 16.0, but the computer does not do real arithmetic exactly, because it is often impossible to do real arithmetic exactly. When adding one-third three times, we would get 1 if we did it using fractions, and 0.99999 if we did it using decimals.*   The computer does real arithmetic in

---

* To 5 decimal places, one-third is 0.33333, so adding it three times would result in 0.99999. This is called *round-off error*.

binary; therefore, for calculations we could do exactly in decimal, the computer sometimes gives slightly higher or lower results.

Exercises

1. Write a program that computes the area of a circle given the radius. The formula is $area = \pi radius^2$.
2. Write a program that computes the volume of a sphere given the radius. The formula is $volume = \frac{4}{3}\pi radius^3$.
3. Write a program that determines how long it takes a body to fall a given distance from rest. Use the function Sqrt (*real expression*) to obtain the square root of a real expression. For example, Sqrt (2.0) = 1.414.... (Sqrt, a built-in function, will be explained in greater detail in Chapter 9.)

5-4 TYPE CONVERSION

It often desirable to convert integer to real or vice versa. For example, when computing an average of real numbers, you would want to divide the sum of the real numbers, which is real, by the quantity of these real numbers, which is integral. PASCAL has certain rules for allowing us to do this.
1. Integer expressions will automatically be converted to real.
2. Real expressions must be explicitly converted to integer.

```
realVariable := 5 + 10.0;
average := sum / quantity;
realVariable := 1 / 2;
```

Let us consider these statements. In the first, the number 5 is converted to 5.0 since it is to be added to the real value 10.0. In the second statement, the integer quantity is converted to real since it is to be used as the denominator of real division. The last statement is rather interesting. Both 1 and 2 will be converted to real because real division was specified. The value 0.5 will be assigned to realVariable.

Let us now consider some *wrong* examples.

```
integerVariable := realVariable;
realVariable := 5.0 + 10 DIV 2.5;
realVariable := 5.0 + 10.0 DIV 2.5;
```

In the first statement, we are asking a real value to be stored in an integer variable. In the second statement, 10 is to be divided by 2.5. This is incorrect because integer division is specified. The third statement is even worse; both operands to DIV and MOD must be integer expressions.

How do we convert from real to integer? That depends on the kind of answer you want. That is, do you want to round or truncate? For example, given 4.7, do you want 4.0 or 5.0? If you want 4.0, you want to truncate. To obtain the truncate of a real expression, we can say

```
integerVariable := Trunc (real expression);
```

The function `Trunc` takes the greatest integer less than or equal to the value of *real expression*. (Hence, it is also called the *greatest integer function*.) Similarly, to round off a real expression, we can say

```
integerVariable := Round (real expression);
```

The function `Round` takes the nearest integer to the value of *real expression* One-half is rounded up to the next integer. Negative real numbers are handled the same way as in `DIV` and `MOD`. That is,

```
Trunc (-expression) = - Trunc (expression)
Round (-expression) = - Round (expression)
```

In other words, we truncate toward 0 and round away from 0. (In mathematics, we usually truncate down and round up.) Some examples might be useful.

value	Trunc (value)	Round (value)
5.0	5	5
4.5	4	5
4.999999	4	5
4.499999	4	4
4.2	4	4
4.7	4	5
-5.0	-5	-5
-4.5	-4	-5
-4.2	-4	-4
-4.7	-4	-5

Exercise

1. Write a program that gives the real average of a list of integer values read from a file.

Program Correctness

In this chapter, we will talk about correcting programs. It is not very easy to write programs that are correct the first time. Initially, programs usually have some errors. For example, the program may not compile properly or it may not produce the correct output. We will consider some kinds of errors, how to fix them, and how to verify that our program is actually correct. Much of this chapter is based on work by Rich Pattis.

6-1 PROGRAM DEBUGGING

We spend much time finding and correcting errors in programs. This is called *debugging*. Let us explore this process of debugging programs.

There are three phases in debugging. The first phase is the detection of an error. The second phase determines the cause of the error. The third phase determines how to fix the error. For most problems, determining the location of the error is more difficult than determining how to fix it. We will concentrate first on this type of debugging. We call this *error localization*.

When we write programs, it is important not to try to keep the whole program in our head at once. Studies of short-term memory have shown that it is impossible to keep track of more than 7 to 9 facts at once. This is why using procedures is so important. We can write a procedure to solve a problem, and then we can forget how the procedure was written (including such things as variable names, etc.). When we are dealing with another part of the program, we only have to remember what the procedure does and how to use it, not how it does it. In this way, we only concern ourselves with a small part of the program at a time.

Program debugging uses a similar strategy. We cannot effectively debug an entire program. We must determine the approximate location of the error and then concentrate on this area. We ignore areas of the program that appear to be working correctly. When we finally narrow the location of the error down to, say, one instruction, we can then proceed to the final phase of debugging—actually fixing the error.

Rather than telling how to debug a program, we will present some tools and techniques for debugging. Debugging, like programming, is more of an art than a science. We have to choose our tools based on the particular program and its symptoms. With practice, we will learn to debug programs more efficiently. We can learn from our mistakes and the steps needed to correct them.

6-2 SYNTAX ERRORS

We differentiate between two types of errors in programs. The first is called a *syntax error*. This occurs when you write a PASCAL program that uses poor grammar, such as faulty punctuation, misspelled words, forgotten declarations, etc. PASCAL is very good in spotting these errors, although the error messages generated are sometimes cryptic.

PASCAL can often spot an error, but does not usually know how to correct it. Let us consider some examples.

```
foo := bar + * 3;          (* error *)
```

This statement is clearly incorrect since you cannot have a plus sign followed by an asterisk. Did the programmer want to omit the plus or the asterisk, or to insert something between the two? The computer has no way of knowing the programmer's intention, but is aware of the error. It would report something akin to "error in factor."

```
diameter := pi * raduis * raduis;        (* note spelling *)
```

If `raduis` was not declared, did the programmer mean to declare it or was it instead misspelled? We could infer that it was probably misspelled—especially if `radius` was declared with the correct spelling—but the computer is unlikely to be programmed to do that. PASCAL, however, might say "identifier not declared." Misspellings are relatively easy to detect, because the error message tells what is wrong and locates the error.

Let us consider errors in our programs. Many errors are caused by missing or additional semicolons. Semicolons can appear at the end of every statement, but never before an `ELSE`. Other common syntax errors include unbalanced parentheses or quotes, type incompatibilities, and undeclared variables.

Some errors cause correct things to be flagged as errors. For example, if we make an error in a variable declaration, attempts to use that variable may be met by messages stating that the variable has not been declared. Other errors may result in cryptic messages. For example, if certain types of errors appear in a procedure declaration, PASCAL may think it has completed the declarations and will expect the body of the main procedure. It will then become quite "upset" if it finds a procedure declaration, even if the declaration is valid. This can also happen if the `BEGIN`s and `END`s do not match up.

We should take error messages with a grain of salt. Obtaining an explicit error message is better than having PASCAL say, "I'm sorry, Dave. I'm afraid

I can't do that."* The existence of an error message simply means that there is an error. (Conversely, the absence of a message means that *if* there is an error, it has not been detected.) At best, the error message gives the location and the nature of the error. At worst, it indicates that an error has occurred somewhere before this. Thus, if we correct something in a program, it is possible that error messages that we cannot figure out will also be eliminated. Rerunning a program without changing *anything* will *never* work. But changing one part of a program may cause another, seemingly unrelated, part of the program to fail.

With most error messages, the cause will be obvious; with some, the cause will not be clear at all. If we detect an error and cannot determine its cause after a while, take a break and return to the problem later, or ask someone else. People often think about a program in one frame of mind, which can obscure the cause of an error. A fresh look at the program usually results in spotting the cause of the error message.

To debug syntax errors, obtain a listing of your program and the error messages. This list of messages should be scanned quickly, in conjunction with a listing of the program, to locate and determine the cause of all obvious syntax errors. These errors should then be fixed. It is not necessary to look at every error message, since some messages are redundant and others are caused by previously incorrect instructions that have now been fixed. However, you should try to fix several errors in each pass; otherwise, you will unnecessarily prolong the debugging process.) Once this is done, the entire process should be repeated until all syntax errors—and error messages—have been eliminated.

PASCAL will not run any program with a syntax error. When a program has no syntax errors, PASCAL will then attempt to run it. This brings us to the next class of errors.

6-3 HOW TWO SYNTAX ERRORS BECOME TEN

We will now do a case study of a program with two syntax errors.† The compiler diagnoses 10 errors. The program follows, with line numbers on the left.

```
00100    PROGRAM Test
00200    VAR
00300      i:integer;
00400      x:real;
00500    BEGNI
00600      Read(i);
00700      Write(i); Writeln;
00800      FOR i:= 1 TO 10 DO Write('I am a duck');
00900
01000    END.
```

The messages from the compiler follow. The messages you obtain from other compilers may vary; however, virtually every compiler gives error messages that do not correspond to the "true" underlying errors.

```
PASCAL/LOTS: TEST
--------   PROGRAM TEST
00200/ 1  VAR
TEST            ∧
1.∧:  ";" EXPECTED     *** CHECK ALSO PREVIOUS LINE ***
--------   BEGNI
00600/ 1    READ(I);
TEST             ∧*∧  ∧
1.∧:  ILLEGAL SYMBOL  *** CHECK ALSO PREVIOUS LINE ***
2.∧:  IDENTIFIER ALREADY DECLARED
3.∧:  ":" EXPECTED
00700/ 1    WRITE(I); WRITELN;
TEST             ∧∧  ∧       ∧∧
1.∧:  ILLEGAL SYMBOL
2.∧:  IDENTIFIER ALREADY DECLARED
3.∧:  ":" EXPECTED
4.∧:  MORE THAN FOUR ERRORS IN THIS SOURCELINE
00800/ 1    FOR I:= 1 TO 10 DO WRITE('I AM A DUCK');
TEST              ∧
1.∧:  "BEGIN" EXPECTED     *** CHECK ALSO PREVIOUS LINE ***

  10 ERROR(S) DETECTED

  COMPILE RUNTIME: 00:00.756   ELAPSED: 00:00:02.8     134 CHARS
EXECUTION SUPPRESSED.


EXIT
```

As you can see, it took the compiler a long time to figure out that we had misspelled BEGIN in line 500. Since it never saw a BEGIN, the compiler thought we were still trying to define more variables, so it printed many spurious error messages. Out of the 10 errors detected, only the first and the last were real errors! The moral of the story: skim your error messages, write down the line numbers on which the compiler thinks there are problems, and carefully check those lines (and the surrounding lines) for errors. Do not worry about all of the error messages; simply fix a few of the problems, and try executing the program again.

Here is a detailed explanation of what happened and why:

1. We omitted the semicolon after PROGRAM TEST. The compiler does not realize this until it sees VAR. It prints line 200 along with the preceeding line. The dashes (--------) are printed instead of a line number for the preceeding line. The caret (∧) points to the place where the compiler first spotted the error. On the next line, 1.∧: ";" EXPECTED tells us what the compiler thinks the problem is. The *** CHECK ALSO PREVIOUS LINE *** is printed because the compiler thinks the problem may have occurred in the preceeding line.

2. We misspelled BEGIN, but since we are in the middle of our VAR declarations, the compiler thinks we were trying to define a new variable called BEGNI. Thus, not until the Read does the compiler realize that something is wrong. Again, it prints the preceeding line, and then line 600. The first caret points to Read and the line below it tells us that this first caret (1.∧:) is pointing

to an illegal symbol (since the compiler was expecting either a comma or a colon). Well, the compiler is confused, so it ignores the opening parenthesis (the things it ignores are underlined with asterisks) and examines the next word: I. Now, the compiler thinks we are trying to define a variable called I, but that variable is already defined, so we obtain the next message: 2.∧: IDENTIFIER ALREADY DECLARED. Still, the compiler does not give up. It looks ahead for a colon, which would continue the variable definition, but instead it finds a semicolon. The compiler then gives up and prints the third message: 3.∧":" EXPECTED.

3. Line 700 is misinterpreted in the same way as line 600. Notice that the compiler gives up after finding four errors on one line.

4. When the compiler sees the reserved word FOR it finally figures out that we are no longer declaring variables—we are trying to give instructions. It correctly concludes that we had left out a BEGIN so it prints the error: 1.∧: "BEGIN" EXPECTED. It prints the same error twice for some stupid reason!

After we fixed all of the errors, we executed the program, but typed the letters "ab" instead of an integer number. The computer prints the error message %? INPUT DATA ERROR IN FILE INPUT AT USER PC 514301 to tell us that the input data (the letters **ab**) on the file was incorrect. It then aborts the execution of our program!

```
PASSGO/LOTS: TEST    [ TEST       ] PAGE  1..
   O ERROR(S) DETECTED

   COMPILE RUNTIME: 00:00.185   ELAPSED: 00:00:01.7    218 CHARS
TEST      : EXECUTION

TO CONTINUE, HIT THE RETURN KEY *
ab

%?      INPUT DATA ERROR IN FILE INPUT AT USER PC 514301

EXIT
```

6-4 SEMANTIC ERRORS

The next classification of errors is semantic errors. A *semantic error* is not one of grammar but of *meaning*. Observe the difference between syntax and semantic errors in the following analogy. If someone asks you for directions you might say, "Go blocks 3 down, and more go turn 4 left blocks." This would be a syntactic error; the driver cannot understand what you are saying. On the other hand you might say, "Go down 3 blocks, turn left, and go 4 more blocks." These would be syntactically correct directions, but they could still be in error.

The first way that these instructions could be wrong is if it were physically impossible to follow the instructions. For example, the street could be only 2 blocks long. In this case, the driver could understand the instructions, but would be unable to carry them out. This type of error is called an *execution error* or a *runtime error*. Division by 0 is an example of this type of error in PASCAL.

The second way that the above directions could be wrong is if they directed the driver to the wrong location. The driver could understand and carry out the directions, but the end result would not be the desired one. We will call this type of error an *intent error*. The computer cannot detect intent errors. After all, it has no idea what we want it to do, but only what we tell it to do. For example, suppose we asked a grade school student to balance a checking account. We would have to tell the student how to do it. If the instructions were wrong, the student might have no way of knowing that. But when we looked at the results, we would have to verify that it was correct.

First, we have to detect that the results are wrong. This is not easy if we do not know what the results are supposed to be. (That is why we wrote the computer program in the first place!) Thus, we always test programs on simple data first, so that we can detect any semantic (runtime) errors. We will soon consider useful techniques for finding which instructions in a program are wrong, once we know that the computed results were in error.

6-5 INVARIANT ASSERTIONS

Although the title of this section is somewhat forbidding, we will discuss how to reason about what our programs do and how they do it. We will do this by making claims about the values of program variables at different times. These claims are called *invariant assertions*.

Let's consider the following program fragment.

```
statement₁;
baz := 8;                (* this is statement₂ *)
statement₃;
```

We can assert at the start of $statement_3$ that all variables other than **baz** have the same values as at the end of $statement_1$. The variable **baz**, on the other hand, has the value 8. Immediately after $statement_2$ (or immediately before $statement_3$), we can assert that **baz** = 8, regardless of the original value of **baz**.

Now, let us consider another program fragment.

```
statement₁;
foo := bar + 7;          (* this is statement₂ *)
statement₃;
```

Once again, only **foo** is changed by $statement_2$. That is, $statement_2$ does not change the value of **bar**, but only changes the value of **foo**. Immediately after $statement_2$, we can assert that **bar** = **foo** − 7, regardless of the original value of **bar**.

Let us consider the following problem.* A boy breeds goldfish as a hobby. He decides to sell all his fish. He does this in five steps:
1. He sells one half of his fish plus half a fish.
2. He sells a third of what remains, plus one third of a fish.
3. He sells a fourth of what remains, plus one fourth of a fish.
4. He sells a fifth of what remains, plus one fifth of a fish.

---

* From Martin Gardner, *aha! insight*, W. H. Freeman, San Francisco, 1978.

5.   He now has 11 goldfish left, which he sells.

Of course, no fish is divided or injured in any way. How many did he start with?

   To solve this problem, we first consider the problem of fractions of a fish. Suppose that we have 23 fish. One-fourth of that is $5\frac{3}{4}$ fish. That plus one-fourth of a fish is 6 fish. The second important realization is that you can go through the steps backward. Now, we need to determine the starting number x when we take away one-fifth of x and another one-fifth and get y, where $y = 11$. That is,

$$x - \left(\frac{1}{5}x + \frac{1}{5}\right) = y$$

Or, solving for x,

$$x = \frac{5y + 1}{4}$$

We can now write a program to compute the answer.

```
PROGRAM FishStory (input, output);
    VAR stepOne, stepTwo, stepThree, stepFour, start: integer;
BEGIN
    Read (start);
    Write ('Ending up with', start);
    stepFour := (5 * start + 1) DIV 4;
    (* stepFour - 1/5 stepFour - 1/5 = start *)
    stepThree := (4 * stepFour + 1) DIV 3;
    (* stepThree - 1/4 stepThree - 1/4 = stepFour *)
    stepTwo := (3 * stepThree + 1) DIV 2;
    (* stepTwo - 1/3 stepTwo - 1/3 = stepThree *)
    stepOne := (2 * stepTwo + 1) DIV 1;
    (* stepOne - 1/2 stepOne - 1/2 = stepTwo *)
    Writeln (', he started out with', stepOne);
END (* FishStory *).
```

The comments between pairs of statements are true assertions that we make after execution of the preceding statement. As we did with the first assertion, all assertions can be derived from the statements that precede them. We can read the assertions backward to see the steps described in the problem. In that way, we have *proven* that the answer of 59 must be the original number.

   We will return to the concept of invariant assertions in later chapters. Now, we will discuss other tools for debugging programs.

6-6 DEBUGGING TECHNIQUES

When we know that an answer is wrong, how do we find out the cause? To answer that, we should consider how the answer is wrong. Is it wrong for all input? Do some cases work and others fail? Were intermediate calculations correct?

   Let us first consider intermediate calculations. We can insert **Write** and **Writeln** instructions throughout the program to print the intermediate results. However, unless this is done carefully, a mass of incomprehensible numbers will be printed out. We should label the intermediate results much the same way we label ordinary output. It is also important to indicate which statement wrote which output. Here is an example:

```
IF debugging
   THEN Writeln ('In procedure Foo, before FOR bar loop: ',
       'x=', x, ', quad=', quad);
```

Notice that we have described where the statement was inserted. Also, we have labeled the printing of **x** and **quad**. Furthermore, we have made the **Writeln** statement conditional based on the value of **debugging**, a boolean constant. This way, when the program is debugged, we do not have to delete the **Writeln** statement from our program. We simply define **debugging** to be **true** or **false** depending on whether or not we want the debugging code executed. Notice that since **debugging** is boolean, it is already the right type for use in an IF condition. It is redundant to say IF **debugging** = **true**; IF **debugging** will do just fine.

The main advantage of this method is that possibly relevant information never has to be removed from a program once it has been added. We will never make the mistake of thinking a program is debugged, removing the debugging instructions, and then finding that the program is still in error! At this point, we would have to edit the program and resupply all of the instructions that printed out the debugging information.

To debug different kinds of things, we can condition the **Writeln** statement on one of several boolean constants. Alternately, the debugging code can be placed inside comments.

We can use a similar technique to verify that invariant assertions hold. Suppose we wanted to verify the assertion

```
(* stepThree - 1/4 stepThree - 1/4 = stepFour *)
```

from the previous section. We could use the following test.

```
IF NOT ( (stepThree - 1) * 3 DIV 4 = stepFour )
   THEN Writeln ('Assertion 2 failed: stepThree=',
       stepThree, ', stepFour=', stepFour);
```

Note that we have slightly modified the assertion to take into account the problems of integer arithmetic. Also, the assertion is always tested; we do not do it only when debugging.

Inclusion of assertion verification is an important way to ensure correct and reliable programs. It also makes the program check itself, and this is especially useful when the program is altered.

6-7 DEBUGGING PROCEDURES

There is a special technique for debugging well-procedurized programs. It is a variant of the IF-debugging method mentioned in the previous section. There is a school of thought that says that main programs (the executable part of our programs) should contain only very simple PASCAL instructions and procedure calls. Thus, debugging a program will consist mainly of debugging each procedure. As we have seen many times before (when procedures are involved), this school of thought splits one hard problem into several smaller ones that are easier to solve.

One useful way to debug a program composed of procedures is the *trace* method. For this method, each procedure has (at least) two sections that print debugging information. The first section appears at the beginning of the procedure body; the second appears at the end. When a procedure is called, it should print its name, the fact that it is entering the procedure, and the values of the variables to be used. Just before the procedure exits, it should print its name, the fact that it is exiting, and the values of the variables that were altered. For example, such a procedure might appear as

```
PROCEDURE Bazola;
    VAR declarations...
BEGIN
    Writeln ('Bazola - start');
    code for Bazola
    Writeln ('Bazola - end');
END (* Bazola *);
```

Depending on the nature of the declarations, code, and context, other things may be printed as well.

6-8 REWRITING PROGRAMS

Programmers learn much about a problem by writing a program to solve it. Frequently, while debugging a program, massive revisions are made. If this happens too often, the original "thread of reasoning" that the program was designed around will be lost. The program starts to look patched together and its structure will be lost. This would be an appropriate time to rewrite the program totally. Keep in mind that total rewriting of a program will not be as difficult as the original writing, since we have gained much useful information in our first attempt.

It takes considerable time to rewrite a program. It is difficult to say when a program has become so patched together that it needs rewriting. But, in the long run, it is frequently easier to rewrite a cleaner version of the program and debug that than to try to debug a hopelessly patched together program. This is especially true for programs that we are going to modify extensively.

6-9 INVARIANT ASSERTIONS AND IF STATEMENTS

We will now explore the use of invariant assertions when we are using IF statements. Consider the following statement template:

```
(* preassertion *)
IF condition
    THEN (* preassertion AND condition *)
        statement₁
        (* THEN-postassertion *)
    ELSE (* preassertion AND NOT condition *)
        statement₂
        (* ELSE-postassertion *);
(* IF-postassertion *)
```

Assume that the preassertion is true before executing the IF statement. Then before *statement*$_1$, we can assert both the preassertion and the condition. Similarly, before *statement*$_2$, we can assert both the preassertion and the negation of the condition. Anything that we can assert if we execute either *statement*$_1$ or *statement*$_2$, we can also assert as a IF-postassertion. That is, if something is true regardless of which branch we take of the IF statement, then it is true after the IF statement. In other words, the IF-postassertion is THEN-postassertion OR ELSE-postassertion.

Let us consider the example of printing three numbers in sorted order. Assume that there are values in **a**, **b**, and **c**. In order to find the smallest number, we need to compare these numbers. We first compare **a** with **b**. If **a** is less than **b**, either **a** or **c** is the smallest, so we compare them. Whichever is the smallest, we then compare the other two to find out the next smallest. Code to do this follows, with assertions in comments:

```
IF a < b
    THEN (*  a  <  b  *)
        IF a < c
            THEN (*  a  <  b,  a  <  c, a is smallest *)
                IF b < c
                    THEN (*  a  <  b  <  c  *)
                        Writeln (a, b, c)
                    ELSE (*  a  <  c  ≤  b  *)
                        Writeln (a, c, b)
                ELSE (*  c  ≤  a  <  b  *)
                    Writeln (c, a, b)
    ELSE (*  b  ≤  a  *)
        IF b < c
            THEN (*  b  ≤  a,  b  <  c, b is smallest *)
                IF a < c
                    THEN (*  b  ≤  a  <  c  *)
                        Writeln (b, a, c)
                    ELSE (*  b  <  c  ≤  a  *)
                        Writeln (b, c, a)
                ELSE (*  c  ≤  b  ≤  a  *)
                    Writeln (c, b, a);
```

Notice how an assertion from an enclosing IF statement is inherited by an inner IF statement. That is, the inner THEN clause knows the results of both tests. Of course, this is simply a formal way of explaining something we already knew.

Suppose, instead, that we wanted to sort four numbers. Clearly, such a sequence of IF statements could get quite unwieldy before too long. Another technique is to swap two numbers if they are out of order. We can do as many comparisons and swaps as needed to sort the numbers.

Assume that the four numbers are in **a**, **b**, **c**, and **d**, and that we want them printed in ascending order. Also assume that someone gives us the following code fragment, which we should verify.

```
IF a > b                   (* a b c d *)
   THEN SwapAB;            (* X       *)
IF b > c                   (* a b c d *)
   THEN SwapBC;            (*   X     *)
IF c > d                   (* a b c d *)
   THEN SwapCD;            (*     X   *)
IF a > b                   (* a b c d *)
   THEN SwapAB;            (* X       *)
IF b > c                   (* a b c d *)
   THEN SwapBC;            (*   X     *)
IF a > b                   (* a b c d *)
   THEN SwapAB;            (* X       *)
                           (* a b c d *)
Writeln(a, b, c, d);
```

We need to consider how to swap two values. We can swap **x** and **y** by

```
temp := x;
x := y;
y := temp;
```

Let us try to prove this program fragment. We need to prove two things. First, the resulting numbers must match the original numbers. Since the only thing we do is swap them, they must be the same numbers, although probably reordered. Second, the resulting numbers must be in ascending order. Looking at the first **IF**, we can assert that **a** must exceed **b** if the swap is done. After the swap, **a** is less than **b**. On the other hand, the swap is not done if **a** does not exceed **b**. Thus, whether or not the **THEN** part is done, we can assert that **a** is less than or equal to **b** after the first **IF** test. Similarly, we can assert **b** <= **c** after the second **IF** and **c** <= **d** after the third. We can write our program fragment now as the following:

```
IF a > b
   THEN SwapAB;
        (* Assert: a ≤ b *)
IF b > c
   THEN SwapBC;
        (* Assert: a ≤ c, b ≤ c *)
IF c > d
   THEN SwapCD;
        (* Assert: a ≤ d, b ≤ d, c ≤ d *)
IF a > b
   THEN SwapAB;
        (* Assert: a ≤ b, a ≤ d, b ≤ d, c ≤ d *)
IF b > c
   THEN SwapBC;
        (* Assert: a ≤ c, b ≤ c, a ≤ d, b ≤ d, c ≤ d *)
IF a > b
   THEN SwapAB;
        (* Assert: a ≤ b, a ≤ c, b ≤ c, a ≤ d, b ≤ d, c ≤ d *)
```

The first step looks straightforward, but the second assertion is not. Suppose we were to swap b and c. Then a is less than or equal to the old b, which is now c. Also, b is less than c because of the swap. If a swap was not done, then b is less than or equal to c. Furthermore, since a was less than b, by transitivity, it is less than or equal to c. We have succeeded in *proving* that our code for sorting actually works. We will use this technique of invariant assertions to reason about other constructs as we learn them.

Indefinite Loops

We have seen how to execute instructions a variable number of times. But we always had to know the number of iterations before entering the loop. In this chapter, we will learn another method for looping.

7-1 WHILE STATEMENT

We have already written a program that reads in a variable amount of data. We did that by first reading in a number telling how much data would be read. However, this technique is prone to error, because we have to count the amount of data. Since the computer is so much better at it, we should say, "Do it until there is no more data." Before we do this, though, we need a way of marking the end of the data. We can do this by choosing some value that cannot be a valid piece of data and testing for its occurrence. But we now need a way to repeat some code an unknown number of times. We have seen how the FOR statement does something a variable number of times, but we have to know beforehand the value of that variable number. What we want is a way to say, "While something is true, do it again." We do this by the WHILE statement:

```
WHILE condition DO
    statement;
```

Some examples are:

```
WHILE tired DO
    sleep;
WHILE NOT bored DO
    work;
WHILE timeLeft DO
    play;
```

There is a difference between the **IF** statement and the **WHILE** statement. The **IF** statement says, "Test the condition and, if it is true, do the statement *once*." The **WHILE** statement says, "Test the condition and, if it is true, do the statement and then test the condition again. If it is still true, do the statement again. Do this repeatedly until the condition is false. Then, continue with the first statement *following the loop*."

Let us look at an example:

```
number := 1;
WHILE number <> 5 DO
    BEGIN
        Write (number);
        number := number + 1;
    END; (* WHILE number <> 5 *)
Writeln (' Foo');
```

```
1       2       3       4 Foo
```

Notice that the variables in the condition must be initialized before entering the loop. Also notice that the loop is executed each and every time until the condition becomes **false**. If the condition were **false** to begin with, the loop would not be executed.

Suppose we want to print the odd numbers up to 10. Let us try:

```
number := 1;
WHILE number <> 10 DO
    BEGIN
        Write (number);
        number := number + 2;
    END (* WHILE number <> 10 *);
```

```
1       3       5       7       9       11      13...
```

Notice that **number** would *never* have the value 10. Therefore, the loop would execute forever! This is called an *infinite loop*. Instead, we should say

```
WHILE number < 10 DO ...
    or
WHILE number <= 10 DO ...
```

Never use <> when < or > will suffice.

Consider the following program fragment.

```
x := 5.0;
WHILE x > 0.0 DO
    BEGIN
        x := x - 1.0;
        Write (10.0 / x);
    END (* WHILE x > 0.0 *);
```

What is wrong with it? First, **x** is 5.0. Then, **x** > 0.0 so we go through the loop. We subtract 1.0 from **x** and get 4.0. We print 10.0 / 4.0 or 2.5. Then, **x** > 0.0 so we go through the loop. We subtract 1.0 from **x** and get 3.0. We print 10.0 / 3.0 or 3.333333. Then, **x** > 0.0 so we go through the loop. We subtract 1.0 from **x** and get 2.0. We print 10.0 / 2.0 or 5.0. Then, **x** > 0.0 so we go through the loop. We subtract 1.0 from **x** and get 1.0. We print 10.0 / 1.0 or 10.0. Then, **x** > 0.0 so we go through the loop. We subtract 1.0 from **x** and get 0.0. We then divide 10.0 / 0.0 and get a *divide exception* for dividing by 0. Notice that the test is done only *before* executing the loop each time. To make this work, we should do

```
x := 4.0;
WHILE x > 0.0 DO
    BEGIN
        Write (10.0 / x);
        x := x - 1.0;
    END (* WHILE x > 0.0 *);
```

Notice that the test is now done between computing a new **x** and using it. Why does reversing the order of the two statements in the WHILE loop put the test in the correct location? What we want is

compute new **x**
test
write
compute new **x**
test
write
compute new **x**
test
write

Therefore, what goes between successive tests is

```
Write (10.0 / x);
x := x - 1.0;
```

which is thus what goes in the loop.

It is important to note the following paradigm in using the WHILE loop.

Generate first value
WHILE *there are more*
   Process that value
   Generate the next one

In this way, we ensure that only *tested* values are processed.

  Some people view the **WHILE** loop as a combination of some of the properties of the **FOR** loop and the **IF** statement. It has the repetition and iteration properties of the **FOR** statement, but it also has a test similar to the **IF** statement. Most importantly, we know how many times a **FOR** statement will execute before it starts, but we do not know how many times the body of a **WHILE** loop will be executed. This is similar to not knowing *a priori* which branch of an **IF** statement will be executed.

Exercises

1. What is the output of the following section of code? Assume that the variables **sum** and **counter** have been declared to be **integer**s.

```
sum := 33;
counter := 1;
WHILE  counter < 12  DO
    BEGIN
        sum := sum + counter;
        counter := counter + 2;
    END;  (* WHILE counter < 12 *)
Writeln ('Some interesting numbers are:', counter,
    ' and', sum);
```

2. What is output by the following? Assume **number** has type **integer**.

```
number := 0;
WHILE  number <= 5  DO
    BEGIN
        number := number + 1;
        Write (number);
    END;  (* WHILE number <= 5 *)
```

3. What is the output? All variables have type **integer**.

```
number := 17;
exponent := 0;
power := 1;
WHILE  power < number  DO
    BEGIN
        exponent := exponent + 1;
        power := power * 2;
    END (* WHILE power < number *);
Writeln ('2 to the exponent ', exponent :1, ' exceeds ',
    number :2);
```

4. What is the output? All variables have type `integer`.

```
number := 1;
WHILE  number <> 10  DO
    BEGIN
        Writeln (number);
        number := number * 2;
    END;  (* WHILE number <> 10 *)
Writeln (number);
```

5. What is output from the following? Assume that variables `arrived1` and `arrived2` have type `boolean`, and all other variables have type `integer`.

```
dest1 := 15;       dest2 := 27;        (* destinations *)
locat1 := 20;      locat2 := 20;       (* locations *)
arrived1 := false; arrived2 := false;  (* whether arrived *)
WHILE  (NOT arrived1) AND (NOT arrived2)  DO
    BEGIN
        locat1 := locat1 - 1;    (* moves one unit per time *)
        locat2 := locat2 + 2;    (* moves twice as fast! *)
        arrived1 := (locat1 <= dest1);
        arrived2 := (locat2 >= dest2);
        Writeln ('Travelers are at ', locat1 : 2, ' and ',
            locat2 : 2);
    END;  (* WHILE (NOT arrived1) AND (NOT arrived2) *)
Writeln ('The final positions of the two travelers are ',
        locat1 : 2, ' and ', locat2 : 2);
```

6. Here is a misconception some people have. What does this segment print?

```
t := 1;
WHILE t = 1 DO
    BEGIN
        Write ('Afghanistan');
        t:= 2;
        Write (' Banana Stand');
    END; (* WHILE t = 1 *)
```

7. What can we conclude about a WHILE loop body that does not alter any of the variables mentioned in the condition?

7-2 REASONING ABOUT PROGRAMS

It might be helpful to consider WHILE loops in a more formal way. We will consider the following template in this discussion

$statement_1$;

$\qquad$ (* assert: *invariant* *)

WHILE *condition* DO

$\qquad$ (* assert: *invariant* AND *condition* *)

$\qquad statement_2$

$\qquad$ (* assert: *invariant* *);

$statement_3$;

$\qquad$ (* assert: *invariant* AND NOT *condition* *)

First, we can assert that the condition is true at the beginning of the body of the WHILE loop, that is, immediately before $statement_2$. This is similar to observing that the IF condition must be true at the beginning of the THEN clause of an IF statement. Of course, this is due to the fact that we only execute the loop when the condition is true. Second, we can assert the negation of the condition just after the WHILE loop, because we stop executing the loop only when the condition is false.

The invariant is more complicated. Suppose that we know the invariant is true right before the loop. This means that the first time through the loop, just before the loop body, the invariant will still be true, and so will the condition. Suppose that we also know that if the invariant and condition are true before the loop body, then the invariant will be true at the end of the loop body. This means that all subsequent times through the loop, the invariant and condition will be true at the start of the loop. It also means that the invariant will be true and the condition false right after the WHILE loop.*

Consider the problem of finding the greatest common divisor of two numbers. Historically, this problem is very important; it gave rise to the first algorithm ever devised explicitly. This was done by Euclid over 2000 years ago. The greatest common divisor of two numbers is the largest number that divides both numbers. We will use $\gcd(a,b)$ to symbolize the greatest common divisor of two numbers. For example, $\gcd(10,15) = 5$, $\gcd(120,336) = 24$, and $\gcd(5,9) = 1$.

The algorithm has a structure similar to that of Fibonacci numbers. Assume we want to determine $\gcd(a,b)$. Of course, a and b must both be positive. If q is the quotient b DIV a, and r is the remainder b MOD a, then we know that

$$b = aq + r \qquad (0 \le r < a)$$

If $r = 0$, then $\gcd(a,b) = a$. Otherwise, we determine $\gcd(r,a)$.

There are three things we will have to prove.

1. The algorithm terminates.
2. The number obtained divides both original numbers.
3. The number obtained is the largest such number; that is, any number that divides both original numbers also divides our presumed greatest common divisor.

A few simple facts from number theory will be useful in our proof. First, we use the notation $a \mid b$ to mean a divides b evenly (that is, with no remainder).

---

* Readers familiar with mathematical induction will notice the similarity of the first and second "supposes" to the basis and induction steps of mathematical induction, respectively. The basis step proves something for the initial case, such as $n = 1$. The induction step assumes it true for $n = i$, and proves it for $n = i + 1$.

Second, if $a \mid b$ and $b \mid c$, then $a \mid c$. Third, if $g \mid a$ and $g \mid b$, then $g \mid a + b$ and $g \mid a - b$. Fourth, if $a \mid b$, then $a \mid bx$ for all integers x. Fifth, if $a \mid b$ and $b \mid a$, then $a = b$ or $a = -b$. From the third and fourth facts, we know that $\gcd(a, b)$ divides $b - aq$, since it divides both a and b.

Now, we can proceed to programming and proving the algorithm.

```
PROGRAM GCD (input, output);
    VAR olda, oldb, a, b, r: integer;
BEGIN
    Read (olda, oldb);
    WHILE (olda > 0) AND (oldb > 0) DO
        BEGIN
            Write ('GCD (', olda, ',', oldb, ')=');
            a := olda;
            b := oldb;
            r := b MOD a;
            (* assertion 1: gcd(a,b) = gcd(olda,oldb) *)
            WHILE r > 0 DO
                BEGIN
                    (* assertion 2: r > 0 and
                        gcd(a,b) = gcd(olda,oldb) *)
                    (* assertion 3: gcd(r,a) = gcd(olda,oldb) *)
                    b := a;
                    (* assertion 4: gcd(r,b) = gcd(olda,oldb) *)
                    a := r;
                    (* assertion 5: gcd(a,b) = gcd(olda,oldb) *)
                    r := b MOD a;
                    (* assertion 6: gcd(a,b) = gcd(olda,oldb) *)
                END (* WHILE r <> 0 *);
            (* assertion 7: r = 0 and gcd(a,b) = gcd(olda,oldb) *)
            (* assertion 8: a = gcd(olda,oldb) *)
            Writeln (a);
            Read (olda, oldb);
        END (* WHILE we have valid input *);
END (* GCD *).
```

Assertion 1 is true since **a** equals **b** and **olda** equals **oldb**. Assertion 2 derives from assertions 1 and 6, as well as the condition of the WHILE loop. For assertion 3, we must do a little mathematics. Since $r = b - aq$, we know that $\gcd(a, b)$ divides r. Since $b = aq + r$, we know that $\gcd(r, a)$ divides b. This means that $\gcd(a, b) = \gcd(r, a)$.* We can conclude $\gcd(r, a) = \gcd(olda, oldb)$. Assertion 4 substitutes b for a, as they are equal. Assertion 5 does the same with a for r. Assertion 6 is the same as assertion 5. From assertions 2 and 6, and the WHILE condition, we get assertion 7. Since $r = 0$, $a \mid b$. Since $a \mid a$, and nothing bigger does,

$$a = \gcd(a, b) = \gcd(olda, oldb)$$

and this is assertion 8. We have proven that if the euclidean algorithm terminates, it will produce the correct solution.

---

* We can show this by considering that $\gcd(a, b)$ divides r and a and, therefore, $\gcd(r, a)$. Similarly, $\gcd(r, a)$ divides $\gcd(a, b)$. That means they are equal.

We still need to prove that the algorithm terminates. Notice that each time through the loop, we compute **r** to be less than **a**. We then set **a** to the value **r**. This means that each time through the loop, **a** has a smaller value. Since **r** cannot be negative, it must eventually become 0, and that is when the algorithm terminates.

Due to its difficulty, we usually do not go through a formal proof like the one we just did. But the concepts can be used in informal reasoning about the program.

Let us summarize the most important facts about **WHILE** assertions. First, just inside the loop, we can assert that the condition is true. Second, just after the loop, we can assert that the condition is false. Third, we can often conclude other things being true at the end of the loop.

Exercises

1. Notice that in the body of the loop, **b** becomes **a** and **a** becomes **r**. What if we replaced the body of the loop by

    ```
    b := r;
    r := b MOD a;
    ```

    Would the algorithm still be correct? That is, would it terminate and produce the correct value?

2. What happens if we replace the body of the loop by

    ```
    b := r;
    r := a MOD b;
    ```

    Would the algorithm still be correct? That is, would it terminate and produce the correct value? Is the correct value in **b** at the end of the loop, instead of in **a**?

7-3 VARIABLE-LENGTH INPUT: SIGNAL-VALUE METHOD

Our programs must often read data from an input file without knowing the size of the file beforehand. For example, suppose that we want to write a program that reads in a list of real numbers from an input file and averages them. We have seen how to do this by first reading how many numbers there will be.

It is usually a much better idea to set up a program so that it simply continues to read data values until there are no more, regardless of the exact number. One technique for doing this makes use of a *signal value*, which is a special data value placed at the end of the input file that lets the computer know when the entire file has been processed. This signal value is also known as a *sentinel*.

For example, if the data values to be averaged are exam scores in the range 0.0 to 100.0, then a value of -1.0 could be placed at the end of the input file to indicate that there is no more data. We might write this as

```
PROGRAM Average (input, output);
    (* This version uses the SIGNAL VALUE technique INCORRECTLY *)
    CONST
        endOfData = -1.0;

    VAR
        sum,                        (* the running sum of the nos. *)
        score:    real;            (* an individual data value *)
        count:    integer;         (* the no. of data values in *)
                                    (* the input file *)

BEGIN    (* main program *)
    sum := 0.0;
    count := 0;
    WHILE score <> endOfData DO
        BEGIN
            (* this loop will compute the sum *)
            (* and count data values *)
            Read (score);
            Writeln ('The data value is ', score);
            sum := sum + score;
            count := count + 1;
        END; (* WHILE *)
    Writeln ('There are ', count, ' values.');
    IF count > 0
        THEN Writeln ('The average is ', sum / count);
END  (* Average *).
```

However, we have a problem. First, the variable **score** is not initialized when the **WHILE** loop is first executed. We can fix this by preceding the **WHILE** loop with the instruction **Read (score)**. This will initialize **score** to the first data value in the input file.

There is *still* something wrong, though! If we run our program after this modification, we notice that the first input value has been ignored. The signal value is also included in the sum. The **Read (score)** instruction inside the loop should be moved to the end. Now, each time through the loop, we read the data value that will be processed the *next* time through the loop. This also corrects the error of adding the signal value into the sum. Convince yourself that the correct version of the program appears as

```
PROGRAM  Average  (input, output);
    (* This version uses the SIGNAL VALUE technique CORRECTLY *)
    CONST
        endOfData = -1.0;

    VAR
        sum,                (* the running sum of the nos. *)
        score:    real;    (* an individual data value *)
        count:    integer; (* the no. of data values in the *)
                            (* input file *)
```

```
BEGIN     (* main program *)
    sum := 0.0;
    count := 0;
    (* Let's read in the first data value and echo it *)
    Read (score);
    WHILE score <> endOfData DO     (* "<>" means "not equal to" *)
        BEGIN         (* This loop will compute the sum and count *)
                      (* data values.  Each time thru, the NEXT  *)
                      (*  data value is read in and echoed.       *)
            Writeln ('The data value is ', score);
            sum := sum + score;
            count := count + 1;
            Read (score);
        END; (* WHILE *)
    Writeln ('There are ', count, ' values.');
    IF count > 0
        THEN Writeln ('The average is ', sum / count);
END (* Average *).
```

7-4 REPEAT STATEMENT

The WHILE statement tests each and every time before executing the loop. What happens if you want to do something once and then test. For example, suppose we want to compute our own square root using Newton's method. To do this, we start with a guess. To obtain the next guess, we take the average of the previous guess and the number whose square root we want divided by the previous guess. We iterate this way until two consecutive guesses are closer than a certain threshold. One way to test whether two consecutive guesses are close enough is to see if they differ by at most epsilon, an appropriate small threshold. We do this by taking the absolute value of the difference and comparing it to epsilon. The absolute value of a number has the same magnitude as the number but a nonnegative sign. For example, Abs (5) is 5, Abs (-5) is 5, and Abs (0) is 0. We could say

```
number := 3.0;
guess := 1.0;
prevGuess := 0.0;
WHILE Abs (guess - prevGuess) > epsilon DO
    BEGIN
        prevGuess := guess;
        guess := (number/prevGuess + prevGuess) / 2.0;
    END (* WHILE guesses not close *);
```

Well, instead we could say

```
number := 3.0;
guess := 1.0;
REPEAT
    prevGuess := guess;
    guess := (number/prevGuess + prevGuess) / 2.0;
UNTIL Abs (guess - prevGuess) <= epsilon;
```

Note that the form of the statement is

```
REPEAT
    statement₁;
    statement₂;
    statement₃;
        ⋮
    statementₙ;        (* semicolon optional *)
UNTIL condition
```

Note that the following is redundant.

```
REPEAT
    BEGIN
        statement₁;
        statement₂;
        statement₃;
            ⋮
        statementₙ;        (* semicolon optional *)
    END (* REPEAT *);        (* semicolon optional *)
UNTIL condition
```

Also notice that the sense of the test is reversed; we do the loop as long as the test is **false**. Furthermore, **WHILE** does *test-loop, test-loop,* etc., whereas **REPEAT** does *loop-test, loop-test,* etc. The **REPEAT** loop ensures that the instructions are executed at least once regardless of the conditions.

Exercise

1. If there wasn't a **REPEAT** loop, how could you use a **WHILE** loop to do the same thing?

More Input and Output

We will now concern ourselves with the finer points of input and output. These include formatted output, character input and output, and other topics.

8-1 FORMATTED OUTPUT

Suppose we say

```
Write ('The number is', 15, 'but the real number is', 15.0, '.');
```

```
The number is        15but the real number is 1.500000000E+01.
```

Notice that there is no space between `15` and `but`, nor is there one between `1.500000000E+01` and period. We probably do want a space in the first case, and do not want a space in the second. Also notice the large amount of space between `is` and `15`. Each integer is allocated 10 columns even though it may need less. (The number of allocated columns may differ from implementation to implementation, but is constant for any particular implementation.) It is printed *right-justified* in its field. (A *field* is the columns allocated to a particular value.) This fixed field width is useful for printing tables, since all of the numbers will line up. Consider what would happen if you wrote 9 numbers in a square. Certainly,

```
        1       234        12
     4096       497      3227
  1234567         2        12
```

looks better than

```
1  234 12
4096 497 3227
1234567 2 12
```

We can change the allocation of columns. We say,

Write (*value* : *number of columns*);

to print the value with the specified number of columns. For example, **Write** (15:2) will print 15, while **Write** (15:3) will print ⊔15, where ⊔ is the symbol for a space. This is referred to as the *colon convention*. If the number needs more columns to print than specified, the number of columns is expanded enough to contain the number, according to the new standard. For example, **Write** (123:1) will print 123.

Real numbers print in *scientific notation*. Thus, the real number 15.0 prints as 1.500000000E+01. The E means "times 10 to the"; the above number really means 1.5×10^1, or 15.0. In some PASCAL implementations, the E+00 does not print. There is also a colon convention for real numbers. We say,

Write (*value* : *total number of positions* : *number of decimal places*);

Therefore, **Write** (15.123 : 6 : 2) will print ⊔15.12.

Let us consider further the format of real numbers printed using double colons. The number after the first colon—call it t—tells how many columns the number is to take up. The number after the second colon—call it d—tells how many digits are to be printed after the decimal point. From t and d, we can derive the number of columns to the left of the decimal point: there are $t - d - 1$ columns to the left of the decimal point. The sign—if negative—and the integral part of the real number go in these columns. As with integers, the field is expanded as necessary if there aren't enough columns. If there are too many decimal places (significant digits to the right of the decimal point), the additional ones are ignored. The following table illustrates these rules.

```
Write ( 15.126: 3: 2);     prints 15.12
Write ( 15.126: 4: 2);     prints 15.12
Write ( 15.126: 5: 2);     prints 15.12
Write ( 15.126: 6: 2);     prints ⊔15.12
Write ( 15.126: 7: 2);     prints ⊔⊔15.12
Write (-15.126: 3: 2);     prints -15.12
Write (-15.126: 4: 2);     prints -15.12
Write (-15.126: 5: 2);     prints -15.12
Write (-15.126: 6: 2);     prints -15.12
Write (-15.126: 7: 2);     prints ⊔-15.12
```

Some old PASCAL implementations print asterisks if not enough columns are allocated to the left of the decimal point to handle the integral part of the number. In this nonstandard case, the entire field is filled with the number of asterisks specified by the number between the colons. Similarly, these nonstandard versions print asterisks if there are not enough columns to print an integer.

8-2 READ AND READLN

There is an input cursor that indicates where the computer will next read. We will symbolize this input cursor by ☞, occasionally with a subscript to denote the location of the input cursor at different times. When you read an integer, real, or boolean, all leading blanks and ends of lines are skipped until a nonblank is reached. If we are reading an integer, the nonblank character must be a sign or digit; otherwise, the program abnormally terminates with an error message. After the optional sign, all successive numeric characters are read until a nonnumeric character is reached. The input cursor then points to the first nonnumeric character. If we are reading a real number, the same is true except that a decimal point may appear within the number and it may contain an E followed by an optional sign and an integer exponent. If we are reading a boolean, the input must contain either **true** or **false**. (Many implementations do not allow reading of booleans, as it is not required in standard PASCAL.) The string **true** or **false** must be followed by a blank, a carriage return, or some other non-alphanumeric character.*

The **Readln** statement differs from the **Read** statement in that it causes the remainder of the current line to be ignored after the requested variables have been read. For example, assume that **r1** is a real variable, **b1** is boolean, and **i1**, **i2**, and **i3** are integer variables.

```
Read (r1);              (* location 1 *)
Readln (b1);            (* location 2 *)
Write (r1, b1);         (* location 3 *)
Read (i1, i2, i3);      (* location 4 *)
Writeln (i2);           (* location 5 *)
Write (i3);             (* location 6 *)
```

Assume the previous program fragment is given the following input data.

```
        5.0 ☞₁ true garbage
☞₂     6    7
       8 ☞₄ 9 10
```

```
       5.000000000     true ✎₃ 7
✎₅           8    ✎₆
```

---

* An alphanumeric character is a letter or a number. On some systems, letters are considered to include $, #, and @ for historical reasons.

The variables will have these values at the end of the fragment.

r1 = 5.0   b1 = true   i1 = 6   i2 = 7   i3 = 8

The input cursors, 👁, and output cursors, ✎, tell where they will be after executing the statements listed above at the end of the corresponding location. For example, after doing the `Read (r1)` instruction, the input cursor will be at 👁₁; after doing the `Write (r1, b1)` instruction, the output cursor will be at ✎₃.

Exercises

In order to save space, only the relevant segments of the program are given. Specify what is printed, if anything, and the value of each variable at the end of the fragment. Also annotate the input to indicate where the input cursor is at the end of each `Read` or `Readln` instruction and where the output cursor is at the end of each `Write` or `Writeln` instruction. *Remember that type checking is done on input, so be sure to point out type errors.* Use the example in the text as a model. Assume the following declarations:

```
VAR
     re1, re2, re3: real;
     in1, in2, in3: integer;
     bo1, bo2, bo3: boolean;
```

1. **Fragment**
```
Read (in1); (* 1 *)
Readln;  (* 2 *)
FOR i := 1 TO in1 DO
    Readln (in3);  (* 3 *)
```
Input
```
2  5  6  7  GEORGE
6  9
1
17  false
```

2. **Fragment**
```
Read (bo1, in1, bo2, in2);  (* 1 *)
Readln (re1); (* 2 *)
Read (in3);  (* 3 *)
Read (re2);  (* 4 *)
```
Input
```
false  6true
9  5.0E3  7
4  false
99
```

3. **Fragment**
```
Read (in1, in2);  (* 1 *)
Readln (in3);  (* 2 *)
Read (re1);  (* 3 *)
Read (in1);  (* 4 *)
```
Input
```
1  5  9  5.0E3
5.0 E3
17
```

4. **Fragment**
```
Read (in1);  (* 1 *)
Write (in1);  (* 2 *)
in2 := in1 * 7;
Write (in1, in2);  (* 3 *)
Read (in1);  (* 4 *)
Write (in1, in2);  (* 5 *)
Read (in3);  (* 6 *)
```
Input
```
5  7  9
```

5. **Fragment**   **Input**
```
Read (in1);  (* 1 *)                    6
FOR i := 1 TO in1 DO                     3.14159
   IF i = 1                              1.7E1    690.0E-1
      THEN Read (re1)   (* 2 *)
   ELSE IF i = 2
      THEN Read (re2)   (* 3 *)
   ELSE IF i = 3
      THEN Read (re3)   (* 4 *)
   ELSE Writeln ('i = ', i, ' is too big');  (* 5 *)
Write ('error');  (* 6 *)
```

8-3 CHARACTER VARIABLES AND INPUT-OUTPUT

We have alluded to the existence of character variables. Let us consider them now. You can declare a variable to be of type **char**.

```
VAR
    ch: char;
```

Each character variable can hold a single character at a time. Just as numeric variables can hold only one number, putting a new character into a character variable obliterates the old one. We write a character value or *literal* by enclosing the single character in single quotes, such as **'Q'**. Characters are ordered, so relational operators can be applied to them.

```
'A' < 'B' < 'C' < 'D' < ... < 'Z'
'0' < '1' < '2' < '3' < ... < '9'
```

However, these characters do not have to be consecutive; for example, on some IBM machines there are several characters between **'I'** and **'J'**. The numbers *are*, however, consecutive. We can use character variables in **FOR** loops.

```
FOR ch := 'A' TO 'Z' DO
    Write (ch);
```

ABCDEFGHIJKLMNOPQRSTUVWXYZ

The result may be different on IBM machines.

8-3-1 Reading and Writing Characters

To read a single character, we say **Read (ch)**, where **ch** is a character variable. The character to which the input cursor is pointing is read into **ch** and the input cursor is advanced one column. If the character is the last one on the line, the input cursor now points to the end-of-line character. We should generally *not* read the end-of-line character.*   If you do, you will get a space and move to the first character on the next line according to the new PASCAL standard. Instead, we *should* do a `Readln` to get to the beginning of the next line.

Now that we have been able to get this character into our computer, we may also want to write it. We do that by saying `Write (ch)`. The single character in `ch` will be written where the output cursor is and the output cursor will be advanced one column.

For example, suppose we want to read in and print a list of words. Each word is followed by a space, and the last word is followed by a space and a period. We want the output words to be on separate lines. A program to do this might appear as

```
WHILE we haven't reached a period yet DO
    WHILE we haven't reached a space yet DO
        BEGIN
            Read (ch);
            Write (ch);
        END; (* WHILE no space *)
    Writeln;
```

There are several problems with this approach. First, we cannot test against `ch` the first time into the two `WHILE` statements because we have not initialized it yet. It then seems appropriate to put a character other than a blank or period into `ch`. The next problem is that we read the character, write it, and *then* test whether or not it is a blank. Instead, we should test it after reading it but before writing it. Thus, we want the following sequence:

read
test
write
read
test
write
read
test
write
etc.

Notice that there is a write and a read between successive tests. Strange as it may seem, reversing the order of the read and the write statements will fix *that* problem. But now, we have introduced another problem! We write a character without having read one. Instead of priming the loop with any arbitrary character, why not read a real one from the input? Now our program appears as

---

* Soon we will learn how to test for end of line using `Eoln`.

```
PROGRAM CopyWords (input, output);
    VAR
        ch: char;
BEGIN
    Read (ch);        (* prime the pump *)
    WHILE ch <> '.' DO      (* not end of input *)
        BEGIN
            WHILE ch <> ' ' DO       (* not end of word *)
                BEGIN
                    Write (ch);
                    Read (ch);
                END; (* WHILE not space *)
            Writeln;
        END; (* WHILE not period *)
END (* CopyWords *).
```

There is still a bug in the program. What happens when we read a space? We then fall out of the WHILE ch <> ' ' loop, do a Writeln, and test for a period. It is not a period; it is still a blank. We then test for a blank, and lo and behold, it still is, so we do not do that loop at all, but go straight through to Writeln. It is in an *infinite loop*. We forgot to go on to the next character. The repaired program becomes

```
PROGRAM CopyWords (input, output);
    VAR
        ch: char;
BEGIN
    Read (ch);        (* prime the pump *)
    WHILE ch <> '.' DO      (* not end of input *)
        BEGIN
            WHILE ch <> ' ' DO       (* not end of word *)
                BEGIN
                    Write (ch);
                    Read (ch);
                END; (* WHILE not space *)
            Writeln;
            Read (ch);        (* read the char after space *)
        END; (* WHILE not period *)
END (* CopyWords *).
```

Consider the following input.

```
Pascal is a good language to learn .
```

```
Pascal
is
a
good
language
to
learn
```

8-4 EOF AND EOLN

Notice that the input format in the last example differs from the output format. Suppose we want to copy text, character for character, line for line. We should first consider the format of a file.

A text file consists of a series of lines. Each line consists of a series of characters terminated by a special end-of-line character. At the end of the file—after the last end-of-line character—is an end-of-file character. On an interactive system, the end-of-line character is usually entered by typing a carriage return, and there is some designated end-of-file character, such as control-Z. On a batch system using cards, an end-of-line character is automatically considered to follow the last character on the card; after the last card in the file, an end-of-file character is appended to the end of the file.

We need a way to test for being at the end of the line. We can do so by looking at the boolean value of Eoln, which is true when the input cursor points to the end of the line and false otherwise. The boolean Eoln is declared automatically; we should not include it in a VAR section. Thus, to read a line and copy it verbatim, we can do this:

```
WHILE NOT Eoln DO
    BEGIN
        Read (ch);
        Write (ch);
    END; (* WHILE NOT Eoln *)
Readln;
Writeln;
```

Notice the order of read and write. It is attributable to Eoln, which peeks at the next character before we read it. To read it, we must do a Read or a Readln.

We now need a way to test for the end of file. To do this, we look at the boolean Eof, which is true when the input cursor points to the end of the file and false otherwise. Thus, to copy the entire file, we can change the above to

```
WHILE NOT Eof DO
    BEGIN
        WHILE NOT Eoln DO
            BEGIN
                Read (ch);
                Write (ch);
            END; (* WHILE NOT Eoln *)
        Readln;
        Writeln;
    END; (* WHILE NOT Eof *)
```

In computer memory, each line of a file is followed by a special *end-of-line marker* that tells the computer where the line ends. After the last such marker, there is also a special *end-of-file marker* that tells the computer where the file ends. The boolean `Eoln` is **true** when the input cursor is situated exactly at the end-of-line marker. Similarly, the boolean `Eof` is **true** when the cursor is situated exactly at the end-of-file marker.

There is one tricky aspect of `Eof`: it cannot be **true** at the end of the last line, but can only be **true** just after the last end-of-line character is read. Therefore, always make sure each test for `Eof` occurs after a `Readln`. Also, remember not to do a `Read` at the end of the line. Do a `Readln` first. What happens if there are spaces after the last number in the line, which we have just read? We will have `Eoln` **false**, and thus a `Read` will unexpectedly bring us to the next line. This is disastrous if we are on the last line of the input file! The moral is, "Do not put spaces after the last number on any line."*

Suppose we want to write a program to copy integers, keeping them grouped into lines the same way that they were in the input. It is very easy to model this program after the last one.

```
WHILE NOT Eof DO
    BEGIN
        WHILE NOT Eoln DO
            BEGIN
                Read (number);
                Write (number);
            END; (* WHILE NOT Eoln *)
        Readln;
        Writeln;
    END; (* WHILE NOT Eof *)
```

What assumptions have we made? We have assumed that there are no spaces after the last number on each line. What happens if there are spaces after the last number on any line that is not the last line? That line will be joined with its successor in the output. What happens if there are spaces after the last number in the file? The program abnormally terminates because it tries to read a number after the last number in the file.

---

* There is a way to skip over these unwanted spaces, but it involves use of advanced PASCAL features.

8-5 SUMMARY OF INPUT

The input file is read character by character. We will refer to the next character to be read as the location of the input cursor. The way we read input is dependent on the type of variable being read. The four types of variables are `integer`, `real`, `char`, and `boolean`.*

1. `Integer` input. When reading an integer variable, we skip over all blanks and ends of lines until we reach a nonblank character. If this nonblank character is not a digit or a sign (+ or −) or if we have reached the end of the file, then an error will be reported. Otherwise, we then read all digits until we reach a blank or other nonnumeric character. These digits (and sign) taken together form the number. The input cursor is set to the first blank or other non-numeric character.

2. `Real` input. When reading a real variable, we again skip over all blanks and ends of lines until we reach a nonblank character. The next character must be numeric or a sign; otherwise, an error condition is reported. The number may be of the same form as one within a PASCAL program, without any spaces. For example, all of the following are acceptable: `5.0`, `-5.0`, `+5.00E3`, `5.0E-2`. The number must include a decimal point and one digit after the decimal point; otherwise, it will have the syntax of an integer, which is not acceptable. The input cursor is set to the first blank or other character that does not fit.

3. `Boolean` input. When reading a boolean variable, we again skip over all blanks and ends of lines until we reach a nonblank character. The next characters must be `true` or `false`. The input cursor is left pointing to the following character, which must be a blank or other delimiter, such as, a comma or a period. Not all systems allow reading of `boolean` variables, as it is not required in the new standard.

4. `Char` input. When reading a character variable, we read the very next character at the input cursor. We do *not* skip over blank characters. The input cursor is set to the following character. Note that it is not correct to read past the end of the line. Instead, read until `Eoln` and then do a `Readln` to get to the next line. The computer will not warn you when you read past the end of line, but it will warn you when you read past the end of file.†

If there are spaces following the last number or boolean on a line, notice that `Eoln` will not be true after reading that value. Also note that `Eof` will not be true until the last line has been `Readln`ed. After performing a `Readln` on the last line, `Eof` becomes true, but `Eoln` *remains* true.

8-6 VARIABLE-LENGTH INPUT USING EOF METHOD

We have discussed two techniques for handling variable-length input: (1) reading the number of values there are, and (2) following the last value with a signal

---

* This summary is due to Jeff Vitter.

† If you try to read the end-of-line character, you will get a space. You should think long and hard before taking advantage of this fact.

value. Another technique utilizes the idea of the *end-of-line* and *end-of-file* boolean values. We will use these booleans, which we recall are Eoln and Eof, respectively, to rewrite the program from Section 7-3 that takes the average of all values in a data file.

```
PROGRAM  Average (input, output);
    VAR
        sum,                 (*  the running sum of the nos. *)
        score:   real;       (*  an individual data value *)
        count:   integer;    (*  the no. of data values in the *)
                             (*  input file *)

BEGIN  (* main program *)
    sum := 0.0;
    count := 0;
    WHILE NOT Eof DO
    BEGIN   (* the outer loop is executed once for each line *)
            (* in the input file *)
        WHILE NOT Eoln DO
            BEGIN   (* this inner loop is executed once *)
                    (* for each data value *)
                Read (score);
                Writeln ('Data value =  ', score);
                sum := sum + score;
                count := count + 1;
            END; (* WHILE NOT Eoln *)
        Readln;
    END; (* WHILE NOT Eof *)
    Writeln ('There are ', count : 3, ' data values.');
    IF count > 0
        THEN  Writeln ('The average is ',  sum / count);
END (* Average *).
```

The purpose of the **Readln** statement is to skip past the end-of-line marker. For this technique to work, there must be *no* additional blanks following the last data value; **Eof** would still be **false** when the input cursor is situated at an additional blank following the last data value. The computer would then give an error message when the next **Read (score)** instruction is executed, since there are no longer any real numbers to be read.

Procedures,
Parameters, and Scope

We will now learn about some features of procedures. We will explore how to get information into and out of a procedure. We will also learn about the use of main procedure variables by internal procedures.

9-1 PROCEDURES

Thus far we have considered the major ideas of programming languages: variables, control structures, and procedures. Procedures exist even in languages with primitive control structures (such as FORTRAN) and in languages without regular variables (such as pure LISP*).

Why are procedures so important? A typical program is seen by many people other than the original programmer; occasionally, thousands may see it. Some of them even change it. Procedures make life easier for both the programmer and the program reader.

Why use procedures? We use procedures to avoid duplicate code and achieve shorter programs. Procedures are also a conceptual tool to break up a problem into independently solvable subproblems. They also serve as a documentation tool by breaking up the program into pieces which can be read and understood independently.

We subscribe to the black box idea. We want to be able to solve a problem while ignoring what is going on around it. This self-imposed discipline of mind is needed to write programs of any size, especially large ones. Procedures offer a formalism in which that sort of idea can be expressed.

---

* Most LISP programmers, however, use versions that *do* have regular variables.

9-1-1 Procedure Parameters

We have already seen that procedures are a powerful programming tool. In this section, we will discuss an extension to the concept of procedures, called *procedures with parameters.*

The concept of a procedures having parameters is common to everyday life. For example, a cashier knows how to give change from a purchase. To do so, the cashier needs to know how much the items cost and how much the customer has paid. The cashier can then calculate the amount of change to give and what bills and coins to give the customer. Another example is the steps in a recipe. A step such as "fold the egg whites into the batter" takes two parameters, the egg whites and the batter.

Suppose that we wish to write a PASCAL program that prints 10 triangles, alternating between triangles having 6 rows of asterisks and those having 7 rows of X's. We could write

```
PROGRAM TenTriangles (output);
    CONST
        numberOfTriangles = 10;            (* should be even *)

    VAR
        triangleCount: integer;


    PROCEDURE DrawStarTriangle;
        (* Draws a triangle of 6 rows of stars *)
        CONST numberOfRows = 6;
            ch = '*';

        VAR row, column: integer;


    BEGIN
        FOR row := 1 TO numberOfRows DO
            BEGIN
                FOR column := 1 TO row DO
                    Write (ch);
                Writeln;
            END (* FOR row *);
    END; (* DrawStarTriangle *)


    PROCEDURE DrawXTriangle;
        (* Draws a triangle of 7 rows of X's *)
        CONST numberOfRows = 7;
            ch = 'X';

        VAR row, column: integer;
```

```
    BEGIN
        FOR row := 1 TO numberOfRows DO
            BEGIN
                FOR column := 1 TO row DO
                    Write (ch);
                Writeln;
            END (* FOR row *);
    END; (* DrawXTriangle *)


BEGIN (* main procedure *)
    FOR triangleCount := 1 TO numberOfTriangles DIV 2 DO
        BEGIN
            DrawStarTriangle;
            Writeln;
            DrawXTriangle;
            Writeln;
        END (* FOR triangleCount *);
END (* TenTriangles *).
```

Although boring, this program will illustrate simply the points we wish to make. The types of procedures used up to this point are fairly difficult to use in this situation, since we want to print something different for each procedure. We would like to write a procedure that has some "holes" in it (such as the values of some variables) and to be able to fill in the holes differently each time we call the procedure. We could use global variables for this purpose, setting up the values of numberOfRows and ch just before each call, but there is a simpler way. This program could be written with parameterized procedures as

```
PROGRAM TenTriangles (output);
    CONST
        numberOfTriangles = 10;            (* should be even *)

    VAR
        triangleCount: integer;


    PROCEDURE DrawTriangle (numberOfRows: integer; ch: char);
        (* Draws a triangle of numberOfRows rows of ch *)
        VAR row, column: integer;


    BEGIN
        FOR row := 1 TO numberOfRows DO
            BEGIN
                FOR column := 1 TO row DO
                    Write (ch);
                Writeln;
            END (* FOR row *);
    END, (* DrawTriangle *)
```

```
BEGIN (* main procedure *)
    FOR triangleCount := 1 TO numberOfTriangles DIV 2 DO
        BEGIN
            DrawTriangle (6, '*');
            Writeln;
            DrawTriangle (7, 'X');
            Writeln;
        END (* FOR triangleCount *);
END (* TenTriangles *).
```

A parameter is another form of variable. The **PROCEDURE** statement has been augmented to allow for the declaration of parameters. The parameter variables can be used only within the procedure in which they are declared. The procedure also declares the local variables `row` and `column`. It would be incorrect to try to do anything with `row`, `column`, `numberOfRows`, or `ch` in the main procedure of this program.

When a procedure is called, the computer creates a pegboard for the procedure, with holes drilled and named for all the parameters and local variables of that procedure. Then, the parameters are given values from the calling statement. In the above example, `numberOfRows` will be 6 (the first time), so that we write 6 rows; `ch` will be '*', and thus we write asterisks. Notice that we have two parameters in the procedure and two in the calling statement. The order in which parameters in the procedure are matched up with the variables or expressions in the main program is indicated by the order of the parameters appearing in the procedure declaration and the order of the main program items appearing when the procedure is called. That is, the procedure parameters and the values in the procedure calls are matched up first to first, second to second, etc.

This process is similar to having assignment statements that assign the parameter values in the calling statement to the parameters in the procedure. In the above example, it would be like these two statements:

```
numberOfRows := 6;
ch := '*';
```

This means that the parameters must also be type-compatible.

The parameters in the calling statement are called *actual parameters* or *actuals*. The parameters in the procedure are called *formal parameters* or *formals*. The actual parameters may be constants, as in these examples, or may be variables or expressions.

When a program starts execution, a pegboard is made for all the global variables. These are the variables that are declared directly after the **PROGRAM** instruction. The main program is used to hold these variables. When the executable section in the above program starts, it puts the constant 10 into the `numberOfTriangles` hole of the main pegboard. We then start executing the main procedure. The value 1 is put into the hole marked `triangleCount`. We then call the procedure `DrawTriangle` with parameters 6 and '*'. This means that a pegboard with holes for `numberOfRows`, `ch`, `row`, and `column` is created. The holes for `row` and `column` are left empty. The values of the actual parameters (6 and '*') are stored in the holes of the formal parameters (`numberOfRows` and `ch`). The procedure `DrawTriangle` continues execution and, when it is done, we throw away (or recycle) its pegboard and return control to the calling procedure. We then continue with `Writeln`. The next statement calls for the execution of `DrawTriangle` again. This time, however, the actual parameters are different. Thus, when we create the new pegboard, we will put different values into `numberOfRows` and `ch`. The holes for `row` and `column` are once again left empty. The procedure `DrawTriangle` then continues execution normally.

The formal parameters `numberOfRows` and `ch` are similar to ordinary local variables except that they start out with values when the procedure is called. Although values can be stored in these variables, this should not be done for two reasons. First, if you need the original value of the parameter, it will not be available. Second, it confuses the reader of the program. What will happen to the actual parameter if the formal parameter is changed? The actual parameter is not altered because we have made a *copy* of it, and it is the copy that has been changed. It is similar to writing on a photocopy: the original does not change!

9-2 FUNCTIONS

PASCAL *functions* are quite similar to the mathematical idea of a function. A function is used to compute a value from given values. Familiar functions are square root, absolute value, trigonometric functions, etc. We will learn how to write our own special functions in PASCAL.

9-2-1 Built-in Functions

PASCAL has a built-in set of standard functions similar to those found on most engineering calculators. A brief list of these standard functions is contained in Appendix B. Let us look at a short program segment that makes use of two of these functions.

```
im := Sqrt (Abs (discriminant)) / (2.0 * a);
```

PASCAL views functions in a way similar to values. Functions can be used in expressions in much the same way as variables. When PASCAL evaluates a variable, it finds the value stored in that variable hole in the pegboard. When PASCAL evaluates a function, it first evaluates the parameters and then computes the value of the function. In both cases, the end result is a value (whether it was looked up or computed). The main difference between the use of functions and variables is that we cannot assign a number to a function; that is,

```
q := 3.0;           is perfectly legal, while
Sqrt(x) := 3.0;     has no meaning in PASCAL.
```

We still must have only variables on the left-hand side of the assignment operator.

9-2-2 Programmer-Defined Functions

In this section we will discuss PASCAL's mechanism for allowing programmers to define their own functions. The key characteristic of a PASCAL function is that it computes a value from the variables with which it is supplied.

Before we procede to complicated functions, let us look at how we could define the absolute value function on integers and discuss its various components.

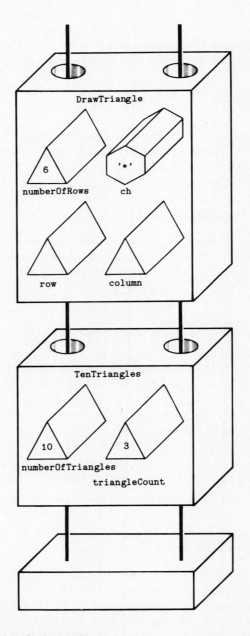

Figure 9-1 Pegboards for procedures.

```
FUNCTION MyAbs(x : integer) : integer;
BEGIN
    IF x >= 0
        THEN MyAbs:= x
        ELSE MyAbs:= -x;
END; (* MyAbs *)
```

First, notice that the punctuation word **FUNCTION** is used to start the definition of a function. The function name follows, in the same manner as a procedure name. Then, the list of parameters follows, again just as in the **PROCEDURE** instruction. After the parameters, we see something applicable only to functions: a colon followed by the word **integer**. This indicates to PASCAL that this function returns a value that is an integer. The form of this is similar to the form in which a variable is declared. PASCAL functions can return integer, real, boolean, and character values.*

A common mistake is to assume that functions taking integers as parameters must return an integer as a result. While this is frequently the case, it is not necessarily so. For example, we might write a function that tells us whether the value of a parameter is prime. The function would be declared as boolean (that is, return a boolean value), while the parameter of the function would be declared as integer. We will see functions that have all different kinds of parameters and return various types of answers.

Following the function header comes the declaration of local variables (the **MyAbs** function has none). This is followed by the function body which, like the body of a procedure, is delimited by a **BEGIN-END** block.

The second new concept is that the function name (**MyAbs** in this case) can be used inside the function body in the same manner as a local variable. The type of this variable is the same as the type of the function, which has been specified after the colon in the **FUNCTION** instruction (integer in this case). *The result of the function is the value that is stored in this variable when the function is finished executing.* This result is the computed value of the function. In the **MyAbs** example, the value stored in this variable is either the original input (if the number was nonnegative) or the negation of the input (if the number was negative).

PASCAL places a restriction on this variable specifying that it must appear in the function body only on the left hand side of an assignment instruction.† Its value may never be looked at within the function; it should only be mentioned when some value is being stored into it. The following function illustrates a common mistake. It is supposed to return the sum of all numbers from 1 to the value represented by the parameter **limit**.

---

* It also allows scalar, subrange, and pointer types to be returned, but not arrays and records. These topics will be covered later.

† Use of the function name in an expression in the function is called a *recursive reference*. Rather than meaning "give the current value of the function," it means "call the function again and compute a new value." If the function has no parameters, such recursive references will result in an infinite loop. If the function has parameters, such recursive references will result in a strange error message that complains about mismatch in the type of parameters.

```
FUNCTION SumUp (limit : integer) : integer;
    VAR number: integer;
BEGIN
    SumUp := 0;
    FOR number := 1 TO limit DO
        SumUp := SumUp + number;
END; (* SumUp *)
```

The error occurs in the addition instruction. To update the value of SumUp, the old value must be added to the next number. This requires looking at the value of SumUp, which violates our rule. The correct way to write this function would be

```
FUNCTION SumUp (limit : integer) : integer;
    VAR number, sum: integer;
BEGIN
    sum := 0;
    FOR number := 1 TO limit DO
        sum := sum + number;
    SumUp:= sum;
END; (* SumUp *)
```

The rule is not violated in this function. This "trick" of using a local variable to represent the answer of a function and then having the last instruction of the function transfer this value to the function name is used quite frequently. In general, all functions should be written that way.

Another common mistake is to use a function in the same way as a procedure. For example, the following three PASCAL instructions are all meaningless (if FunnyFunc has been defined as a function and not as a procedure).

```
15;      x;      FunnyFunc(a,b,c);
```

These are not PASCAL instructions since they do not direct PASCAL to do anything, they only represent values.

The parameter mechanism for functions is the same as that for procedures. Thus the only extension that functions implement is the ability to return a computed value in place of the function call. This is used when we want the function call to appear in an expression. Thus, if we had declared a real function called Cube, we could take the volume of a sphere by the following

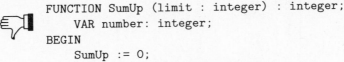

```
volume := 4.0 / 3.0 * pi * Cube (radius);
```

Exercise

1. Explain what is wrong with this function (that is, what rule about writing functions does it violate) and rewrite it correctly.

```
FUNCTION  Factorial (n: integer)  : integer;
    (* this function returns the Nth factorial,
        that is, N*(N-1)*(N-2)* ... *)
    VAR  factor : integer;

BEGIN
    Factorial := 1;
    FOR factor := 2 TO n DO
        Factorial := Factorial * factor;
END; (* Factorial *)
```

9-3 SUMMARY: PROCEDURES VERSUS FUNCTIONS

Both procedures and functions allow parameters that can be used to pass information from the caller to the called procedure. The only difference between
the two is that functions can also return a value. Note that the type of value
returned by the function (also known as the type of the function) must satisfy
the type compatibility rules about its use. Thus, we can use a function call
wherever we can use an expression. But since expressions cannot appear on the
left-hand side of an assignment statement, function calls cannot appear there as
well.

9-4 EXAMPLE: PRIME NUMBERS

Prime numbers are integers greater than 1 with no positive integral divisors
except for themselves and 1. For example, 7, 11, and 13 are prime, but 6 and
9 are not. One interesting observation is that all prime numbers are odd except
for 2. Let us look at one method for determining whether a number is prime.

```
PROGRAM Prime (input, output);
    VAR number: integer;

    FUNCTION IsPrime (theNumber: integer): boolean;
        VAR soFarPrime: boolean;     (* our current guess *)
            candidate: integer;      (* factors to test *)

    BEGIN
        soFarPrime := TRUE;
            (* innocent until proven guilty *)
        FOR candidate := 2 TO theNumber - 1 DO
            IF theNumber MOD candidate = 0
                (* candidate is a factor of theNumber *)
                THEN soFarPrime := FALSE;
        IsPrime := soFarPrime;  (* return the answer *)
    END; (* IsPrime *)
```

```
BEGIN (* main procedure *)
    WHILE NOT Eof DO
        BEGIN
            Readln (number);
            Write (number);
            IF IsPrime (number)
                THEN Writeln (' is prime.')
                ELSE Writeln (' is not prime.');
        END (* WHILE NOT Eof *);
END (* Prime *).
```

First, we notice that the loop gets done (number - 2) times. But we know there is no reason to test if number is even, unless it is 2. Therefore, we can speed up the function to the following.

```
FUNCTION IsPrime (theNumber: integer): boolean;
    VAR soFarPrime: boolean;    (* our current guess *)
        candidate: integer;     (* factors to test *)


BEGIN
    soFarPrime := TRUE; (* innocent until proven guilty *)
    IF (theNumber MOD 2 = 0) AND (theNumber > 2)
        THEN soFarPrime := FALSE (* divisible by 2 *)
        ELSE FOR candidate := 3 TO theNumber - 1 DO
            IF theNumber MOD candidate = 0
                (* candidate is a factor of theNumber *)
                THEN soFarPrime := FALSE;
    IsPrime := soFarPrime;   (* return the answer *)
END; (* IsPrime *)
```

Notice how the loop now starts at 3 because we have already tested whether theNumber is even or odd. We further observe that we need only test for odd divisors, since when we test whether it is divisible by 2, we also decide whether it has any even divisors. But we must have some way of incrementing candidate by 2 each time through the loop. Well, instead of doing that, we can double candidate before using it as a divisor. To be precise, we do not want to double it, but we want to double it and then add 1 to get an odd number. We want the odd numbers from 3 to theNumber - 1. Well, $2 \times 1 + 1$ is 3, and $2 \times (\frac{1}{2}$theNumber $- 1) + 1$ is theNumber - 1, which is what we want. We can change IsPrime to the following.

```
FUNCTION IsPrime (theNumber: integer): boolean;
    VAR soFarPrime: boolean;    (* our current guess *)
        candidate: integer;     (* factors to test *)
```

```
BEGIN
     soFarPrime := TRUE; (* innocent until proven guilty *)
     IF theNumber <> 2    (* do nothing if theNumber is 2 *)
         THEN IF (theNumber MOD 2 = 0)
              THEN soFarPrime := FALSE (* divisible by 2 *)
              ELSE FOR candidate := 1 TO theNumber DIV 2 - 1 DO
                   IF theNumber MOD (2 * candidate + 1) = 0
                       (* candidate is a factor of theNumber *)
                       THEN soFarPrime := FALSE;
         IsPrime := soFarPrime;  (* return the answer *)
END; (* IsPrime *)
```

This algorithm now requires at most one-half of theNumber tests. But now, we will make a further observation. If a divides n, then there is a number b such that $a \times b = n$. We make the claim that one of a and b does not exceed $\sqrt{n}$, while the other is at least $\sqrt{n}$. Thus, we need only test numbers up to $\sqrt{number}$. Our function now becomes the following.

```
FUNCTION IsPrime (theNumber: integer): boolean;
     VAR soFarPrime: boolean;     (* our current guess *)
         candidate: integer;      (* factors to test *)

BEGIN
     soFarPrime := TRUE; (* innocent until proven guilty *)
     IF theNumber <> 2    (* do nothing if theNumber is 2 *)
         THEN IF (theNumber MOD 2 = 0)
              THEN soFarPrime := FALSE (* divisible by 2 *)
              ELSE FOR candidate := 1 TO
                   Trunc (Sqrt (theNumber)) DIV 2 DO
                   IF theNumber MOD (2 * candidate + 1) = 0
                       (* candidate is a factor of theNumber *)
                       THEN soFarPrime := FALSE;
     IsPrime := soFarPrime;  (* return the answer *)
END; (* IsPrime *)
```

Now, we do the test at most $\frac{1}{2}\sqrt{number}$ times. We notice that there is no reason to continue testing once we have found a divisor. If we want to be able to quit early, we cannot use a FOR loop, because the number of times it loops is decided before we enter the loop. Instead, we will use a WHILE loop.

```
FUNCTION IsPrime (theNumber: integer): boolean;
     VAR soFarPrime: boolean;     (* our current guess *)
         candidate: integer;      (* factors to test *)
         lastCandidate: integer; (* last factor to test *)

BEGIN
     soFarPrime := TRUE; (* innocent until proven guilty *)
     candidate := 2;      (* first number to test *)
     lastCandidate := Trunc (Sqrt (theNumber));
             (* calculate lastCandidate once and use it *)
             (* often in the WHILE test *)
```

```
        WHILE soFarPrime AND (candidate <= lastCandidate) DO
            BEGIN
                IF theNumber MOD candidate = 0
                    (* candidate is a factor of theNumber *)
                    THEN soFarPrime := FALSE;
                IF candidate = 2
                    THEN candidate := 3
                    ELSE candidate := candidate + 2;
            END; (* WHILE *)
        IsPrime := soFarPrime;  (* return the answer *)
    END; (* IsPrime *)
```

We observe that there was no reason to specially test for number being even since we will now stop after finding 2 divides theNumber anyway. It works for 2 since Trunc (Sqrt (2)) = 1; therefore, the WHILE loop will not be executed. Notice the code for incrementing candidate: it goes 2, 3, 5, 7, 9, and then the rest of the odd numbers. The above algorithm does the test at most $\frac{1}{2}\sqrt{\text{number}}$ times, and far less for composite (nonprime) numbers. One final observation: we should test only for prime divisors since if a number is divisible by a composite, it is also divisible by the prime divisors of that composite. With a self-satisfied look, we exclaim, "It is too much work to decide whether a number is prime, so it is quicker to divide by it anyway!"

There is one last measure we can take to improve this algorithm. Notice that we test for candidate having the value 2 each time through the loop even though it will only have that value once. By duplicating some code, we obtain the following program.

```
FUNCTION IsPrime (theNumber: integer): boolean;
    VAR soFarPrime: boolean;    (* our current guess *)
        candidate: integer;     (* factors to test *)
        lastCandidate: integer; (* last factor to test *)

BEGIN
    soFarPrime := TRUE; (* innocent until proven guilty *)
    candidate := 3;     (* first number past 2 to test *)
    lastCandidate := Trunc (Sqrt (theNumber));
            (* calculate lastCandidate once and use it *)
            (* often in the WHILE test *)
    IF NOT odd (theNumber) AND (theNumber <> 2)
                    (* easy test for divisible by two *)
        THEN soFarPrime := FALSE
        ELSE WHILE soFarPrime AND (candidate <= lastCandidate) DO
            BEGIN
                IF theNumber MOD candidate = 0
                    (* candidate is a factor of theNumber *)
                    THEN soFarPrime := FALSE;
                candidate := candidate + 2;
            END; (* WHILE *)
    IsPrime := soFarPrime;  (* return the answer *)
END; (* IsPrime *)
```

9-5 REFERENCE OR VAR PARAMETERS

Recently, we have learned about passing parameters to procedures and about obtaining a single value returned in functions. In this section, we will learn how to return multiple values.

The parameters we have already seen are called *value* parameters. These involve only one-way communication: when the procedure (or function) is called, the value of the actual parameter is transmitted to be the value of the formal parameter. If you change the value of the formal parameter in the procedure, the value of the actual parameter does *not* change. Let us first write a function that finds the maximum of two numbers.

```
FUNCTION Maximum (number1, number2: integer): integer;
BEGIN
    IF number1 < number2
        THEN Maximum := number2
        ELSE Maximum := number1;
END; (* Maximum *)
```

But suppose that we want to write a function or procedure that returned the minimum as well as the maximum. We could use global variables, but as we have seen, that is not very good style. Instead, we will use **VAR** parameters as in this example.

```
PROCEDURE MaxMin (VAR maximum: integer;
                  VAR minimum: integer;
                  number1: integer;
                  number2: integer);

BEGIN
    IF number1 < number2
        THEN BEGIN
            maximum := number2;
            minimum := number1;
            END (* IF number1 < number2 *)
        ELSE BEGIN
            maximum := number1;
            minimum := number2;
            END (* IF number2 <= number1 *);
END; (* MaxMin *)
```

The parameters **maximum** and **minimum** are called *reference* or **VAR** *parameters*. These parameters use two-way communication: When we change the formal parameter, we also change the actual parameter. We could rewrite this procedure header as

```
PROCEDURE maxmin (VAR maximum, minimum: integer;
                  number1, number2: integer);
```

Notice that the **VAR** parameters include everything between the **VAR** and the next colon and type name, `integer`. Also, the parameters can appear in any order as long as the procedure call statement and the procedure header are consistent; the **VAR** parameters do not have to precede the value parameters, nor do the **VAR** parameters all have to be together. Simply choose a reasonable style and follow it consistently.

There is another reason to use **VAR** parameters even when we return only one value. If we change the value of a global variable (and there should be a very good reason for not passing the global as another parameter) or if we do input or output in the function or procedure, the procedure is said to have *side effects*—because the procedure or function has some effect other than that seen through its parameters. In general, it is better style to avoid side effects by adding parameters. But if the side effect is performing input or output, we cannot handle this simply by additional parameters. We *try to avoid side effects in functions* even more than avoiding them in procedures. If we must have a side effect, we should use a procedure instead of a function. For example, if we want to write a function that returns the next integer from the input file, we use a procedure instead and can write

```
PROCEDURE ReadInteger (VAR theNumber: integer);
BEGIN
    Read (theNumber);
    IF Eoln
        THEN Readln;    (* Do a Readln to allow Eof testing *)
END; (* ReadInteger *)
```

For the same reason, we generally do not use **VAR** parameters in functions.

Returning once again to our pegboard analogy, let's see how **VAR** parameters work. (This concept is due to Rich Pattis.) When a procedure is called, imagine the creation of a pegboard for all of the local and parameter variables of the procedure. The holes for local variables are left empty. A piece of string is attached to each hole in the pegboard that represents a reference parameter. The other end of each string is tied above the variable hole whose name is specified where the procedure is called. This string tells us the variables to use when the procedure instructs us to do something with reference parameter variables. Each pair of strung-together holes must be type-compatible. The holes for the value parameters are filled with the values of the actual parameters.

When a procedure needs to know the value of a formal reference parameter, it simply follows the string from the hole for that parameter until it finds the variable hole for the actual parameter that the formal represents. The value of the formal parameter is then the value of this actual variable. Likewise, if we wish to store something in a reference parameter hole, we actually put the data into the hole of the actual parameter (the hole to which the string leads). Again, reference parameters are simply names the procedure gives to variables that are elsewhere.*

Since the communication of **VAR** parameters is two-way, we could put a value into the parameters before we call the procedure the first time. For example,

---

* These names are sometimes referred to as aliases, and the process of having two names refer to the same variable is called aliasing.

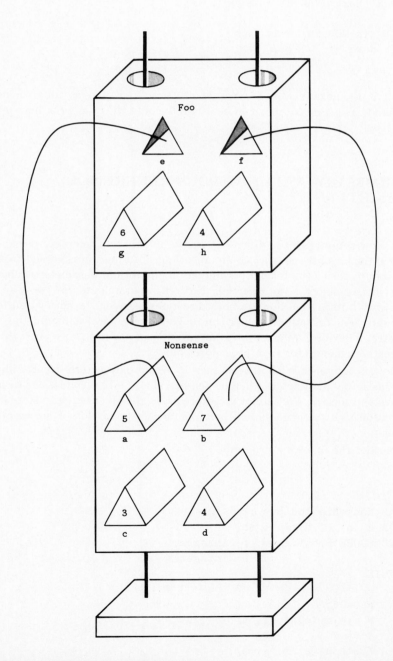

Figure 9-2 Pegboard for VAR parameters.

suppose we wanted to have a variable that counted

$$1, 2, 3, \ldots, 60, 1, 2, 3, \ldots, 60, \ldots$$

We could write the procedure

```
PROCEDURE Next (VAR n: integer);
BEGIN
    n := (n MOD 60) + 1;
END; (* Next *)
```

and call it by `next(number)`. We would have to assign a value to `number` beforehand. This procedure would be useful to count the number of lines printed on the page.

9-6 SUMMARY: VALUE VERSUS REFERENCE PARAMETERS

We will now summarize the difference between value and reference parameters. Value parameters use one-way communication. Information is copied from the actual parameter to the formal parameter. If the formal parameter is changed, the actual parameter is not affected. Reference parameters use two-way communication. Information flows in both directions between the actual and formal parameters. The formal parameter can be viewed as a local name for the actual parameter. They both refer to the same variable on any one procedure call. This identification changes for each procedure call.

Another difference is what we can use as actual parameters. Expressions can be used as actual parameters when passed by value. Only variables can be actual reference parameters. We cannot use expressions as reference parameters for the same reason that we cannot put them on the left-hand side of an assignment statement.

Consider the following program

```
PROGRAM Nonsense (output);
    VAR a, b, c, d: integer;
    PROCEDURE Foo (VAR e, f: integer;
                        g, h: integer);
    BEGIN
        e := 5;
        g := 6;
        Writeln (e, f, g, h);
        f := 7;
        Writeln (e, f, g, h);
    END (* Foo *);
```

```
BEGIN (* main program *)
    b := 2;
    c := 3;
    d := 4;
    Writeln ('              ', b, c, d);
    Foo (a, b, c, d);
    Writeln (a, b, c, d);
END (* Nonsense *).
```

	2	3	4
5	2	6	4
5	7	6	4
5	7	3	4

Notice that the first parameter has not been given a value by the calling procedure. That is permitted because the procedure **Foo** does not use the value of
the first parameter before assigning a new value to it. Notice that the third
parameter is given a value by procedure **Foo**, but since it is a value parameter,
the actual parameter does not get altered.

Exercises

1.   What is output by the following program?

```
PROGRAM Tricky (input, output);
    VAR x, y, z: integer;

    PROCEDURE Sort (VAR first, second, third: integer);
    (* Note: all three formal parameters are VAR parameters *)

        PROCEDURE  Swap (VAR number1, number2: integer);
            (* Both formal parameters are VAR parameters *)
            VAR dummy: integer;   (* local variable *)
        BEGIN
            dummy := number1;
            number1 := number2;
            number2 := dummy;
        END;   (* Swap *)
```

```
            BEGIN (* Body of Sort *)
               IF first > second
                  THEN  Swap (first, second);
               IF second > third
                  THEN
                        BEGIN
                           Swap (second, third);
                           IF first > second
                              THEN Swap (first, second);
                        END;
            END;  (* Sort *)

      BEGIN  (* main program *)
         x:= 90;  y:= 25;  z:= 50;
         Sort (x, y, z);
         Writeln (x, y, z);
         x:= 6;  y:= 2;  z:= 1;
         Sort (x, y, z);
         Writeln (x, y, z);
      END (* Tricky *).
```

2.   What would the above program output if **third** was a value parameter
     instead?

9-7 SCOPE: LOCAL AND GLOBAL VARIABLES

If we have several procedures, it is possible to declare variables in each procedure as well as in the main procedure. The constants and variables declared
immediately after the **PROGRAM** heading and before any procedure declaration are
called *global*. Constants and variables declared immediately after the **PROCEDURE**
heading are called *local*. For example, consider the following program to print
several triangles.


```
PROGRAM PrintTriangles (output);
      (* program to print several triangles *)
   CONST
      numberOfTriangles = 2;      (* print two triangles *)
      size = 6;                   (* size of each triangle *)

   VAR
      countOfTriangles: integer;  (* global variable *)

   PROCEDURE DrawTriangle;
      (* draws one triangle followed by a blank line *)
      VAR
         row, column: integer;   (* local variables *)
         foo: integer;           (* for illustration only *)
```

```
        PROCEDURE RowOfTriangle;
            (* Draws one row of the triangle *)
            VAR
                foo: integer;        (* for illustration only *)
        BEGIN
            FOR column := 1 TO row DO
                Write(countOfTriangles);
            Writeln;
        END; (* RowOfTriangle *)

    BEGIN  (* the body of DrawTriangle *)
        FOR row := 1 TO size DO
            RowOfTriangle;
        Writeln;
    END; (* DrawTriangle *)

(* main procedure *)
BEGIN
    FOR countOfTriangles := 1 TO numberOfTriangles DO
        DrawTriangle;
END (* PrintTriangles *).
```

Notice that there is the program (or main procedure) and two other procedures. The program is said to *contain* the DrawTriangle procedure, which in turn contains the procedure RowOfTriangle. The procedure RowOfTriangle is said to be *nested in* or *embedded in* the DrawTriangle procedure, which in turn is nested in the main procedure. We would also say that RowOfTriangle is nested in the main procedure. Procedures can be nested to an arbitrary number of levels. The *body* of a procedure is composed of the statements enclosed in BEGIN-END brackets that are associated with the procedure. Declarations separate the body of a procedure from the procedure header.

We notice that there are both global and local variables. We wish to know which variables we can access where. We can always reference a variable in the body of the procedure in which it is declared. The first rule is:

> A variable V that can be referenced in a procedure P can also be referenced in a procedure Q that is nested in P, unless there is also a declaration for V in Q.

Thus, we can access countOfTriangles in DrawTriangle and, therefore, in RowOfTriangle. Similarly, we can access row in RowOfTriangle. The foo inside RowOfTriangle is different from that in DrawTriangles. The variable row is the same in both DrawTriangles and RowOfTriangle. In particular, a variable declared in a procedure cannot be referenced in containing procedures.

For any particular reference to a variable, the following algorithm describes how to find where the variable has been declared. We first look at the present procedure. If it is not declared there, we look at the procedure that this procedure is embedded in. If it is not declared there we look at the next containing procedure, and so on, until we find the preceding procedure that declares the variable.

It is possible to have several variables with the same name declared in different procedures. This is possible but not desirable. It tends to confuse the reader. Thus, it is best to choose variable names that describe the use of variable, and desirable to choose distinct names for each variable in the program. Names such as I and J are easy to spell but rather uninformative. The time you invest in typing longer, more informative names will be more than made up by later savings in understanding and debugging your program.

The *nesting level* of a procedure is the number of procedures in which it is contained. The main procedure has nesting level 0. The procedure DrawTriangle has nesting level 1. And the procedure RowOfTriangle has nesting level 2. Notice that the amount of indentation reflects the nesting level of the procedure.

It is possible to have multiple procedures declared within a program at the same level. The rule about them is:

> Variables declared at a given nesting level are not accessible in other procedures of the same level.

Procedures also have associated scopes. A program or procedure named P can call a procedure Q if:

1. Q is declared in P.
2. P is nested in some procedure R, and Q and R are declared in the same program or procedure, provided that the definition of R follows that of Q.
3. P and Q are both declared in R, provided that the definition of P follows that of Q.

The phrase "nested in" means "declared in" or "declared in some procedure that is declared in," etc.

Thus far we have considered only the referencing of variables in the program without worrying about the sequence in which the various procedures are called. Until now, we have addressed *static issues*; these issues do not change with time. When we consider the calling sequence of the various procedures and which procedures are actively being executed at any given time, we are concerned with *dynamic issues*; these issues do change with time.

In Chapter 4, we used the analogy of a pegboard with holes representing variables. We will now use different pegboards to represent the variables of different procedures. The preceding static scope rules tell us when we can access variables on a pegboard other than the variable for the procedure currently being executed.

Let us consider what happens when we enter a procedure. In order to have the local variables for this procedure, we take another pegboard. We place this blank pegboard on top of the pegboard for the calling procedure. (We sometimes call this pile of pegboards a *stack*, and an individual pegboard a *stack frame*.) While executing the procedure, we store values into this pegboard by placing pegs into it. Eventually, the procedure will terminate and control will return to the caller. But now the top pegboard is discarded, along with all values. If we call the procedure again, we get a new pegboard without any values. We do not have access to the values computed during the previous call.*

---

* On some computers, we are not told when we reference uninitialized variables. Instead, the variables have whatever random values happen to be in memory. When we call a procedure repeatedly, its stack frame may be in the same place causing the old values to still be there. When we alternately call two procedures, their stack frames may be in the same place (though not at the same time), so our uninitialized variables will get random values placed there by the other procedure. Values from the previous call to a procedure are not likely to be accessible anymore.

Try "playing computer" by seeing what is done by the program at the beginning of this section. You will notice that each procedure is executed several times. While you are executing the program, simulate the creation of a new pegboard for each procedure call, and its destruction on the procedure exit.

The last issue is one of style. In general, declare your variables nearest to their location of use. Declare them at the deepest (highest-numbered) nesting level possible while still maintaining access to them where necessary. The idea is to make each procedure as self-contained as possible, so that each procedure and its variables can be understood without reference to its containing procedures.

Now let us refer to the diagram below.

```
PROGRAM A;
    PROCEDURE B;
        PROCEDURE D;
            BEGIN
            END; (* D *)
        BEGIN
        END; (* B *)
    PROCEDURE C;
        PROCEDURE E;
            BEGIN
            END; (* E *)
        PROCEDURE F;
            BEGIN
            END; (* F *)
        BEGIN
        END; (* C *)
    BEGIN
    END (* A *).
```

Try to determine which procedures can be called by which other procedures. Also, determine for the variables declared in each procedure (assuming there were any), those procedures that can reference them. What is the nesting level of each procedure?

Now that you have done it for yourself, check your answers below.

Procedure	Can be called by statement in procedures
B	A, C, E, F
C	A
D	B
E	C, F
F	C

Variables declared in	Can be referenced in
A	A, B, C, D, E, F
B	B, D
C	C, E, F
D	D
E	E
F	F

Nesting level	Procedure
0	A
1	B, C
2	D, E, F

Note that even though D and E are on the same nesting level, they are declared (immediately nested) in *different* procedures, B and C. For this reason, procedure D *cannot* be called by procedure E. Note that recursive calls are not listed.

Exercise

1. What is output by the following program? Assume that the input file contains the integers 2 3. This program is not supposed to be meaningful; it is simply a tricky test of your knowledge of parameters and scope.

```
PROGRAM HodgePodge (input, output);
    VAR a, b, x, y : integer;

    PROCEDURE  MixUp  (VAR  q, a: integer;
                            (* Q, A are VAR parameters *)
                        b, r: integer);
                            (* B, R are value parameters *)
        VAR  x, z:  integer;
                            (* X. Z are local variables *)

    BEGIN
        Read (x);
        z := -x;
        x := x + 1;
        q := 2*q + a;
        b := 1 + z - 2*x;
        Writeln (q, a, b, r, x, z);
    END;   (* MixUp *)

BEGIN  (* main program *)
    a := 1;   b := 2;   x := 7;   y := 11;
    Writeln (a, b, x, y);
    MixUp (a, b, x, y);
    Writeln (a, b, x, y);
    MixUp (b, a, x - y, y);
    Writeln (a, b, x, y);
END.
```

HINT: The first three lines of output should look like:

1	2	7	11		
4	2	-7	11	3	-2
4	2	7	11		

Another View of Types

Thus far we have seen that PASCAL lets us declare variables to hold values of all four *standard types*: integer, real, character, and boolean. Actually, it also lets us *declare* types as well as variables. We can specify the values that the type includes and then give the new type a name so that we can declare variables of that type to hold those values.

There are two simple ways to do this (and a host of complicated ways that we will get to shortly): subrange types and enumerated types. We will also learn about arrays.

10-1 SUBRANGE TYPES

Suppose that we are writing a program to process exam scores and want a variable that will hold a score between 0 and 100. We might say

```
VAR score: integer;
```

There are a few disadvantages: the type **integer** permits many values that we will never use because they simply are not legal scores. This means that if we accidentally type

```
score := 1000;
```

(or worse yet, if 1000 appears in the data), it could be disastrous. Someone reading the program may not realize what a legal score is and go through considerable trouble to dig out that information.

Before all **VAR** declarations, PASCAL lets us include **TYPE** *declarations*, which in this case would say

```
TYPE
    legalScore = 0..100;
```

Now, in addition to the standard types, we have a *programmer-defined type* called `legalScore`; therefore, we can declare

```
VAR
    score: legalScore;
```

Now it is obvious from the program text what legal scores are. If we say

```
score := 1000;
```

PASCAL will mark it as a type error, in much the same way as if we had tried to say

```
score := 6.17;   or
score := 'X';
```

This is called a *subrange type* because it is a subrange of another type. We can take subranges of any standard type except reals.

```
TYPE
    letter = 'A'..'Z';
    digit = '0'..'9';
    hour = 1..24;
VAR
    initial: letter;
    time: hour;
```

Notice the form of **TYPE** declarations. The *lower bound* and *upper bound* of the declaration are separated by two dots without a space between them, though one or more spaces may surround them. An equal sign separates the type name from the type. Note the continued use of the colon in **VAR** declarations.

There is a shorthand notation for declaring variables of subrange types. This method specifies the type in the variable declaration itself.

```
VAR
    score: 0..100;
    time: 1..24;
    initial: 'A'..'Z';
```

This is usually perfectly reasonable and often better. Occasionally, it is clearer to explicitly declare a type in the **TYPE** declaration—for example, if we declare many variables of the same type or if giving the type name makes the program clearer. For example, a variable declared to be type **courseGrade** is more easily understood than one declared to be type 'A'..'F'. Only type names can appear in procedure and function headers.

```
TYPE
    courseGrade = 'A'..'F';
VAR
    hour: 1..24;
    grade: courseGrade;
⋮
```

Right
```
PROCEDURE foo (grades: courseGrade; number: integer);
```

Wrong
```
PROCEDURE foo (grades: 'A'..'F'; number: 1..10);
```

10-2 ENUMERATED TYPES

We have seen the various standard data types. We can store integers, characters, booleans, and real numbers. Integers can be restricted to a particular range of values. However, not everything we wish to store in a computer is easily thought of in these simple terms. For example, suppose that you want to record whether someone was a student or a member of the faculty. You could have a boolean variable **student**, which would be **true** if the person was a student and **false** if the person was a faculty member. However, colleges also need staff to run them. We need a variable that is capable of storing only three values. A subrange of integers, say 1 to 3, would do. But the values 1 for student, 2 for faculty, and 3 for staff are not mnemonic.* For many years, programmers using such languages as FORTRAN and COBOL had no choice. PASCAL, however, supports another data type.

In PASCAL, we can create our own type, called an *enumerated type*, whose values are identifiers. For example, we could create the type **status**, with values **student**, **faculty**, and **staff**. We do this with the following declaration:

```
TYPE status = (student, faculty, staff);
```

Notice that the type name is followed by an equal sign, as in the subrange types. The list of acceptable values appears in parentheses, separated by commas. We can also declare variables of this type.

```
VAR instructor: status;
```

This declaration defines the variable **instructor** to be of type **status**. We can thus assign values, such as **faculty**, to the variable **instructor**, as this example does.

---

* We could use constants **student** = **1**, etc., but assigning integers to identifiers is a tedious, error-prone task.

```
instructor := faculty;
```

The values `student`, `faculty`, and `staff` are automatically declared when the type `status` is declared. This means that it is *wrong* for these values to be declared otherwise. For example, we could not declare a variable called `student`. In the same way that the type of `'A'` is `char`, the type of `staff` is `status`. Except for the first one, the following are all incorrect:

```
TYPE status = (student, faculty, staff); (* this is ok *)
     nonAdministrative = (student, teacher);
                 (* duplicate declaration of student *)
VAR  faculty: status;
                 (* duplicate declaration of faculty *)
BEGIN
    student := x;       (* student is a value *)
```

Values of enumerated types are ordered in PASCAL; using the above example, `faculty` < `staff`. They can also be used in `FOR` loops. For example, suppose we counted the preferences for favorite colors in a class. We could have an enumerated type to list some common colors:

```
TYPE color = (red, blue, yellow, green, orange,
    brown, white, black);
```

If the counts are in the same order, the following program prints out the total number of votes, as well as the number of votes for primary colors (that is, red, blue, yellow).

```
PROGRAM ColorCount (input, output);
    (* total the counts of color preferences *)
    TYPE color = (red, blue, yellow, green, orange,
        brown, white, black);
    VAR primaryColorCount: integer;
        totalColorCount: integer;
        count: integer;
        theColor: color;

BEGIN
    primaryColorCount := 0;
    totalColorCount := 0;
    Writeln ('Counts follow:');
```

```
    FOR theColor := red TO black DO
        BEGIN
            Read (count);
            Writeln (count);
            totalColorCount := totalColorCount + count;
            IF theColor <= yellow
                THEN primaryColorCount :=
                    primaryColorCount + count;
        END (* FOR theColor *);
    Writeln ('Primary color count:', primaryColorCount);
    Writeln ('Total color count:', totalColorCount);
END (* ColorCount *).
```

If the input is 1, 2, 4, 8, 16, 32, 64, 128, the output will be:

```
Counts follow:
        1
        2
        4
        8
       16
       32
       64
      128
Primary color count:        7
Total color count:      255
```

10-3 THE PRED, SUCC, ORD, AND CHR FUNCTIONS

We have learned to use enumerated types to define our own values. Within a type, these values have an order and can be used in comparisons as well as in FOR statements. It would also be useful to determine the predecessor and successor values for that type. Suppose that we have the following type:

```
TYPE digits = (zero, one, two, three, four, five,
    six, seven, eight, nine);
```

Then, the functions Pred and Succ are defined to have exactly one argument and give a value of the same type that is the predecessor and successor, respectively. For example, Pred (two) = one and Succ (five) = six. These functions may have an argument of any scalar type except real; recall that the scalar types are integer, real, boolean, char, enumerated types, and their subrange types. For example, Pred (6) = 5 and Succ (false) = true. Note that Pred is not defined if its argument already has the lowest value possible. Therefore, Pred (zero) is undefined. Similarly, Succ is undefined if its argument already has the highest value possible. Thus, Succ (nine) is undefined.

Notice that Pred (Succ (foo)) is usually foo. When would it not be foo? If foo is the highest possible value in its enumerated type, then Succ (foo) is undefined.

Some PASCAL compilers include a nonstandard extension to read and write enumerated types. Although your PASCAL compiler may not support this (ask your instructor), the following examples illustrate the use of Pred and Succ.

Suppose that we want to read a digit and determine its predecessor and successor. A program to do this could appear as

Read digit
IF *digit is not* zero
    THEN *print predecessor*
IF *digit is not* nine
    THEN *print successor*

We could convert this to the following PASCAL program.

```
PROGRAM PlayWithDigit (input, output);
    (* Read digit and print predecessor and successor *)
    TYPE digits = (zero, one, two, three, four, five,
            six, seven, eight, nine);
    VAR digit: digits;
BEGIN
    WHILE NOT Eof DO
        BEGIN
            Readln (digit);
            Writeln ('Digit is ', digit);
            IF digit > zero
                THEN Writeln ('Predecessor is ', Pred (digit));
            IF digit < nine
                THEN Writeln ('Successor is ', Succ (digit));
        END (* WHILE NOT Eof *);
END (* PlayWithDigit *).
```

Consider the following input.

```
zero
five
nine
```

```
Digit is zero
Successor is one
Digit is five
Predecessor is four
Successor is six
Digit is nine
Predecessor is eight
```

Now suppose that we want to read in a digit and print it in both words and numbers. We would need a way to get the ordinal position of the value in the enumerated type. The `Ord` function takes one argument and returns its ordinal value. For example, `Ord (two) = 2`. PASCAL always numbers enumerated types from 0 regardless of the value names used. For example, in the type

```
TYPE digitsGerman = (eins, zwei, drei, vier, fünf, sechs,
    sieben, acht, neun);
```

`Ord (eins)` is still 0, and `Ord (sechs)` is still 5.

```
PROGRAM PlayWithDigit (input, output);
    (* Read digit and print predecessor and successor *)
    TYPE digits = (zero, one, two, three, four, five,
            six, seven, eight, nine);
    VAR digit: digits;
BEGIN
    WHILE NOT Eof DO
        BEGIN
            Readln (digit);
            Writeln ('Digit is ', digit, ' = ', Ord (digit));
            IF digit > zero
                THEN Writeln ('Predecessor is ', Pred (digit));
            IF digit < nine
                THEN Writeln ('Successor is ', Succ (digit));
        END (* WHILE NOT Eof *);
END (* PlayWithDigit *).
```

Consider the following input.

```
zero
five
nine
```

```
Digit is zero =         0
Successor is one
Digit is five =         5
Predecessor is four
Successor is six
Digit is nine =         9
Predecessor is eight
```

It would also be useful to convert from an integer to an enumerated type value. Unfortunately, PASCAL supports this only for the type **char**. This is done through the **Chr** function, which takes an **integer** argument and returns a **char**. For example, if **ch** is a character variable, **Chr (Ord (ch)) = ch**. If **int** is an integer variable with an acceptable value, **Ord (Chr (int)) = int**. Also, **Chr (Ord (ch) + 1) = Succ (ch)** and **Chr (Ord (ch) - 1) = Pred (ch)**. When we first covered the type **char**, we mentioned that the letters do not have to be consecutive, but that the numbers must be. Thus, if **int** is between 0 and 9, then **Chr (Ord ('0') + int)** gives the character that corresponds to the value of **int**. The following program illlustrates this fact.

```
PROGRAM PlayWithDigit (input, output);
    (* Read digit and print predecessor and successor *)
    TYPE digits = (zero, one, two, three, four, five,
            six, seven, eight, nine);
    VAR digit: digits;
        int: 0..9;
BEGIN
    WHILE NOT Eof DO
        BEGIN
            Readln (digit);
            int := Ord (digit);
            Writeln ('Digit is ', digit, ' = ', int, ' or ',
                Chr (Ord ('0') + int) );
            IF digit > zero
                THEN Writeln ('Predecessor is ', Pred (digit));
            IF digit < nine
                THEN Writeln ('Successor is ', Succ (digit));
        END (* WHILE NOT Eof *);
END (* PlayWithDigit *).
```

Consider the following input.

```
zero
five
nine
```

```
Digit is zero =          0 or 0
Successor is two
Digit is five =          5 or 5
Predecessor is four
Successor is six
Digit is nine =          9 or 9
Predecessor is eight
```

Exercise

1.   What is the value of Succ (Pred (foo))? When would it not be foo?

10-4 THE CASE STATEMENT

The IF statement can only distinguish between two cases. That is, it can do one of two things depending on the value of the condition. It is often useful to distinguish between multiple, similar conditions.

Suppose we want to read in expressions that each involve two integers and an operator, and then print out the value of the expression. For example, the input could appear as **5*6** and program print out **30**. A program to do this could appear as

```
WHILE there is more input
     Read an integer
     Read the operator
     Read the other integer
     Perform the correct operation
     Print the result
```

We already know how to do the WHILE loop and the reads of integers. Reading the operator is a little tricky if we want to skip the leading spaces, but that only involves a WHILE or REPEAT loop. However, performing the correct operation involves a complicated, nested IF statement, unless we can find a better way.

The CASE statement allows us to execute one of an arbitrary number of statements depending on the value of a variable or expression. The form of the CASE statement is

```
CASE expression OF
     value₁: statement₁;
     value₂: statement₂;
     ⋮
     valueₙ: statementₙ;
END (* CASE expression *);
```

The expression is evaluated and the statement with the appropriate *case label* is executed. The following example uses the CASE statement to perform the correct operation, as desired above.

```
CASE operator OF
    '+': Writeln (int1 + int2);
    '-': Writeln (int1 - int2);
    '*': Writeln (int1 * int2);
    '/': Writeln (int1 DIV int2);
END (* CASE operator *);
```

Note that the *case expression* must be the same type as the case labels.

Let us continue with our program.

```
PROGRAM ExpressionEvaluation (input, output);
    (* Read and evaluate a series of expressions involving
        two integers and an operator (+, -, *, /) *)
    VAR int1, int2: integer;
        operator: char;

    FUNCTION GetOperator: char;
        (* Returns the next nonblank *)
        VAR ch: char;
    BEGIN
        REPEAT
            Read (ch);
        UNTIL ch <> ' ';
        GetOperator := ch;
    END (* GetOperator *);

BEGIN
    WHILE NOT Eof DO
        BEGIN
            Read (int1);
            Write (int1);
            operator := GetOperator;
            Write (operator);
            Readln (int2);
            Write (int2, '=');
            CASE operator OF
                '+': Writeln (int1 + int2);
                '-': Writeln (int1 - int2);
                '*': Writeln (int1 * int2);
                '/': Writeln (int1 DIV int2);
            END (* CASE operator *);
        END (* WHILE NOT Eof (input *);
END (* ExpressionEvaluation *).
```

The input follows.

```
5 + 6
3 - 7
4*  9
12/3
10 * 0
```

```
5+        6=        11
3-        7=        -4
4*        9=        36
12/       3=         4
10*       0=         0
```

Chapter 11

Arrays

Suppose we want to read in a list of scores from a file counting the frequency of each score. This is very difficult to solve with the PASCAL we have seen thus far. Let us try to decompose the problem anyway.

Initialize counters
WHILE *there is more input*
        Read a number
        Add one to the appropriate counter
Print out counters

Suppose that the scores range from 0 to 20. Currently, we can only solve this problem by having 21 separate variables. To initialize them, we would need 21 separate assignment statements. To "add one to the appropriate counter," we would need a very cumbersome **IF** statement or a **CASE** statement with 21 cases. We would also need to list 21 separate variables to print out all of the counters. Writing such a program would be more of an exercise in typing or text editing than programming. Furthermore, after finishing the program, imagine being asked to modify the program to handle scores from 0 to 100!

We need the ability to "add one to the ith variable." The solution is to use an *array*. An array is a structure made up of many variables of the same type. We can refer to an array as a whole, or to any of its elements.

11-1 USING ARRAYS

Arrays are a generalization of the concept of a variable. Whereas one variable name can denote at most one value, a single array name can denote a collection of values. We can view an array as a peg that balloons out of the pegboard into a shape similar to a TV picture tube. The name of the array appears over the hole in the pegboard in which this TV tube peg is inserted. The shape of this peg is discussed in the next section.

The front of this picture tube acts as a miniature pegboard itself. The variables on the picture tube are called the *elements* of the array. This miniature pegboard must conform to the following restrictions.

1. Each hole in the miniature pegboard must be of the same shape. Remember that a shape specifies the *type* of the values that can be stored there. The types we have seen thus far are integer, real, character, boolean, and enumerated and subrange types. Thus, we can speak of an array of integers, an array of reals, an array of characters, an array of booleans, or even arrays of enumerated or subrange types. The type of elements of the array is called the *base type*; it describes the kinds of values to be stored in the array.

2. Each variable hole on the miniature pegboard has a *name* that can be an integer (regardless of what type of value can be put in the hole).* This name is called the *index* of the array.

To refer to any specific array variable, we must specify both the array name (which TV tube on the pegboard) and the index or element number (which hole number on the TV screen). For example, we might specify element number 2 of the array, which is named **z** (see Figure 11-1 for a graphic illustration). This is done by writing `z[2]`. That is, the array name **z**, followed by a left square bracket [, followed by the element number 2, followed by an ending right square bracket]. We speak of this as *accessing* the second element of **z**. The most important fact to know about arrays is that *we can use an array name with an index value anywhere we can use a simple variable*. By this rule, we can legally write the following PASCAL instructions.

```
z[1] := 3;        x := z[3];              z[1] := z[2];
Read (z[2]);      Write ('ANSWER=', z[1]);   Foo(x, y, z[2]);
```

Thus far, we have only put constants between the brackets, [and]. But, as we have seen many times before, PASCAL generalizes concepts. *Any expression that evaluates to the index type of the array can appear within the square brackets.* This allows us to *compute* the element of the array we wish to use.

Let us go back to the problem in the previous section: tallying frequencies of scores. The expansion of "add one to the appropriate counter" is now

```
counter[score] := counter[score] + 1;
```

We also need to initialize the array of counters. We wish to loop through all array elements. This can be done with a **FOR** loop.

```
FOR score := lowScore TO highScore DO
    counter[score] := 0;
```

Similarly, we can print out the values of the array.

```
FOR score := lowScore TO highScore DO
    Writeln ('There are ', counter[score],
        ' occurrences of the score ', score);
```

---

* We will generalize this shortly.

```
VAR z: ARRAY [1..2] OF integer;
    r1: real;
    r2: real;
    b: boolean;
    ⋮
z[1] := 3;
z[2] := 7;
r1 := 1.6;
r2 := 2.5;
b := true;
```

Figure 11-1 Pegboard for Arrays.

Thus, FOR loops are useful in programs that compute with arrays. We have seen that the index of a FOR loop can be used directly to access an array element by *indexing* into the array.

We must also consider the kinds of values used to index the array. Notice that there must be a separate variable in the array for each value of the index. If the index value is an integer, there would be millions of elements in the array unless we constrain the index value. Instead, we declare two extreme index values to be the *bounds* of the array. We will speak of the *lower bound* and the *upper bound* of an array. (For most of our purposes, we will use arrays with a lower bound of 1.) Our problem uses scores of 0 to 20 to index the array; consequently, the bounds are 0 and 20. All values within this range are also index values of the array; that is, the range of index values for a given array is contiguous.

To read in some test scores and count the frequency of each score, we could use the following program.

```
PROGRAM TallyScores (input, output);
    (* tallies occurrences of scores *)
    CONST
        lowScore = 0;
        highScore = 20;

    TYPE
        scoreRange = lowScore..highScore;
        arrayType = ARRAY [scoreRange] OF integer;

    VAR
        testScore: scoreRange;
        testCount: arrayType;

    BEGIN

        FOR testScore := 0 TO highScore DO
            testCount[testScore]:= 0;

        WHILE NOT Eof DO
            BEGIN
                Readln (testScore);
                testCount[testScore] := testCount[testScore] + 1
            END; (* FOR tests *)

        FOR testScore := 0 TO highScore
            Write (testCount[testScore] : 4,
                ' people got a test score of', testScore : 4)
    END (* TallyScores *).
```

What would happen in the preceding example if the user had input a test score of 21? It would be rejected, since **testScore** is constrained to the bounds of **scoreRange**. However, if we had declared **testScore** to be an ordinary **integer**, the value would not be rejected upon input. But we would have a problem when we accessed **testCount[21]**.

If the expression within the brackets evaluates to an integer that is not in the array bounds (too low or too high), PASCAL will stop the program and remark, "ARRAY INDEX OUT OF BOUNDS," or some such equivalent. A common source of programming errors when dealing with arrays are bugs that cause out-of-bounds array accesses.

Exercise

1. Write a code fragment to read in the elements of the array **listnum** with bounds of 1 and 8.

11-2 DECLARING ARRAYS

Arrays are declared in much the same manner as ordinary variables, but additional information must be present to fully specify an array.

```
TYPE
    baseType = (red, green, blue);
    indexType = 1..100;
    arrayType = ARRAY [indexType] OF baseType;
VAR
    arrayName: arrayType;
```

An array type, such as the type of **arrayType**, has two types that compose it: the *index type* and the *base type.* The index type tells the number of values in the array, and how to refer to them. In **arrayType**, the index type is **indexType**. The variable **arrayName** has 100 elements, named **arrayName[1]**, **arrayName[2]**,..., **arrayName[100]**. Thus far we have used only subranges of integers as index types of arrays. We can use any scalar type, **char**, **boolean**, or subranges of them or of **integer**s. The base type is the type of value that can be stored in any element of the array. In **arrayName**, the base type is **(red, green, blue)**. The shape of the peg that fits into the TV tube is that of the base type. As we have noticed, we can use a type name instead of the subrange notation to declare the index type of an array.

We can pass array elements to procedures; from the procedure's point of view, it is the same as passing an ordinary variable as a parameter. We can also pass an entire array to a procedure.

If we had an array in the main program whose type was an array from 1 to 10 of integer, we would like to be able to pass this array to a procedure with its parameter declared as

```
                  (* wrong *)
PROCEDURE TakeArray (myname : ARRAY [1..10] OF integer);
                  (* wrong *)
```

PASCAL does not let us do this. The restriction placed on parameters is that the type specification following the colon must be a type name. Thus, we need to use a type definition.

```
TYPE
    arrayType = ARRAY [1..10] OF integer;

PROCEDURE TakeArray(myname : arrayType);
```

As an example, the following declaration can be used to declare the two integer variables: **count** and **limit**, the real variable **xcoord**, the two integer arrays **xcount** and **ycount**, and a real array called **zplex**. The elements of arrays **xcount** and **ycount** are named by the integers 1 to 8. The elements of the array **zplex** are named by the integers 1 to 100.

```
TYPE
    countIndex = 1..8;
    countArray = ARRAY [countIndex] OF integer;

VAR
    count, limit: countIndex;
    xcoord: real;
    xcount, ycount: countArray;
    zplex: ARRAY [1..100] OF real;
```

When passing an array to a procedure as a value parameter, a copy is made of the array (see the end of Section 9-2-1). This may be wasteful of memory and time; therefore, it is usually preferred to pass arrays by reference to avoid using the additional memory for the copy.

11-3 ARRAYS: AN EXAMPLE

Instead of tallying numerical scores, the following program illustrates arrays indexed by an enumerated type to tally the occurrences of favorite color.

```
PROGRAM Rainbow (input, output);
    (* program to count occurrences of favorite colors *)
    TYPE
        color = (red, blue, green, orange, yellow, black, white);
        countType =  ARRAY [color] OF 0..100;

    VAR
        count: countType;
        favoriteColor: color;

    PROCEDURE Initialize (VAR theCount: countType);
        (* initializes counters to 0 *)
        VAR aColor: color;

    BEGIN
        FOR aColor := red TO white DO
            theCount[aColor] := 0;
    END; (* Initialize *)

    PROCEDURE ProcessFavoriteColor (theColor: color;
                                    VAR theCount: countType);
        (* adds 1 to the appropriate counter *)
    BEGIN
        theCount[theColor] := theCount[theColor] + 1;
    END; (* ProcessFavoriteColor *)
```

```
    PROCEDURE PrintResults (VAR theCount: countType);
        (* prints totals of occurrences *)
        VAR aColor: color;

    BEGIN
        FOR aColor := red to white DO
            Writeln ('There were', theCount[aColor],
                ' occurrences of ', aColor);
    END; (* PrintResults *)

BEGIN (* Main procedure body *)
    Initialize (count);
    WHILE NOT Eof DO
        BEGIN
            Readln (favoriteColor);
            ProcessFavoriteColor (favoriteColor, count);
        END; (* WHILE NOT Eof *)
    PrintResults (count);
END (* Rainbow *).
```

Exercises

1.   Write a program that reads a list of numbers and prints them in reverse order. Use a constant to define the maximum number of input values to handle. The program should give a message if there are too many input values, indicating that the additional ones are being ignored.

2.   Modify the above program so that when there are too many input values, it reports the current maximum allowed as well as how many input values there actually are. This allows someone to change the constant in the program to the desired value without having to guess what the new value should be.

11-4 STANDARD DEVIATION

When faced with large quantities of real values, such as the longevity of a particular brand of 60 watt lightbulbs, two summary values are interesting: the average value and an estimate of the variation. One measure of the variation is the *standard deviation*. Since we are unable to test all of the items, we will take a representative sample and calculate estimates of the average (or mean) and standard deviation using this sample. If x_i is the ith number and $\bar{x}$ is the average value of x_i, then the standard deviation is well estimated by the formula

$$\sigma = \sqrt{\sum (\bar{x} - x_i)^2 / (n-1)}$$

This means that we should make two passes over the data, the first to compute the average and the second to compute the sum of squares.

Read numbers
Compute Average
Compute Sum of Squares
Compute Standard Deviation

This converts to the following PASCAL program.

```
PROGRAM StandardDeviation (input, output);
    (* compute standard deviation of a list of numbers *)

    CONST maxCount = 100;
    TYPE range = 1..maxCount;
         rangeZero = 0..maxCount;
         valueArray = ARRAY [range] OF real;
    VAR values: valueArray;
        count: rangeZero;
        average: real;
        sumOfSquares: real;
        standardDeviation: real;


    PROCEDURE ReadNumbers (VAR theCount: rangeZero;
                           VAR theValues: valueArray);
        (* Read numbers into array *)
    BEGIN
        theCount := 0;  (* no numbers read so far *)
        WHILE NOT Eof DO
            BEGIN
                theCount := theCount + 1;
                Readln (theValues[theCount]);
            END; (* WHILE NOT Eof *)
    END; (* ReadNumbers *)


    FUNCTION ComputeAverage (    theCount: rangeZero;
                             VAR theValues: valueArray): real;
        (* Compute average of array *)
        VAR sum: real;
            counter: range;
    BEGIN
        sum := 0;
        FOR counter := 1 TO theCount DO
            sum := sum + theValues[counter];
        ComputeAverage := sum / theCount;
    END; (* ComputeAverage *)


    FUNCTION ComputeSumOfSquares (    theAverage: real;
                                      theCount: rangeZero;
                                  VAR theValues: valueArray):
            real;
        (* compute sum of squares *)
        VAR sum: real;
            counter: range;
    BEGIN
        sum := 0;
        FOR counter := 1 TO theCount DO
            sum := sum +
                Sqr(theAverage - theValues[counter]);
        ComputeSumOfSquares := sum;
    END; (* ComputeSumOfSquares *)
```

```
BEGIN (* StandardDeviation *)
    ReadNumbers (count, values);
    average := ComputeAverage (count, values);
    Writeln ('Average=', average);
    IF count = 1
        THEN Writeln ('Standard Deviation is undefined')
        ELSE BEGIN
            sumOfSquares :=
                ComputeSumOfSquares (average, count, values);
            Writeln ('Standard Deviation=',
                Sqrt (sumOfSquares / (count - 1) ) );
            END (* more than one value *);
END (* StandardDeviation *).
```

There are a number of subtle points in this program. Notice that there are two similar ranges, **range** and **rangeZero**. Before we have read any values, we have read zero values, but we have not read a *zeroth* value. Therefore, we need to handle more values in the index than than in the array.

Notice that the array is always passed as **VAR** parameters even when it is not being altered. This is because a copy of the parameter is made when it is passed by value. Whereas this is acceptable and desirable for simple parameters, making a copy of an array wastes both space and time. Therefore, arrays are usually passed as **VAR** parameters.

11-5 CODE CONVERSION

Suppose we want to compute grade point averages. We would read in a series of letter grades and then have to compute arithmetic based on them. Suppose the grades are A, B, C, D, and F, which are 4, 3, 2, 1, and 0 points, respectively. We could decompose the problem as follows:

```
WHILE there is more input
        Set sum and count to zero
        WHILE there are more grades for this student
                Read a letter
                Add 1 to count
                Add points to sum
        Compute average
```

We need to be able to convert from letters to numbers. To do this, we can index an array by letters whose values are integers. That is,

```
VAR gradePoints: ARRAY ['A'..'F'] OF 0..4;
```

We could initialize this array with a series of assignment statements.

```
gradePoints['A'] := 4;
    ⋮
gradePoints['F'] := 0;
```

What should we initialize gradePoints['E'] to? We either make sure not to access that element or test for the presence of a strange value there. Since there is only one value, it is easy to test for 'E', but consider the problem of computing grade point averages using E (excellent), G (good), M (mediocre), P (poor), and F (failure).

```
PROGRAM GPAs (input, output);
    (* Compute Grade Point Averages *)
    TYPE gradeRange = 'A'..'F';
        points: -1..4;
    VAR gradePoints: ARRAY [gradeRange] OF points;

    PROCEDURE Initialize;
    BEGIN
        gradePoints['A'] := 4;
        gradePoints['B'] := 3;
        gradePoints['C'] := 2;
        gradePoints['D'] := 1;
        gradePoints['E'] := -1;
        gradePoints['F'] := 0;
    END (* Initialize *);

    PROCEDURE ProcessAStudent;
        VAR grade: char;
            sum: integer;
            count: integer;
    BEGIN
        sum := 0;
        count := 0;
        WHILE NOT Eoln DO
            BEGIN
                Read (grade);
                IF (grade < 'A') OR (grade > 'F')
                    THEN Writeln ('Grade ', grade,
                            ' out of range')
                ELSE IF gradePoints[grade] = -1
                    THEN Writeln ('Grade ', grade,
                            ' invalid')
                ELSE BEGIN
                    sum := sum + gradePoint[grade];
                    count := count + 1;
                END (* grade in range and valid *);
            END (* WHILE there are more grades *);
        Writeln ('GPA = ', sum / count);
        Readln;
    END (* ProcessAStudent *);

BEGIN
    Initialize;
    WHILE NOT Eof DO
        ProcessAStudent;
END (* GPAs *).
```

Chapter 12

Records

We have seen how to aggregate data into arrays. There is another technique for aggregating data—*records*. Like arrays, records are variables that can hold more than one data value. Unlike arrays, records can hold data of different types. The individual components of an array are called *elements*; the individual components of a record are called *fields*.

Suppose that we want to store information about a person. We might want to keep track of height, weight, birthday, etc. We could create variables for these values (`height`, `weight`, `monthOfBirth`, etc.). Rather than having individual variables for each of these values, we might want to somehow put them into one large variable with many slots. We can do this by creating a record.

```
TYPE
    months = (jan, feb, mar, apr, may, jun, jul, aug, sep,
        oct, nov, dec);
    dayOfMonth = 1..31;
    date = RECORD
        month: months;
        day: dayOfMonth
        END; (* date RECORD *)
    heightValue = RECORD
        feet: 0..7;
        inches: 0..11
        END; (* heightValue RECORD *)
    person = RECORD
        height: heightValue;
        weight: integer;
        birthday: date
        END; (* person RECORD *)

VAR
    myBirthday: date;
    me: person;

BEGIN
    myBirthday.month := jan;
    myBirthday.day := 14;
    me.height.feet := 5;
    me.height.inches := 10;
    me.weight := 170;
    me.birthday := myBirthday;
    Write(me.birthday.day);
```

A record contains fields that resemble ordinary variables. These fields may be of any type, including another record. We refer to a field within the record by giving the record name followed by a period and the field name. We can use the field of a record the same way as we use an ordinary variable: we can assign into it or use its value in an expression. We can also assign whole records if, of course, they are of the same type. We can use records as the base type of an array, or have an array as a field of a record.

12-1 RECORDS: AN EXAMPLE—BUBBLE SORT

Suppose that we have a file containing a list of students in a class, with each name followed by a grade. The file contains records in random order, but we want the output to be a list of students in descending order of grade; that is, we want to list the student with the highest grade first and the one with the lowest grade last. This problem falls under the general category of sorting.

There are many algorithms for sorting. In fact, entire books have been devoted to analysis of sorting algorithms. We will use an algorithm called the *bubble sort*.

Since it is possible for the highest grade to be last in the file, we will have to delay printing anything until all input values have been read. Thus, we need an array to store all of the input values. We will be ordering the student information by the student's grade. The category by which the ordering occurs is called the *sort key*. Associated with each key—or grade—is some information, often called *data*; in this case, the data is the student's name. If we have an array containing all of the grades, the result should be an array containing the grades in descending order. Since the grades will be rearranged, we will need to maintain a correlation between the keys and the data. One way to do this is to have two parallel arrays, one containing the keys and the other containing the data. Then, the matching key and data pairs will have the same index value in both arrays. For some applications, this may actually be the best method. However, a clearer alternative is to have a single array of records, with each record containing both the key and the data.

We can sort the array by rearranging it in place or by making a copy of it. Let us consider the case of rearranging it in place. When we move one of the elements of the array, we will have to relocate the old value to make room for the new one. We can do this simply by *swapping* values.

We first compare the first two elements of the array and swap them if they are out of order. After these are in order, we can compare element (say, the second one) with the third, and swap them if they are out of order. Next, we compare the third and fourth elements, and swap them if necessary. We continue comparing, and optionally swapping, adjacent elements of the array until we reach the end with high index values. In this process, small elements tend to move to higher index values, while larger elements tend to move to lower index values. That is, small elements bubble up to the right, hence the name *bubble sort*.

Consider sorting the following five numbers:

        10   12   8   10   14

We want the numbers to print in descending order. After comparing the first two elements we obtain

        12   10   8   10   14

The order remains unchanged when we compare the second and third elements. Comparing the third and fourth elements causes a swap with the following results:

        12   10   10   8   14

Next, we compare and swap the last two elements of the array.

        12   10   10   14   8

The array is not yet sorted, but it is closer; perhaps a few more passes will help. The second pass produces

        12   10   14   10   8

The third pass gives

12	14	10	10	8

The fourth pass produces

14	12	10	10	8

Absence of swaps on the fifth pass confirms that the array is in sorted order.

Let us proceed to writing a general algorithm for sorting in descending order. We do repeated passes over the data until no swaps are performed.

```
REPEAT
    one bubble-sort pass
UNTIL NOT swapDone;
```

Each bubble-sort pass involves going through all pairs of adjacent elements and swapping those that are out of order.

```
REPEAT
    swapDone := false;
    FOR index := 1 TO size - 1 DO
        IF key[index] < key[index + 1]
            THEN BEGIN
                Swap (key and data[index],
                    key and data[index + 1]);
                swapDone := true;
            END (* records out of order *)
UNTIL NOT swapDone;
```

We must now consider how to declare our array of records containing the grades and names, and how to refer to the key part—the grade—or to the entire thing. To hold the name, we can use an array of characters. Thus, the record declaration would be

```
TYPE nameString = ARRAY [1..nameLength] OF char;
     studentRecord = RECORD
        name: nameString;
        grade: integer;
        END (* studentRecord *);

VAR studentList: ARRAY [1..numberOfStudents] OF studentRecord;
```

To refer to an entire particular student's record, say studentList[index], where index specifies the desired student record. To obtain that student's grade, we say studentList[index].grade. Now, our program becomes

```
REPEAT
    swapDone := false;
    FOR index := 1 TO size - 1 DO
        IF studentList[index].grade <
            studentList[index + 1].grade
            THEN BEGIN
                Swap (studentList[index],
                    studentList[index + 1]);
                swapDone := true;
            END (* records out of order *)
UNTIL NOT swapDone;
```

We should now complete the rest of the program.

```
PROGRAM SortGrades (input, output);
(* This program sorts a list of students in descending order of
   grade *)

    CONST nameLength = 20;
        studentCount = 100;


    TYPE nameString = ARRAY [1..nameLength] OF char;
        studentRecord = RECORD
            name: nameString;
            grade: integer;
            END (* studentRecord *);
        studentArray = ARRAY [1..studentCount] OF studentRecord;
        countType = 0..studentCount;


    VAR studentList: studentArray;
        numberOfStudents: countType;


    PROCEDURE Sort (VAR listOfStudents: studentArray;
                        countOfStudents: countType);
        (* does the actual sorting *)
        VAR index: 1..studentCount;
            swapDone: boolean;


        PROCEDURE Swap (VAR rec1, rec2: studentRecord);
            (* swaps a pair of student records *)
            VAR temp: studentRecord;
        BEGIN
            temp := rec1;
            rec1 := rec2;
            rec2 := temp;
        END (* Swap *);
```

```
BEGIN (* body of Sort *)
    REPEAT
        swapDone := false;
        FOR index := 1 TO countOfStudents - 1 DO
            IF listOfStudents[index].grade <
                listOfStudents[index + 1].grade
                THEN BEGIN
                    Swap (listOfStudents[index],
                        listOfStudents[index + 1]);
                    swapDone := true;
                END (* records out of order *)
    UNTIL NOT swapDone;
END (* Sort *);




PROCEDURE ReadData (VAR listOfStudents: studentArray;
                    VAR countOfStudents: countType);
    (* reads student records from a file *)
    VAR charCount: 1..nameLength;

BEGIN
    countOfStudents := 0;
    WHILE (NOT Eof) AND (countOfStudents < studentCount) DO
        BEGIN
            countOfStudents := countOfStudents + 1;
            FOR charCount := 1 TO nameLength DO
                Read (listOfStudents[countOfStudents].
                    name[charCount]);
            Readln(listOfStudents[countOfStudents].grade);
        END (* WHILE more students to read *);
    IF NOT Eof
        THEN Writeln ('More than ', studentCount,
            ' students, rest ignored.');
END (* ReadData *);




PROCEDURE WriteData (listOfStudents: studentArray;
                     countOfStudents: countType);
    (* reads student records from a file *)
    VAR charCount: 1..nameLength;
        studentNumber: countType;

BEGIN
    FOR studentNumber := 1 TO countOfStudents DO
        BEGIN
            FOR charCount := 1 TO nameLength DO
                Write (listOfStudents[studentNumber].
                    name[charCount]);
            Writeln(listOfStudents[studentNumber].grade);
        END (* FOR each student *);
END (* WriteData *);
```

```
BEGIN (* main procedure *)
    ReadData (studentList, numberOfStudents);
    Sort (studentList, numberOfStudents);
    WriteData (studentList, numberOfStudents);
END (* SortGrades *).
```

Strings

Much of the character manipulation we may want to do involves the use of strings of characters. We would like to be able to read in text from a file, massage it as we see fit, and then write it back out again. Users of interactive systems employ text editors that work in just that way. In this chapter, we will consider ways of manipulating strings.

13-1 FIXED-LENGTH CHARACTER STRINGS

In the previous chapter, we wrote a program that sorted a list of names and grades in descending order by grade. The names were all exactly 20 characters long. In the input, we were going to find 20 characters for the name; in the output, we were going to output exactly 20 characters. This is the simplest form of string manipulation. We did not do anything to the names besides reading, writing, and assigning them. We first encountered fixed-length character strings in Section 12-1.

However, people may put long or short lines in the input. Handling short lines is easy: we can pad them with blanks. That is, we can extend them on the right (high index values) with spaces up to the size of the array. Long lines are more of a problem. We can truncate them, printing an error message if appropriate.

Let us consider the problem of reading in a list of magazine subscriptions and printing two-up labels for the list. (Two-up labels print in two adjacent columns.) Graphically, if our input labels are 1, 2, 3, . . . , our output will be

```
1       2
3       4
5       6
etc.
```

Our input file consists of many subscriptions; each subscription takes up 4 lines and contains the subscription number, name, address, and city/state/zip, respectively. The labels are $3\frac{1}{2}$ inches wide and 1 inch high, corresponding to 35 characters by six lines. Since the labels will not be positioned on the printer exactly, we will not print the top and bottom lines of each label, nor the first or last five columns of each line. Thus, each line will be 25 characters long.

Our program might appear as

```
WHILE NOT Eof DO
    BEGIN
    Read one label
    IF even
        THEN print last two labels
    END
IF odd
    THEN print one label
```

An alternative is to have the read routine return a blank label if end of file has been reached.

```
WHILE NOT Eof DO
    Read one label
    Read another label
    Print two labels
```

We decide to use the second algorithm, so that we now have to write the procedure to read a label.

```
Do 4 times
    Read one line
```

How should we read a line? The lines could be any length.

```
WHILE NOT Eoln DO
    Read a character
    Stuff the character into an array
```

We also have to keep track of the character count to know where to fill the array. Furthermore, we have to test when the array becomes full so that we will stop stuffing characters into the array.

```
charCount := 0;
WHILE NOT Eoln DO
    BEGIN
        charCount := charCount + 1;
        Read (ch);
        IF charCount <= lineLength
            THEN someArray [charCount] := ch;
    END (* WHILE NOT Eoln *);
```

Unfortunately, if the line is short we have to pad it with blanks, that is, fill the high end of the array with blanks.

```
FOR charCount := charCount + 1 TO lineLength DO
    someArray [charCount] := ' ';
```

This seems a bit complicated. Perhaps there is a simpler way.

We could say that we have to stuff `lineLength` characters into the array.

```
FOR charCount := 1 TO lineLength DO
    Read a character, if there is one
    Stuff the character into the array
```

Converting into code, we obtain

```
FOR charCount := 1 TO lineLength DO
    IF Eoln
        THEN someArray [charCount] := ' '
        ELSE BEGIN
                Read (ch);
                someArray [charCount] := ch;
            END (* NOT Eoln *);
```

We forgot to remove the additional characters on the line.

```
Readln;
```

Which is better? That depends on what is meant by better. The second solution is easier to read and understand—or at least the author thinks so. The first solution avoids testing for end of line once it is reached by exiting the first loop and going into a **FOR** loop (which does nothing if the line is not short). However, the first solution reads in the characters one by one even after `lineLength` characters have been read; the second solution does a `Readln` to skip over these characters. (Another alternative is to first blank out the array with a **FOR** loop and then read in the entire line with a **WHILE** loop, which also terminates when the array is full.)

A first solution is not always the best way to do something. Although you may get something to work, speed, elegance, and understanding may have been sacrificed. The time to think about the efficiency or elegance of your algorithm is before you put it into code. This way, you can change it before you have expended much effort. You *will not* want to change it once it works!

Now back to the program. We are now ready to write the complete program.

```
PROGRAM TwoUpLabels (input, output);
(* reads in a file of 4-line labels and
   prints them two-up on gummed labels *)

    CONST lineLength = 25;
        margin = 5;
        numberOfLines = 4;

    TYPE string = ARRAY [1..lineLength] OF char;
        mailingLabel = ARRAY [1..numberOfLines] OF string;

    VAR left, right: mailingLabel;

    PROCEDURE BlankLine(VAR str: string);
        VAR charCount: 1..lineLength;
    BEGIN
        FOR charCount := 1 TO lineLength DO
            str [charCount] := ' '
    END (* BlankLine *);

    PROCEDURE ReadLine(VAR str: string);
        VAR charCount: 1..lineLength;
            ch: char;
    BEGIN
        FOR charCount := 1 TO lineLength DO
            IF Eoln
                THEN str [charCount] := ' '
                ELSE BEGIN
                        Read (ch);
                        str [charCount] := ch;
                    END (* NOT Eoln *);
        Readln;
    END (* ReadLine *);

    PROCEDURE WriteLine(str: string);
        VAR charCount: 0..lineLength;
    BEGIN
        Write (' ' : margin);   (* left margin *)
        FOR charCount := 1 TO lineLength DO
            Write (str [charCount]);
        Write (' ' : margin);   (* right margin *)
    END (* WriteLine *);

    PROCEDURE ReadLabel (VAR lab: mailingLabel);
        VAR line: 1..numberOfLines;
    BEGIN
        FOR line := 1 TO numberOfLines DO
            IF Eof
                THEN BlankLine (lab [line])
                ELSE ReadLine (lab [line]);
    END (* ReadLabel *);
```

```
    PROCEDURE WriteLabels (lft, rt: mailingLabel);
        VAR line: 1..numberOfLines;
    BEGIN
        Writeln;                   (* top margin *)
        FOR line := 1 TO numberOfLines DO
            BEGIN
                WriteLine (lft [line]);
                WriteLine (rt [line]);
                Writeln;
            END (* FOR line *);
        Writeln;                   (* bottom margin *)
    END (* WriteLabels *);
BEGIN
    WHILE NOT Eof DO
        BEGIN
            ReadLabel (left);
            ReadLabel (right);
            WriteLabels (left, right);
        END;
END (* TwoUpLabels *).
```

Notice that the program handles the case of the number of lines in a file that does not correspond to an integral number of labels, that is, not a multiple of 4. This is done by putting the Eof test inside the FOR loop of ReadLabels. In general, programs should be resilient to errors in the data. However, if the first line is missing, all labels produced will be wrong. The program does handle an even or odd number of labels. Simple changes can often improve the "user friendliness" of a program.

13-2 VARIABLE-LENGTH STRINGS

We might want to have character strings of variable length and also keep track of their length. For example, suppose we want to read in sentences and test whether they are palindromes. A palindrome is a sentence that reads the same forward and backward when punctuation is ignored. The following sentences are palindromes: "Aha!" "Madam, I'm Adam." "A man, a plan, a canal, Panama." "Doc, note I dissent; a fast never prevents a fatness. I diet on cod." "Eros? Sidney, my end is sore!" "Rise to vote, sir."

First, we must define a data structure capable of holding a string. An array alone cannot do because we must keep track of its length. Thus, we will use a record containing an array and an integer field for length. We must make the array a fixed size, say 128.

```
CONST
    maxStrLength = 128;
TYPE
    stringSize = 0..maxStrLength;   (* A string can be null *)
    string = RECORD
        length: stringSize;
        text: ARRAY [1..maxStrLength] OF char;
        END; (* string RECORD *)
```

Our algorithm can be

```
WHILE NOT Eof DO
    Read a string
    Write the string
    IF it is a palindrome
        THEN Writeln (' is a palindrome')
        ELSE Writeln (' is not a palindrome');
```

We need a way to read a string.

```
PROCEDURE ReadString (VAR theString: string);
BEGIN
    theString.length := 0;
    WHILE (NOT Eoln) AND (theString.length < maxStrLength) DO
        BEGIN
            theString.length := theString.length + 1;
            Read (theString.text [theString.length]);
        END (* WHILE NOT Eoln *);
    Readln;
END (* ReadString *);
```

We also need a way to write a string.

```
PROCEDURE WriteString (theString: string);
    VAR
        index: stringSize;

BEGIN
    FOR index := 1 TO theString.length DO
        Write (theString.text [index]);
END (* WriteString *);
```

Determining whether or not a string is a palindrome is a little harder. We want to compare the characters starting from both ends of the string. We also want to skip nonalphabetic characters.

```
Set indexes at each end
WHILE more characters to compare
    AND so far a palindrome DO
        Skip nonalphabetic characters at both ends
        Test whether the two characters match
        Advance to next pair of characters
```

Skipping over non-alphabetic characters at each end can be done with a WHILE or REPEAT loop. If we use a REPEAT loop, we can also do the operation of advancing to the next pair of characters.

```
REPEAT
    left := left + 1;
UNTIL Letter (theString.text [left]);
```

This assumes that **Letter** is a boolean function that tests whether its argument is a letter.

```
FUNCTION Letter (ch: char): boolean;
BEGIN
    Letter := (ch >= 'A') AND (ch <= 'Z');
END (* Letter *);
```

Of course, this assumes that there are no extraneous characters between A and Z. This is not the case on some IBM systems, but since none of these extraneous characters will appear in the input, we are relatively safe. If they do, they will be considered as letters.

We can now write the palindrome tester.

```
FUNCTION IsPalindrome (theString: string): boolean;
    VAR left, right: stringSize;
        soFarPalindrome: boolean;
BEGIN
    left := 1;
    right := theString.length;
    soFarPalindrome := true;
    WHILE (left < right) AND soFarPalindrome DO
        BEGIN
            (* skip nonalphabetic characters on left *)
            REPEAT
                left := left + 1;
            UNTIL Letter (theString.text [left]);
            (* skip nonalphabetic characters on right *)
            REPEAT
                right := right - 1;
            UNTIL Letter (theString.text [right]);

            soFarPalindrome :=
                (theString.text [left] = theString.text [right]);
        END (* WHILE still a palindrome and more chars to test *);
    IsPalindrome := soFarPalindrome;
END (* IsPalindrome *);
```

Note that the test for completion is **left < right**. We are finished when **left = right** since two characters in the same position must be equal. This program handles null strings properly, but it will fail if the string does not contain any letters. However, there is a more important bug in this program: it ignores the first and last characters of the line. This can be fixed by initializing **left** to 0 and **right** to one more than **theString.length**. Unfortunately, it no longer handles null strings. This may be considered an error; correcting it is left as an exercise to the reader.

The complete program follows.

```
PROGRAM PalindromeTester (input, output);
    (* tests input lines for being palindromes *)

    CONST
        maxStrLength = 128;

    TYPE
        stringSize = 0..maxStrLength;   (* A string can be null *)
        string = RECORD
            length: stringSize;
            text: ARRAY [1..maxStrLength] OF char;
            END; (* string RECORD *)

VAR pal: string;



PROCEDURE ReadString (VAR theString: string);
BEGIN
    theString.length := 0;
    WHILE (NOT Eoln) AND (theString.length < maxStrLength) DO
        BEGIN
            theString.length := theString.length + 1;
            Read (theString.text [theString.length]);
        END (* WHILE NOT Eoln *);
    Readln;
END (* ReadString *);



PROCEDURE WriteString (theString: string);
    VAR
        index: stringSize;

BEGIN
    FOR index := 1 TO theString.length DO
        Write (theString.text [index]);
END (* WriteString *);



FUNCTION IsPalindrome (theString: string): boolean;
    VAR left, right: stringSize;
        soFarPalindrome: boolean;

    FUNCTION Letter (ch: char): boolean;
    BEGIN
        Letter := (ch >= 'A') AND (ch <= 'Z');
    END (* Letter *);
```

```
    BEGIN (* body of IsPalindrome *)
        left := 0;          (* 0 because of REPEAT loop *)
        right := theString.length + 1;
        soFarPalindrome := true;
        WHILE (left < right) AND soFarPalindrome DO
            BEGIN
                (* skip nonalphabetic characters on left *)
                REPEAT
                    left := left + 1;
                UNTIL Letter (theString.text [left]);
                (* skip nonalphabetic characters on right *)
                REPEAT
                    right := right - 1;
                UNTIL Letter (theString.text [right]);

                soFarPalindrome :=
                    (theString.text [left] =
                    theString.text [right]);
            END;  (* WHILE still a palindrome
                    and more chars to test *)
        IsPalindrome := soFarPalindrome;
    END (* IsPalindrome *);

BEGIN
    WHILE NOT Eof DO
        BEGIN
            ReadString (pal);
            WriteString (pal);
            IF IsPalindrome (pal)
                THEN Writeln (' is a palindrome.')
                ELSE Writeln (' is not a palindrome.')
        END (* WHILE NOT Eof *);
END (* PalindromeTester *).
```

Exercises

1. In the last program, what happens if there is no alphabetic character in the middle of the array?
2. In the last program, correct the program to handle null strings.

13-3 FILLING TEXT

Suppose that we want to read in a paragraph of text, and output as many words as we can on each line without going past the right margin. There may be additional spaces between words, and these are to be removed. There also may be blank lines, and these are to be ignored. We read words repeatedly until we find one that will not fit on the line. We can then output this line and start a new line with the word that did not fit. When we reach the end of the file, we output the partially filled line. We can describe this as follows:

Read a word
WHILE NOT Eof
    WHILE *this word fits on the line*
        Put this word on the end of the line
        Read a word
    Print the line

Consider what happens when we reach the end of the file. We put the last word on the end of the last line and attempt to read the next word, which does not exist. Let the word-reading routine return a "null" word when it reaches the end of the file. But then we will never exit the inner WHILE loop. We can have both the inner and outer loop test for the end of the file.

Read a word
WHILE NOT Eof
    WHILE *this word fits on the line* AND NOT Eof
        Put this word on the end of the line
        Read a word
    Print the line

We need a procedure to read a word.

Skip over spaces and ends of line
Read all characters until a space or end of line is reached

Before we proceed with writing the program, we should consider what happens if we read a character when Eoln is **true**. The PASCAL standard specifies that a space is read, which has the effect of doing a Readln; that is, we are now on the next line of the file. Thus, we can effectively ignore ends of line and rely on spaces to terminate all words. This translates to

```
REPEAT
    Read (ch);
UNTIL ch <> ' ';
theString.length := 0;
REPEAT
    theString.length := theString.length + 1;
    theString.text [theString.length] := ch;
    Read (ch);
UNTIL ch = ' ';
```

Unfortunately, we have not taken care of end of file. End of file can only be reached when we have done a Readln, or otherwise read over the last end-of-line mark by an ordinary Read. Another problem is what the program fragment will do if it encounters too long a word. It will increment theString.length beyond its bounds—a runtime error. We can exit from the second REPEAT loop when we reach a space or the end of the array. The following fragment corrects this problem by assuming that there is a space when we fill up the array. A better approach is to print an error message when this occurs, and we have left this change as an exercise for the reader.

```
REPEAT
    IF Eof
        THEN ch := '*'
        ELSE Read (ch);
UNTIL ch <> ' ';
theString.length := 0;
IF NOT Eof
    THEN REPEAT
            theString.length := theString.length + 1;
            theString.text [theString.length] := ch;
            Read (ch);
        UNTIL (ch = ' ') OR (theString.length = maxStrLength);
```

We need a way to append the word to the end of the line. The reader should write such a procedure with the following specification:

```
PROCEDURE AppendString (VAR result: string;
                        word: string);
```

The remainder of the program is left as an exercise to the reader.

Exercises

1. Complete the program to fill a paragraph.

2. Modify the program to right-justify the paragraph. A paragraph is right-justified when each line (except the last one) is stretched so that all lines are the same length. Additional spaces are inserted to stretch the lines as necessary. These spaces should be distributed evenly throughout the line to achieve a visually appealing result.

13-4 STRING-HANDLING PROCEDURES

String manipulation is very useful for many applications. Much of this manipulation can be made easier by creating a package of string-handling procedures. We have already considered one such procedure: AppendString. Other useful procedures are Substring, Find, Verify, Deposit, Extract, Concatenate, and Length.

The Substring procedure takes a group of consecutive characters out of the middle of a string. We give it the original string, the starting location, and the desired length, and obtain the resultant string. Copying the characters can easily be done by a FOR loop. However, the problem is that the starting location could be beyond the end of the string. Also, there may not be enough characters after the starting location to satisfy the desired length. We can remove this problem by specifying that blanks are used when the original string is too short; that is, we assume that the original string is padded to the right with blanks as needed.

Find out how many characters we can copy
Copy those characters
Fill on the right to achieve desired length

This translates to

```
PROCEDURE Substring (VAR resultantString: string;
                         originalString: string;
                         startingLocation: stringSize;
                         substringLength: stringSize);
    VAR
        amountAvailable: stringSize;
            (* Amount of input string available past *)
            (* starting location *)
        position: stringSize;

BEGIN
    amountAvailable := Max (0,
        originalString.length - startingLocation + 1);
            (* calculate how much of the string is beyond
                startingLocation.  Since the user may have
                asked for characters beyond the end of
                originalString, we need to ignore negative
                values *)
    FOR position := 1 TO Min (substringLength, amountAvailable) DO
        resultantString.text [position]
                            (* copy one character *)
            := originalString [position + startingLocation - 1];
                            (* length starts at 1 *)
    FOR position := amountAvailable + 1 TO substringLength DO
        resultantString.text [position] := ' ';
                            (* blank out all characters
                                we cannot copy from the
                                input *)
    resultantString.length := substringLength;
END; (* Substring *)
```

The function **Find** has two string parameters and finds the position of the first character in the first string that is in the second string.

```
FUNCTION Find (s: string; chars: string): stringLength;
```

The function **Verify** also has two string parameters and locates the position of the first character in the first string that *is not* in the second string.

```
FUNCTION Verify (s: string; chars: string): stringLength;
```

If there is no such character for **Find** or **Verify**, the function returns 0.

The procedure **Deposit** has three parameters: a string, a number, and a character. The character is deposited in the position represented by the number. If the position is beyond the end of the string, the string is extended by one character only if the new character immediately follows the previous end of the string. Otherwise, it has no effect.

```
PROCEDURE Deposit (VAR result: string;
                        ch: char;
                        where: stringLength);
```

The function **Extract** returns the character in the position represented by the number.

```
FUNCTION Extract (result: string;
                    where: stringLength): char;
```

The procedure **Concatenate** takes two strings and produces a resultant string having all of the characters from one input string followed by all those from the other. It is similar to copying the string and then **AppendString**.

```
PROCEDURE AppendString (VAR result: string;
                            s1, s2: string);
```

The function **Length** returns the length of a string.

```
FUNCTION Length (s: string): stringLength;
```

Exercises

1. Write the procedures and functions specified above.
2. Write a program that reads in an essay and determines how often each word is used.

Recursion

In this chapter, we will not learn any new features of PASCAL. Rather, we will learn a new technique for using the features we already know.

Consider a rectangular grid populated with cells that are either marked or unmarked. We define a *blob* as a group of connected marked cells. Two cells are *connected* if there is a path of adjacent cells that leads from one to the other. We consider cells to be adjacent if they share a side as a boundary, so that each cell has four adjacent cells. Cells touching at the corner are not considered adjacent.

What are the blobs in this figure? Marked cells contain an asterisk and unmarked cells are blank.

```
*** * ***
 * *** *
*** * ***
```

There are three blobs; two resemble the shape of the letter I, and one resembles a plus sign. If we put numbers identifying which cell belongs to which blob, it would appear as

```
111 2 333
 1 222 3
111 2 333
```

Let us look at another example.

```
***** *** ***
*     * * * *
* * * * *** *
* *   *
*****  *****
```

Again there are three blobs:

```
11111 333 333
1    1 3 3 3 3
1 2 1 3 333 3
1    1   3
11111   33333
```

Suppose that we want to "kill a blob." That is, given a particular cell, we want to unmark all cells in the same blob. We kill all neighbors of that cell, and then all neighbors of those neighbors, and so on until we have killed all cells in the blob.*

Kill portion of blob to the right
Kill portion of blob to the left
Kill portion of blob above
Kill portion of blob below

We forgot to kill the cell we are at!

Kill portion of blob to the right
Kill portion of blob to the left
Kill portion of blob above
Kill portion of blob below
Unmark current cell

Let us consider what killing the portion of blob to the right is.

Kill portion of blob to its right
Kill portion of blob to its left
Kill portion of blob now above
Kill portion of blob now below
Unmark current cell

This seems the same as killing the original blob.

In order to convert this to PASCAL, we have to declare the necessary data structures. We need to declare the appearance of a cell:

```
TYPE cell = (dead, alive);
```

We also need to declare the appearance of the board:

```
CONST size = 10;
TYPE range = 1..10;
     grid = ARRAY [range, range] OF cell;
VAR board: grid;
```

---

* This example is due to Jim McGrath.

Now we can proceed to the program.

```
PROCEDURE KillBlob (row, col: range);
BEGIN
    KillBlob (row, col+1);      (* to the right *)
    KillBlob (row, col-1);      (* to the left *)
    KillBlob (row-1, col);      (* above *)
    KillBlob (row+1, col);      (* below *)
    board [row, col] := dead;
END (* KillBlob *);
```

Let us try it on a simple example.

```
 123456789
1*       *
2* ***** *
3*       *
```

Suppose we pass `KillBlob` the parameters 2 and 5. We have **row** set to 2 and **col** set to 5. Moving to the right, we then call `KillBlob` with the parameters 2 and 6. We now have another **row** set to 2 and another **col** set to 6. Once again, we move to the right and call `KillBlob` with 2 and 7. We now have yet another **row** set to 2 and yet another **col** set to 7. As expected, we move to the right and call `KillBlob` with 2 and 8. We are now off the end of the blob, but the code says to move right again. In fact, we will move right *forever*, since there are no tests! Let us change the program so that we move back (by returning) if we reach a dead cell.

```
PROCEDURE KillBlob (row, col: range);
BEGIN
    IF board [row, col] = alive
        THEN BEGIN
            KillBlob (row, col+1);      (* to the right *)
            KillBlob (row, col-1);      (* to the left *)
            KillBlob (row-1, col);      (* above *)
            KillBlob (row+1, col);      (* below *)
            board [row, col] := dead;
            END (* cell is alive *);
END (* KillBlob *);
```

Let us try `KillBlob` again with the parameters 2 and 5. We have **row** set to 2 and **col** set to 5. Since we are at a live cell, we move to the right, and then call `KillBlob` with the parameters 2 and 6. We now have another **row** set to 2 and another **col** set to 6. Once again we are at a live cell, so that we move to the right and call `KillBlob` with 2 and 7. We now have yet another **row** set to 2 and yet another **col** set to 7. As expected, we are still at a live cell, so that we move to the right and call `KillBlob` with 2 and 8. We are now off the end of the blob, but this time we simply return. Here comes the tricky part. We return to the most recent caller of `KillBlob`, which was `KillBlob` with **row** set to 2 and **col** set to 7. This is exactly what we wanted.

Let us digress here to understand *why* we returned to the previous `KillBlob`. Each time a procedure is called, something called a stack frame is created. A *stack frame* contains all of the variables declared in the procedure as well as information about the parameters. Furthermore, it keeps track of the location of the procedure call instruction in calling procedure, and also the values of the old variables. (The old variables are actually in the previous procedure's stack frame.) When the latest procedure is running, we look in its stack frame for the values of variables. Thus, we obtain the latest values of these variables. Now consider what happens when this procedure returns to its caller. Its stack frame with local variables and value parameters is thrown away. We now find the stack frame of the caller with that procedure's variables. You can think of stack frames as pieces of paper on a stack, each of which contains a list of variables declared in a particular procedure and the values of those variables as far as that procedure was concerned. Or you can think of them as a stack of pegboards. Two procedures can have declared variables with the same name. These variables are different: they can have different values, but only one of them is accessible at a time. The same thing happens when a procedure calls itself. It is as if the procedure makes a clone of itself, with a new copy of all of the variables. The old ones are no longer accessible while we are in the clone. But when the clone returns, the old values are restored. Now we are ready to proceed with tracing the `KillBlob` procedure.

Recall that we had just returned to `KillBlob` with `row` set to 2 and `col` set to 7. At what statement in `KillBlob` are we? We had called `KillBlob` with `row` and `col+1`, and this it is time to call `KillBlob` with `row` and `col-1`; that is, we have just looked to the right, so now we will look to the left. Therefore, we call `KillBlob` with 2 and 6. This cell is alive, so that we call `KillBlob` again with 2 and 7. We appear to be back where we started.

We have an infinite loop. `KillBlob` at `row` set to 2 and `col` set to 7 will first look to the right at $(2, 8)$ by calling a `KillBlob`, which returns immediately. Then, it will call `KillBlob` at $(2, 6)$. This appears to be a mistake, since the new `KillBlob` will call yet another `KillBlob` at $(2, 7)$ again. This mutual calling sequence appears to go on forever.

How do we fix this infinite loop? Consider that the only test we have is whether a cell is alive or dead. We want to make sure that we do not visit a cell twice. If we kill each cell as soon as we visit it, the next time we visit it, it will be dead; thus, we will simply return. This correction involves a simple change to the program.

```
PROCEDURE KillBlob (row, col: range);
BEGIN
    IF board [row, col] = alive
        THEN BEGIN
                board [row, col] := dead;   (* shoot first *)
                KillBlob (row, col+1);      (* to the right *)
                KillBlob (row, col-1);      (* to the left *)
                KillBlob (row-1, col);      (* above *)
                KillBlob (row+1, col);      (* below *)
                END (* cell is alive *);
END (* KillBlob *);
```

We can now trace the execution of the program. To do so, we could use a notation for describing the state of the current procedure's variables as well as those in the chain of calling procedures, including our present position in each procedure. Since all of the procedures in this example are the same, each having its own copy of the same variables, we will use a simple table with each row representing a different call of the procedure `KillBlob` and with columns representing the variables and their values as well as our present location in the procedure.

We start by calling `KillBlob` with the parameters 2 and 5. The program state is now

```
  123456789        row      col      position
1*        *         2        5        start
2* ***** *
3*        *
```

We then kill the current cell, $(2, 5)$, and call `KillBlob` recursively with $(2, 6)$.

```
  123456789        row      col      position
1*        *         2        5        right
2* ** ** *          2        6        start
3*        *
```

Once again, we kill the current cell and call `KillBlob` recursively with the cell to the right.

```
  123456789        row      col      position
1*        *         2        5        right
2* **  * *          2        6        right
3*        *         2        7        start
```

After killing the new current cell and calling `KillBlob` recursively with the cell to the right, the picture is

```
  123456789        row      col      position
1*        *         2        5        right
2* **     *         2        6        right
3*        *         2        7        right
                    2        8        start
```

This time we have moved off the end of the blob. `KillBlob` then checks that the cell is alive. It is not, so that we simply return.

```
  123456789        row      col      position
1*        *         2        5        right
2* **     *         2        6        right
3*        *         2        7        right
```

We now proceed to the next statement, which is to call `KillBlob` passing the cell to the left.

123456789	row	col	position
1* *	2	5	*right*
2* ** *	2	6	*right*
3* *	2	7	*left*
	2	6	*start*

This cell was killed recently, so that we simply return.

123456789	row	col	position
1* *	2	5	*right*
2* ** *	2	6	*right*
3* *	2	7	*left*

We then look above.

123456789	row	col	position
1* *	2	5	*right*
2* ** *	2	6	*right*
3* *	2	7	*above*
	1	7	*start*

This cell is also dead; thus, we return.

123456789	row	col	position
1* *	2	5	*right*
2* ** *	2	6	*right*
3* *	2	7	*above*

The next step is to look below.

123456789	row	col	position
1* *	2	5	*right*
2* ** *	2	6	*right*
3* *	2	7	*below*
	3	7	*start*

Once again, we have reached a dead cell; thus, we return.

123456789	row	col	position
1* *	2	5	*right*
2* ** *	2	6	*right*
3* *	2	7	*below*

We have now reached the end of this `KillBlob` procedure, causing us to return to its caller.

123456789	row	col	position
1* *	2	5	*right*
2* ** *	2	6	*right*
3* *			

This procedure looks left, above, and below to no avail.

```
  123456789      row    col      position
1*         *      2      5        right
2* **      *      2      6        end
3*         *
```

It too returns.

```
  123456789      row    col      position
1*         *      2      5        right
2* **      *
3*         *
```

This procedure now looks to the left.

```
  123456789      row    col      position
1*         *      2      5        left
2* *       *      2      4        after  kill
3*         *
```

Going to the right proves fruitless now; therefore, we go to the left again.

```
  123456789      row    col      position
1*         *      2      5        left
2*         *      2      4        left
3*         *      2      3        after  kill
```

The entire blob is now killed, but we do not realize it yet. We must first look at all neighbors and notice that they are dead.

```
  123456789      row    col      position
1*         *      2      5        left
2*         *      2      4        left
3*         *      2      3        end
```

This procedure now returns.

```
  123456789      row    col      position
1*         *      2      5        left
2*         *      2      4        left
3*         *
```

We note that the neighbors above and below are both dead; thus, we return.

```
  123456789      row    col      position
1*         *      2      5        left
2*         *
3*         *
```

Again, the neighbors above and below are dead; thus, we return, certain that we are finished.

Exercises

1. Trace the `KillBlob` procedure given the first example and parameters $(2, 5)$, the center of the $+$.
2. Trace the `KillBlob` procedure given the first example and parameters $(3, 10)$, the center of blob 3, the Υ-like figure.

14-1 GENERATING PERMUTATIONS

A permutation of a sequence of objects is a rearrangement of the objects. For example, the permutations of 123 are 123, 132, 213, 231, 312, and 321. Anagrams of words are also permutations. For example, "chum" and "much" are anagrams.

Assume that we have a sequence of n objects. How many permutations of n objects are there? There are n possibilities for the first position. Any object except that used in the first position can be used in the second position. Thus, there are $n - 1$ possibilities for the second position. Similarly, there are $n - 2$ possibilities for the third position. Eventually, we will have only two possibilities of the next to the last position, and only one left for the last. Multiplying these together, we obtain $n \times n - 1 \times n - 2 \times \cdots \times 2 \times 1$ or $n!$ (n factorial).

Let us write a program to write the permutations of 1234. First, we need a **FOR** loop that chooses the first digit of the permutation.

```
FOR first := 1 TO 4 DO
```

Similarly, we can have **FOR** loops for the second, third, and fourth digits of the permutation.

```
FOR first := 1 TO 4 DO
    FOR second := 1 TO 4 DO
        FOR third := 1 TO 4 DO
            FOR fourth := 1 TO 4 DO
```

There is now much duplication between **first**, **second**, **third**, and **fourth**. We can write a massive expression that compares them all.

```
FOR first := 1 TO 4 DO
    FOR second := 1 TO 4 DO
        FOR third := 1 TO 4 DO
            FOR fourth := 1 TO 4 DO
                IF (first = second) OR
                   (first = third) OR
                   (first = fourth) OR
                   (second = third) OR
                   (second = fourth) OR
                   (third = fourth)
                    THEN sequence is not a permutation
                    ELSE sequence is a permutation;
```

This program does $4 \times 4 \times 4 \times 4$, or 4^4 iterations. This is 256 iterations, while $n!$ is only 24. Note that if **second** matches **first**, there is no need to try all possibilities for **third** and **fourth**. Let us distribute our tests for matching.

```
FOR first := 1 TO 4 DO
    FOR second := 1 TO 4 DO
        IF (first <> second)
            THEN FOR third := 1 TO 4 DO
                IF (first <> third) AND
                   (second <> third)
                THEN FOR fourth := 1 TO 4 DO
                    IF (first <> fourth) AND
                       (second <> fourth) AND
                       (third <> fourth)
                    THEN Writeln (first:1, second:1,
                        third:1, fourth:1);
```

Suppose we want to handle permutations of 12345. We would have to add another **FOR** loop. A new, longer **IF** test would also have to be added.

This approach breaks down if we want to handle permutations of arbitrary length. We cannot put in a variable number of **FOR** statements or a variable-length **IF** statement. Here is another opportunity for recursion.

Each step of generating a permutation consists of a **FOR** loop and an **IF** statement.

```
FOR variable := 1 TO size of permutation
    IF variable does not match any previous value
        THEN call recursively
```

Since there will be an arbitrary number of these variables, we should store them in an array.

```
TYPE range = 1..length;
VAR permutation: ARRAY [range] OF range;
```

The **IF** condition can be handled by a boolean function that tests whether the value in the current position matches any previous value.

```
PROCEDURE Permute (position: range);
VAR temp: range;
BEGIN
    FOR temp := 1 TO length DO
        BEGIN
            permutation [position] := temp;
            IF NoMatch (position)
                THEN Permute (position + 1);
        END (* FOR temp *);
END (* Permute *);
```

Let us trace the program for `length` equal to 2. We give `permutation [1]` the value 1. This does not match any previous value; thus, we call `Permute` passing the value 2. We then give `permutation [2]` the value 1, but find that it matches `permutation [1]`. Thus, we give `permutation [2]` the value 2. Since this does not match any previous value, we proceed to calling `Permute` with the parameter 3. We have a problem, since there is no `permutation [3]`. We need a test for when `position` is equal to `length`.

```
PROCEDURE Permute (position: range);
BEGIN
    FOR permutation [position] := 1 TO length DO
        IF NoMatch (position)
            THEN IF position = length
                THEN PrintPermutation
                ELSE Permute (position + 1);
END (* Permute *);
```

Now we can write `NoMatch`. This is a function that returns a boolean value. We first assume that a match does not exist. With a `FOR` loop, we can test each value of the prefix of the permutation.

```
FUNCTION NoMatch (position: range): boolean;
    VAR index: range;
        result: boolean;
BEGIN
    result := true;
    FOR index := 1 TO position - 1 DO
        IF permutation [position] = permutation [index]
            THEN result := false;
    NoMatch := result;
END (* NoMatch *);
```

Our complete program follows.

```
PROGRAM GeneratePermutations (output);
    CONST length = 4;
    TYPE range = 1..length;
    VAR permutation: ARRAY [range] OF range;

    PROCEDURE PrintPermutation;
        VAR index: range;
    BEGIN
        FOR index := 1 TO length DO
            Write (permutation [index] : 1);
        Writeln;
    END (* PrintPermutation *);
```

```
    FUNCTION NoMatch (position: range): boolean;
        VAR index: range;
            result: boolean;
    BEGIN
        result := true;
        FOR index := 1 TO position - 1 DO
            IF permutation [position] = permutation [index]
                THEN result := false;
        NoMatch := result;
    END (* NoMatch *);


    PROCEDURE Permute (position: range);
    BEGIN
        FOR permutation [position] := 1 TO length DO
            IF NoMatch (position)
                THEN IF position = length
                    THEN PrintPermutation
                    ELSE Permute (position + 1);
    END (* Permute *);


BEGIN
    Permute (1);    (* compute permutation from first position *)
END (* GeneratePermutation *).
```

```
1234
1243
1324
1342
1423
1432
2134
2143
2314
2341
2413
2431
3124
3142
3214
3241
3412
3421
4123
4132
4213
4231
4312
4321
```

Analysis
of Several
Sorting Algorithms

In this chapter, we will survey several techniques for sorting numbers. We first encountered sorting in Chapter 12, where we wanted to print a list of students in descending order of grade. The sorting algorithm used there is not one of the better sorting algorithms; in fact, it is one of the worst. This chapter contains some equally inefficient as well as some better algorithms.

We study several sorting algorithms for two reasons. First, it is useful to understand how to evaluate the complexity and efficiency of algorithms. In Chapter 9, we tried to improve the speed of an algorithm, when we considered functions for determining whether or not a number was prime. Second, sorting is an important and frequently used operation. It is so important that entire books have been written about it, which also means that it is well understood; thus, that it is useful as an example in an introductory programming course.

There are many reasons for sorting data. One reason is for ease in searching; it is easier to search a sorted list than an unsorted one. Think how painful it would be to use a nonalphabetic phone book or dictionary! Another reason is to find duplicates, but there are other algorithms that can find duplicates.

We will sort a list of numbers. When we sorted a list of students, we wanted them in descending order of grade. The field (or group of fields) used to determine ordering is called the *sort key*, or *key* for short. The remainder of the information kept with each key is called the *data*. In this chapter, the key is a number, and there is no data. We do it this way because we already know one way to handle data when sorting, and because handling data only complicates our algorithms, but in an obvious way. We often want to sort using a key that has some structure. For example, we may want to order by a character string, such as a name, or based on a group of fields, such as department number, course number, and section number. In this case, we have a hierarchy of orderings. For example, we order by department number, and, within that, course number, and, within that, section number. Thus, we compare department numbers, and if they are different, we know in what order to put them. If they are not different, we go to the next field and compare them. We continue until we have found a field that has different values or until we have tested all fields of the both sort keys and they match.

15-1 SELECTION SORT

First, we will consider is the *selection sort*, which is performed by scanning the input for the smallest number. We then place this number in the first position of the output array. We repeatedly scan for the next smallest number and put it into the next position in the output array. We decide the next smallest number by choosing the smallest number that still exceeds the previous number chosen. A moment's reflection will convince you that this means that the input numbers all need to be distinct. (There are ways to avoid this restriction, but they are slightly more complicated.) In the following program we have also taken the liberty of assuming that all of the numbers are positive.

```
PROGRAM SelectionSort (input, output);
    CONST
        maxNumbers = 10;

    TYPE
        indexRange = 1..maxNumbers;
        indexZeroRange = 0..maxNumbers;
        arrayOfNumbers = ARRAY [indexRange] OF integer;

    VAR
        inputArray: arrayOfNumbers;
        outputArray: arrayOfNumbers;
        numberCount: indexZeroRange;
        compares, moves: integer;              (* statistics *)

    PROCEDURE ReadArray (VAR count: indexZeroRange;
                         VAR theArray: arrayOfNumbers);
    BEGIN
        Write ('Input = ');
        count := 0;
        WHILE NOT Eoln DO
            BEGIN
                count := count + 1;
                Read (theArray [count]);
                Write (theArray [count] : 3);
            END; (* WHILE NOT EOLN *)
        Readln;
        Writeln;
    END; (* ReadArray *)
```

```
    PROCEDURE WriteArray (count: indexZeroRange;
                          theArray: arrayOfNumbers);
        VAR index: indexRange;
    BEGIN
        Write ('Output= ');
        FOR index := 1 TO count DO
            Write (theArray[index] : 3);
        Writeln (' Compares = ', compares : 3,
            ', Moves = ', moves : 3);
    END; (* WriteArray *)

    PROCEDURE SortArray (VAR outputArray: arrayOfNumbers;
                         inputArray: arrayOfNumbers;
                         numberCount: indexZeroRange);
        VAR
            index: indexZeroRange;
            scan: indexZeroRange;
            thisNumber: integer;
            lastNumber: integer;

    BEGIN
        lastNumber := 0;
        FOR index := 1 TO numberCount DO
            BEGIN
                thisNumber := maxint;
                FOR scan := 1 TO numberCount DO
                    BEGIN
                        IF (lastNumber < inputArray [scan]) AND
                            (inputArray [scan] < thisNumber)
                            THEN thisNumber := inputArray [scan];
                        compares := compares + 1;
                    END; (* FOR scan *)
                outputArray[index] := thisNumber;
                moves := moves + 1;
                lastNumber := thisNumber;
        END (* FOR index *);
    END; (* SortArray *)

BEGIN
    WHILE NOT Eof DO
        BEGIN
            ReadArray (numberCount, inputArray);
            compares := 0; moves := 0;
            SortArray (outputArray, inputArray, numberCount);
            WriteArray (numberCount, outputArray);
        END (* WHILE NOT Eof *);
END (* SelectionSort *).
```

Let us analyze this program. Each pass through the array to find the next number involves n comparisons, where n is the amount of numbers in the input. Since we need n passes through the array, this algorithm requires n^2 comparisons and n moves. Execution of this program shows these statistics.

```
INPUT =   1  7  4 92  8 12
OUTPUT=   1  4  7  8 12 92 COMPARES =  36, MOVES =   6
INPUT = 92 12  8  7  4  1
OUTPUT=   1  4  7  8 12 92 COMPARES =  36, MOVES =   6
INPUT =   1  4  7  8 12 92
OUTPUT=   1  4  7  8 12 92 COMPARES =  36, MOVES =   6
```

15-2 INSERTION SORT

We will next analyze the algorithm *insertion sort*. In insertion sort, at each step of the sort, we have a sorted list of the first few numbers into which we insert the next number. We do this repeatedly until all numbers have been inserted into the list.

Let us consider the insertion step further. We can scan the list sequentially until we find the first element greater than the one we want to insert. We then want to move this number and those to its right each one position to the right. This has been programmed by a "right-to-left" scan due to the lack of temporary variables. For each scan, to insert a number into a list of i numbers, we do up to i compares for $i + 2$ compares and moves total. Thus, we do a total of between $\frac{n(n+1)}{2}$ and $\frac{n(n+1)}{2} + n$ compares and moves. We demonstrate this by executing the following procedure, which produces the output shown below. (Assume that the parts of the program not shown are the same as in the previous program.)

```
PROCEDURE SortArray (VAR outputArray: arrayOfNumbers;
                         inputArray: arrayOfNumbers;
                         numberCount: indexZeroRange);
    VAR index: indexZeroRange;

    PROCEDURE Insert (VAR theOutputArray: arrayOfNumbers;
                         size: indexRange; newNumber: integer);
        (* inserts newNumber into the appropriate position in *)
        (* theOutputArray *)
        VAR position: indexZeroRange;
            placeFound: boolean;
            backscan: indexZeroRange;

    BEGIN
        position := 1;
        placeFound := false;
        WHILE (position < size) AND NOT placeFound DO
            BEGIN
                IF theOutputArray [position] > newNumber
                    THEN placeFound := true
                    ELSE position := position + 1;
                compares := compares + 1;
            END; (* WHILE *)
                (* position now has the position where *)
                (* newNumber is to be inserted *)
```

```
        FOR backscan := size DOWNTO position + 1 DO
            BEGIN
                theOutputArray [backscan] :=
                    theOutputArray [backscan - 1];
                (* move up the elements to the right *)
                (* of the insert position *)
                moves := moves + 1;
            END; (* FOR backscan *)
        theOutputArray [position] := newNumber;
        moves := moves + 1;
    END; (* Insert *)


BEGIN (* SortArray *)
    FOR index := 1 TO numberCount DO
        Insert (outputArray, index, inputArray[index]);
END; (* SortArray *)
```

```
INPUT =    1   7   4  92   8  12
OUTPUT=    1   4   7   8  12  92  COMPARES =  15, MOVES =    9
INPUT =   92  12   8   7   4   1
OUTPUT=    1   4   7   8  12  92  COMPARES =   5, MOVES =   21
INPUT =    1   4   7   8  12  92
OUTPUT=    1   4   7   8  12  92  COMPARES =  15, MOVES =    6
```

15-3 BINARY SEARCH

Several search techniques can be used to determine the correct position. The one used in the previous section is called a *sequential search* because it searches the data sequentially. It also works on unsorted data. Another search technique, but one that works only on sorted data, is called the *binary search*. It uses a strategy known as divide and conquer. Basically, we look at the middle element. If it matches the *search key* (what we are searching for), we are finished. If the middle element is less than the search key, we do it again with the second half of the list; that is, we look at the middle of the second half. Otherwise the search key is in the first half of the list. Thus, we repeatedly divide the list in half until we find the position. We eventually find the element because the repeated dividing by 2 eventually results in 1. If you think about it for a while, you will realize that the number of times we need to divide a number by 2 to reach to 1 is the same as the exponent of smallest power of 2 that exceeds the number. The exact exponent for the number n is $\log_2 n$. This algorithm, as programmed below, requires at most $\log_2 n$ comparisons to search a list of n items.

```
low := 1;           (* low is the lower end of range *)
high := n;          (* high is the higher end of range *)
found := false;     (* we have not yet found a match *)
WHILE low <= high DO (* WHILE there is more scanning room *)
    BEGIN
        middle := (low + high) DIV 2;
        IF theArray [middle] < key
            THEN low := middle + 1  (* key on right of middle *)
        ELSE IF key < theArray[middle]
            THEN high := middle - 1 (* key on left of middle *)
        ELSE BEGIN (* key = theArray[middle] *)
            high := low - 1;
            found := true;
            END; (* key found *)
    END; (* WHILE *)
    (* IF found is true, middle points to the matching element *)
    (* Otherwise, middle is near where it belongs *)
```

15-4 BUBBLE SORT

We next study a sorting technique called the *bubble sort*, which swaps adjacent elements that are out of order. The data is sorted when a pass has been made without the occurrence of swaps. Also, the first pass should put the highest number into the last position. In fact, if the last swap in a pass through the data was between the elements in index positions i and $i + 1$, every element in positions $i + 1$ through n are in order and we need only concern ourselves with the elements in positions 1 through i on the next pass. This algorithm has a worst case of $\frac{n(n-1)}{2}$ (or about n^2) compares and swaps as illustrated in the following procedure and output.

```
PROCEDURE SortArray (VAR outputArray: arrayOfNumbers;
                         inputArray: arrayOfNumbers;
                         numberCount: indexZeroRange);
    VAR swapPosition, scanLength: indexZeroRange;

    PROCEDURE DoAPass (VAR lastSwapPosition: indexZeroRange;
                       VAR theArray: arrayOfNumbers;
                           endOfScan: indexRange);
        (* performs a pass on the array swapping adjacent *)
        (* elements that are out of order *)

        VAR index: indexRange;

        PROCEDURE Swap (VAR a, b: integer);
            (* swaps the contents of a and b *)
            VAR temp: integer;
        BEGIN
            temp := a;
            a := b;
            b := temp;
        END; (* Swap *)
```

```
    BEGIN (* body of DoAPass *)
        lastSwapPosition := 0;
        FOR index := 1 TO endOfScan - 1 DO
            BEGIN
                IF theArray [index] > theArray [index + 1]
                    THEN BEGIN
                        Swap (theArray [index],
                            theArray [index + 1]);
                        swaps := swaps + 1;
                        lastSwapPosition := index;
                        END; (* IF out of order *)
                compares := compares + 1;
            END (* FOR index *)
    END; (* DoAPass *)
BEGIN (* SortArray *)
    outputArray := inputArray;
    scanLength := numberCount;
    WHILE scanLength > 0 DO
        BEGIN
            DoAPass(swapPosition, OutputArray, scanLength);
            scanLength := swapPosition;
        END (* WHILE *)
END; (* Sort Array *)
```

```
INPUT =   1  7  4 92  8 12
OUTPUT=   1  4  7  8 12 92 COMPARES =   9, SWAPS =    3
INPUT = 92 12  8  7  4  1
OUTPUT=   1  4  7  8 12 92 COMPARES =  15, SWAPS =  15
INPUT =   1  4  7  8 12 92
OUTPUT=   1  4  7  8 12 92 COMPARES =   5, SWAPS =    0
```

15-5 MERGE BUBBLE SORT

Thus far, all of our sorting algorithms have been of order n^2. To sort 1 million records would require about 1 trillion operations. At an average of 1 million operations per second, 1 million seconds, or $\frac{11}{2}$ days would be required. We will soon describe a sorting algorithm on the order of $n^{1.5}$ (or $n\sqrt{n}$). To sort 1 million records would require only 1 billion operations, or 1000 seconds (17 minutes). The last sorting technique studied will be an $n \lg n$ (or $n \log_2 n$) algorithm. To sort a million records would require 20 million operations, and so only 20 seconds. But this fast algorithm requires additional *overhead* in keeping track of what it is doing, such that the simpler method is often faster on very small sets of data. That is, the number of operations per second varies depending on the complexity of the operations. Clearly, the choice of algorithm is important.

The *merge bubble sort* is a $n\sqrt{n}$ sorting algorithm. We break up the data into lists each $\sqrt{n}$ in size. Each list is sorted. Then, the separate sorted lists are merged together. Each individual bubble sort of $\sqrt{n}$ numbers takes $(\sqrt{n})^2$ or n operations. Since there are $\sqrt{n}$ lists, we have $n\sqrt{n}$ operations. The merge of $\sqrt{n}$ lists of $\sqrt{n}$ numbers each also requires about $n\sqrt{n}$ comparisons. This algorithm follows.

```
PROCEDURE BubbleSortArray (VAR anArray: arrayOfNumbers;
                           startRange: indexRange;
                           endRange: indexRange);
    VAR swapPosition, scanLength: indexZeroRange;

    PROCEDURE DoAPass (VAR lastSwapPosition: indexZeroRange;
                       VAR theArray: arrayOfNumbers;
                       startOfScan: indexRange;
                       endOfScan: indexRange);
            (* performs a pass on the array swapping adjacent *)
            (* elements that are out of order in the range *)
            (* startOfScan to endOfScan *)
        VAR index: indexRange;

        PROCEDURE Swap (VAR a, b: integer);
            (* swaps the contents of a and b *)
            VAR temp: integer;
        BEGIN
            temp := a;
            a := b;
            b := temp;
        END; (* Swap *)

    BEGIN (* DoAPass *)
        lastSwapPosition := 0;
        FOR index := startOfScan TO endOfScan - 1 DO
            BEGIN
                IF theArray [index] > theArray [index + 1]
                    THEN BEGIN
                        Swap (theArray [index],
                            theArray [index + 1]);
                        swaps := swaps + 1;
                        lastSwapPosition := index;
                        END; (* IF out of order *)
                    compares := compares + 1;
                END (* FOR index *);
    END; (* DoAPass *)

BEGIN (* BubbleSortArray *)
    scanLength := endRange;
    WHILE scanLength >= startRange DO
        BEGIN
            DoAPass (swapPosition, anArray,
                startRange, scanLength);
            scanLength := swapPosition;
        END (* WHILE *);
END; (* BubbleSortArray *)
```

```
PROCEDURE SortArray (VAR outputArray: arrayOfNumbers;
                         inputArray: arrayOfNumbers;
                         numberCount: indexZeroRange);
    TYPE arrayOfIndexes = ARRAY [indexRange] OF indexZeroRange;


    VAR sizeOfSubarray: indexRange;
        numberOfSubarrays: indexRange;
        indexOfSubarrays: indexRange;
        startRange, endRange: arrayOfIndexes;
        indexOfOutput: indexRange;
        thisNumber: integer;
        whichSubarray: indexRange;


    BEGIN
        (* sort Sqrt(n) subarrays *)
        sizeOfSubarray := Trunc (Sqrt (numberCount));
        numberOfSubarrays := numberCount DIV sizeOfSubarray;
        IF numberOfSubarrays * sizeOfSubarray < numberCount
            THEN numberOfSubarrays := numberOfSubarrays + 1;
        FOR indexOfSubarrays := 1 TO numberOfSubarrays DO
            BEGIN
                startRange [indexOfSubarrays] :=
                    (indexOfSubarrays - 1) * sizeOfSubarray + 1;
                endRange [indexOfSubarrays] :=
                    MIN (indexOfSubarrays * sizeOfSubarray,
                        numberCount);
                BubbleSortArray (inputArray,
                                startRange [indexOfSubarrays],
                                endRange [indexOfSubarrays]);
            END; (* FOR indexOfSubarrays *)


        (* merge the sqrt(n) (or numberOfSubarrays) subarrays *)
        FOR indexOfOutput := 1 TO numberCount DO
            BEGIN
                thisNumber := maxint;
                FOR indexOfSubarrays := 1 TO numberOfSubarrays DO
                    IF startRange [indexOfSubarrays] <=
                        endRange [indexOfSubarrays]
                        THEN BEGIN
                          compares := compares + 1;
                          IF thisnumber >
                            inputArray
                            [startRange [indexOfSubarrays]]
                            THEN BEGIN
                                thisNumber :=
                                    inputArray [
                                    startRange [indexOfSubarrays]
                                    ];
                                whichSubarray := indexOfSubarrays;
                                END (* IF thisNumber etc. *);
                      END; (* IF and FOR indexOfSubarrays *)
```

```
                    outputArray [indexOfOutput] := thisNumber;
                    moves := moves + 1;
                    IF startRange [whichSubarray] = numberCount
                        THEN endRange [whichSubarray] :=
                            endRange [whichSubarray] - 1
                        ELSE startRange [whichSubarray] :=
                            startRange [whichSubarray] + 1;
                        (* remove thisNumber from its list,    *)
                        (* but if it is from the last list      *)
                        (* and is the last element, we can't    *)
                        (* increment startRange lest we exceed *)
                        (* the limit of the indexRange type,   *)
                        (* so we decrement endRange instead    *)
                        (* to the same effect:                 *)
                        (*     endRange now < startRange        *)
            END (* FOR indexOfOutput *);
    END; (* SortArray *)
```

15-6 MERGE SORT

Lastly, we will study the *merge sort*. Suppose we start out with n numbers. We can treat these as n lists of one element each. Merging these in pairs gives $\frac{n}{2}$ lists with n comparisons. We then merge these lists in pairs repeatedly until we have 2 lists of $\frac{n}{2}$ numbers each. Merging this pair of lists will give a single sorted list. Each merge takes no more than n comparisons, and there are $\lg n$ (or $\log_2 n$) merge steps, for a total of $n \lg n$ operations.

The algorithm programmed below uses a recursive call to itself. We use the divide-and-conquer technique to solve this problem. To sort an array, we sort the first half, sort the second half, and merge the two halves together. To sort the first half (or the second half), we divide it into two halves and merge them. The recursion stops when we have no more than two elements to sort: if there are two left, we simply compare them and swap them if they are out of order. Note that if `start = stop` in the body of `mergeSort`, then we have only one element to sort, which by definition is in order; thus, we do not have to do anything.

```
PROCEDURE MergeSort (VAR arrayToSort: arrayOfNumbers;
                    start, stop: indexZeroRange);
    (* Written by Jeff Vitter *)
    (* this procedure calls itself to sort each half, *)
    (* then merges the two halves *)
    VAR middle : indexZeroRange;
        tempArray : arrayOfNumbers;

    PROCEDURE Merge (VAR arrayToMerge: arrayOfNumbers;
                    left1, right1, right2 : indexZeroRange);
        (* merges the array elements in positions left1,...,right1
           with the elements in positions right1+1,...,right2.
           PTR1 walks thru the first range and PTR2 walks thru the
           second range of indexes.  NEXT is the spot in TEMPARRAY
           where the next smallest element will go            *)
        VAR  left2, ptr1, ptr2, next, i : indexZeroRange;
```

```
BEGIN
    left2 := right1 + 1;
    ptr1 := left1;   ptr2 := left2;  next := left1;
    WHILE (ptr1 <= right1) AND (ptr2 <= right2) DO
        BEGIN
            IF arrayToMerge [ptr1] <= arrayToMerge [ptr2]
                THEN BEGIN
                    tempArray [next] := arrayToMerge [ptr1];
                    ptr1 := ptr1 + 1;
                    END (* IF array1 element smaller *)
                ELSE BEGIN
                    tempArray[next] := arrayToMerge[ptr2];
                    ptr2 := ptr2 + 1;
                    END; (* ELSE *)
            next := next + 1;
        END; (* WHILE not at end of either half *)

    (* if the right half is used up, empty the left half *)
    WHILE ptr1 <= right1 DO
        BEGIN
            tempArray [next] := ArrayToMerge [ptr1];
            next := next + 1;  ptr1 := ptr1 + 1;
        END; (* WHILE leftovers *)
    (* now recopy from TEMPARRAY back to ARRAYTOMERGE *)
    FOR i := left1 TO (next - 1) DO
        arrayToMerge[i] := tempArray[i];
END;  (* Merge *)

PROCEDURE Swap (VAR x, y: integer);
    VAR temp: integer;
BEGIN
    temp := x;  x := y;  y := temp;
END;  (* Swap *)

BEGIN
    IF start < stop - 1
        THEN BEGIN  (* sort each half, then merge together *)
            middle := (start + stop) DIV 2;
            mergeSort (arrayToSort, start, middle);
            mergeSort (arrayToSort, middle+1, stop);
            Merge(arrayToSort, start, middle, stop);
            END (* IF lots more to do *)
        ELSE IF start = stop - 1
            THEN
                IF arrayToSort [start] > arrayToSort [stop]
                    THEN Swap (arrayToSort [start],
                        arrayToSort [stop]);
END;  (* MergeSort *)
```

Sets

Suppose that a group of friends wants to arrange a luncheon date. Unfortunately, each of them has already made commitments on certain days for lunchtime. Incidentally, since these friends all keep their schedules on computer files, they have a file with one line for each person containing the days when that person is available for lunch. Since we know how to write computer programs, we will write one that reports the days that everyone is available.

However, we must decide what data structure to use for storing the days that everyone is available. For each person, we can have an array indexed by day of booleans, where **true** indicates that the person is available. We can then check which index values have the value **true** in every array. We can refine this by having a single array describing the open days so far—this array looks just like the array for a person—and to merge in the data for each person after that person's line has been read in completely. Then we only need to keep one array for the summary of all previous people and one array for the new person's data.

Notice that we want a day to be reported if it appears in all lists. We could **AND** the booleans for the same index and, if the result were true, we would have found a free day. Or, we could treat each person's list as a set, and try to find the intersection of all lists. The latter approach takes advantage of the next feature we are going to learn—sets.

16-1 REVIEW OF SETS

One feature of the so-called new math is sets. We will explore uses for sets and see how they are supported in PASCAL.

A set is a list of items with a given property. In mathematics, we place the list of items in set braces—{ and }. For example, the set of all days of the week is

{Monday, Tuesday, Wednesday, Thursday, Friday, Saturday, Sunday}

The set of all months is

{January, February, March, April, May, June,
July, August, September, October, November, December}

The set of known live unicorns is

{}

This set is known as an empty set. Some other sets are

weekdays = {Monday, Tuesday, Wednesday, Thursday, Friday}

weekends = {Saturday, Sunday}

In PASCAL, we cannot use braces since these are already reserved for comments. We use square brackets instead:

```
[Monday, Tuesday, Wednesday, Thursday, Friday]
```

We might want to do many things with sets. The individual items in a set are called its *elements*. We may want to know whether something is an element of a set. In mathematics, we use ϵ to indicate "is an element of"; therefore, $x\epsilon\{x, y\}$ is true, while $z\epsilon\{x, y\}$ is false. In PASCAL, we do not have the ϵ symbol. Instead, we use the word **IN**:

```
Thursday IN [Monday, Tuesday, Wednesday, Thursday, Friday]
```

The **IN** operator takes an element and a set and gives a boolean value to indicate whether the element is actually in the set.

We will use Venn diagrams to illustrate sets. In Figure 16-1, the circle marked *Weekdays* represents the set containing the days of the week Monday, Tuesday, Wednesday, Thursday, and Friday. This circle is contained in a rectangle representing the *domain* or the *universe*, that is, the set containing all possible elements of a particular category. The domain here is labeled *DaysOfWeek*; it contains Saturday and Sunday, as well as the elements of *Weekdays*.

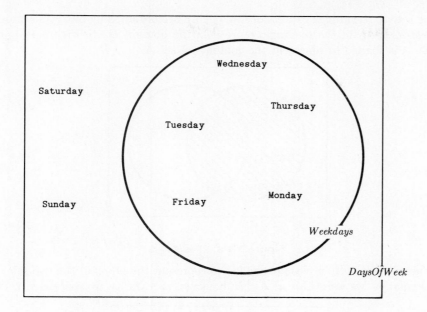

Figure 16-1 A Venn diagram.

There can be several sets in the same domain. For example, the set *Vowels* is {A, E, I, O, U}, as illustrated in Figure 16-2. Another set is *LettersInMyName*, which consists of {A, R, T, H, U, K, E, L}. Note that the order of the elements is irrelevant. Furthermore, each element appears in the set only once.

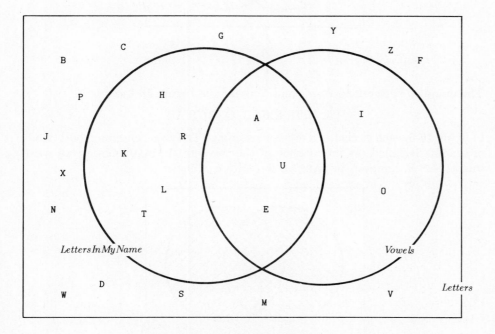

Figure 16-2 Several sets.

We will now consider operations involving two sets. (Operations on more than two sets are accomplished by combining operations on two sets, in much the same way that complex expressions in algebra are obtained by binary arithmetic operators.) Again the rectangle represents the domain D. In Figure 16-3, the circle A is shaded to represent the contents of set A.

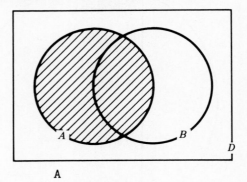

A

Figure 16-3   The set A.

In Figure 16-4, both circles are shaded to represent the *union* of the two sets. In mathematics, we write this as $A \cup B$; however, in PASCAL we write **A + B**.

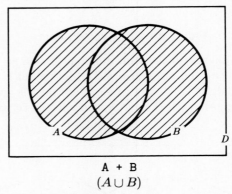

A + B
$(A \cup B)$

Figure 16-4   The set $A \cup B$.

The union of *LettersInMyName* and *Vowels* from Figure 16-2 is

$$\{A, E, H, I, K, L, O, R, T, U\}$$

In figure 16-5, each circle has a different shading. The area containing both kinds of shading is called the *intersection* of the two sets. In mathematics, we write this as $A \cap B$; however, in PASCAL we write **A * B**.

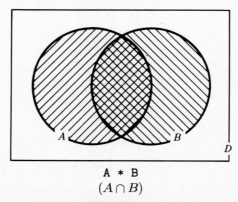

A * B
$(A \cap B)$

Figure 16-5   The set $A \cap B$.

The intersection of *LettersInMyName* and *Vowels* from Figure 16-2 is {A, E, U}. We sometimes want to talk about the elements of *B* that are not in *A*. This is called the *difference* between the two sets. In mathematics and in PASCAL, we write B - A. In Figure 16-5, the area representing $B - A$ is shaded to represent the *difference* between the two sets.

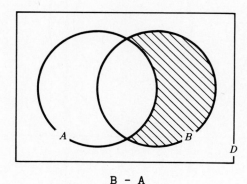

B - A

Figure 16-6   The set $B - A$.

The difference *Vowels* − *LettersInMyName* from Figure 16-2 is {I, O}. All of these operations take two sets and result in a new set.

We can also compare two sets. Two sets are *equal* if they contain precisely the same elements. Set equality can be tested using the equal sign. For example, [A, B] = [B, A] is true and [A, B] = [B, C] is false. Another useful condition to describe is when one set is completely contained in another. The smaller set is considered to be a *subset* of the larger one. (When the two sets are equal, they are both considered to be subsets of each other.) In mathematics, we use the symbol $\subseteq$ to say that one set is a subset of another, as in

$$\{A, B\} \subseteq \{A, B, C\}$$

In PASCAL, no such symbol is available, so we use <= to indicate a subset. For example,

```
   [A, B] <= [A, B, C]  is  true
      [A, B] <= [A, B]  is  true
[A, B, C] <= [A, B]  is  false
```

If $A \subseteq B$, then we say $B \supseteq A$, or *B* is a *superset* of *A*. In PASCAL, we use >= to indicate a superset.

```
   [A, B] >= [A, B, C]  is  false
      [A, B] >= [A, B]  is  true
[A, B, C] >= [A, B]  is  true
```

Figure 16-7 illustrates [A, B] <= [A, B, C, D].

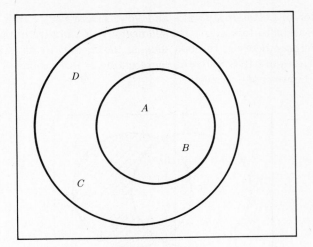

$$[A, B] <= [A, B, C, D]$$
$$(\{A, B\} \subseteq \{A, B, C, D\})$$

Figure 16-7 The sets $\{A, B\} \subseteq \{A, B, C, D\}$.

16-2 SETS IN PASCAL

We make the distinction between the *base type* and the *set type* of a set. The *base type* of a set is the type of elements in a set. The *set type* is the type of set containing the elements. This distinction is similar to that between the base type and the array type of an array. However, unlike an array, there is no distinction between the base type and the index type.

To declare a set, we say SET OF followed by the base type. For example, to declare a set of the days of the week, we can say

```
TYPE
    days = (Monday, Tuesday, Wednesday, Thursday, Friday,
        Saturday, Sunday);
    weekSet = SET OF days;
VAR
    day: days;
    weekdays, weekend: weekSet;
```

Using these declarations, the following are valid assignment statements:

```
day := Monday;
weekdays := [Monday, Tuesday, Wednesday, Thursday];
weekdays := weekdays + [Friday];
weekend := [Friday, Saturday, Sunday];
weekend := weekend - [Friday];
```

Notice that to add an element to a set, we must first place it in a single element set and then union that with the desired set.

The following are all assignment statements incompatible with the declarations given above.

```
day := [Monday];
weekdays := weekdays + Friday;
```

The base type of a set must be a scalar type of limited cardinality; that is, it can be **boolean**, **char**, an enumerated type, or a subrange of these or of **integer**. In particular, we cannot have a **SET OF integer**. Implementations of PASCAL may also place restrictions on the range size of the base type (the maximum cardinality), as well as on the values of the low and high bounds of the base type. Efficiency considerations have motivated these arbitrary restrictions. Ask your instructor or refer to the implementation manual to find out the restrictions on sets in your version of PASCAL.

Sets often contain groups of elements, where a group of elements forms a subrange of the base type. For example, the set **weekdays** above contains the sequence of elements from **Monday** to **Friday**. We can indicate this range the same way we specify subranges in **TYPE** definitions: we use two periods.

```
weekdays := [Monday..Friday];
weekend := [Friday..Sunday];
```

The above statements are equivalent to the following two statements.

```
weekdays := [Monday, Tuesday, Wednesday, Thursday, Friday];
weekend := [Friday, Saturday, Sunday];
```

We can have multiple ranges, and use them with individual elements. For example, the following statement has the same effect as the above assignment to **weekdays**.

```
weekdays := [Tuesday..Thursday, Monday, Friday];
```

The elements of a set may be constants or variables. The following are all valid.

```
TYPE intSet = SET OF 1..10;
VAR s,t,u: intSet;
    i,j,k: 1..10;
BEGIN
    i := 3;
    j := 6;
    k := 5;
    s := [i..j, 9];     (* is [3, 4, 5, 6, 9] *)
    t := [j..k];        (* is [], the empty set *)
    u := [5..k];        (* is [5] *)
```

As demonstrated in the example, variables can even be used in ranges. Then the range indicates a varying number of elements. If the first bound of the range exceeds the second bound, the range is considered empty, but other elements and ranges in the set are still used.

16-3 SETS: AN EXAMPLE

We now return to the example used at the start of this chapter. We have a computer file containing information about when people are available for lunch. There is a line of the file for each person, and it consists of a list of numbers, where each number represents a day of the month when that person is available.

We want to convert the list of numbers for each person into a set, and then take the intersection of all of these sets. Rather than accumulating all of these sets and then taking the intersection, we can use an approach similar to a running sum. We can take the set for the first person and call that the running intersection. With each set, we take the intersection of the new set with the running intersection, and the result becomes the new running intersection. This can be described in the following manner.

Create a set of the first person's free days
Make that the running intersection
WHILE NOT Eof DO
    Create a set of the next person's free days
    Take the intersection of that with running intersection
    Make that the running intersection

The process of creating a set of a person's free days appears twice in the above description and can be further refined.

```
freeDays := [];
WHILE NOT Eoln DO
    BEGIN
        Read (freeDay);
        freeDays := freeDays + [freeDay];
    END (* WHILE NOT Eoln *);
Readln;
```

We now know how to obtain a set consisting of the days that everyone is free, but we do not know how to print that set. We could repeatedly print an element of the set, removing the element from the set, until the set is empty.

```
WHILE everyonesFreeDays <> [] DO
    BEGIN
        Get an element, freeDay, from the set, everyonesFreeDays
        Write (freeDay);
        everyonesFreeDays := everyonesFreeDays - [freeDay];
    END (* WHILE still some free days *);
```

Unfortunately, we have discovered a deficiency in PASCAL: it does not allow us to obtain an element from a set. We could use a FOR loop to enumerate the possible elements of the set. We then test each possible element for membership in the set, and print it if it appears in the set.

```
FOR freeDay := 1 TO 31 DO
    BEGIN
        IF freeDay IN everyonesFreeDays
            THEN Write (freeDay);
    END (* FOR all freeDays *);
Writeln;
```

Unfortunately, if there are no elements in the set, we only write a blank line. If the set is initially empty, we should write out an informative message.

We are now ready to write the complete program.

```
PROGRAM FreeLunch (input, output);
(* Takes the intersection of a list of days when people
   are free for lunch.  Each person's information is one
   line of numbers. *)
  CONST daysPerMonth = 31;
  TYPE day = 1..31;
       daySet = SET OF day;
  VAR freeDays: daySet;              (* one person's free days *)
      everyonesFreeDays: daySet;   (* when everyone is free *)

  PROCEDURE ReadSet (VAR theSet: daySet);
      (* reads a set of days into theSet *)
      VAR freeDay: day;
  BEGIN
      theSet := [];
      WHILE NOT Eoln DO
          BEGIN
              Read (freeDay);
              theSet := theSet + [freeDay];
          END (* WHILE NOT Eoln *);
      Readln;
  END (* ReadSet *);

  PROCEDURE WriteSet (theSet: daySet);
      (* writes the set of days in theSet *)
      VAR freeDay: day;
  BEGIN
      IF theSet = []
          THEN Write ('Empty set')
          ELSE FOR freeDay := 1 TO daysPerMonth DO
              BEGIN
                  IF freeDay IN theSet
                      THEN Write (freeDay);
              END (* FOR all freeDays *);
      Writeln;
  END (* WriteSet *);
```

```
BEGIN
    ReadSet (everyonesFreeDays);
    WHILE NOT Eof DO
        BEGIN
            ReadSet (freeDays);
            everyonesFreeDays := everyonesFreeDays * freeDays;
        END (* WHILE more data *);
    WriteSet (everyonesFreeDays);
END (* FreeLunch *).
```

16-4 PARSING

The compiler into which we feed our PASCAL programs is an ordinary but large PASCAL program. Thus, the compiler must read our programs and try to figure out what they mean. The first step in understanding a program is to separate it into its component parts. At the lowest level, this means determining where the words start and end. Although this seems trivial—people do it easily all the time—it requires some work since not all words are surrounded by spaces. For example, a semicolon may follow a word without an intervening space.

In a computer program there are not only words but also symbols, such as (* and +. We call these objects *tokens*, to mean the words and symbols that comprise a program. These are syntax issues. Reducing the program into tokens is one of the steps in *parsing*, which is the derivation of the syntactic structure of a program (similar to a diagram of the structure of a sentence). We will write the first part of this process, that is, we will read a program and output its constituent tokens, one per line.

The tokens are words, numbers, or special symbols. Words begin with a letter and consist of letters and numbers. Numbers begin with an optional sign and consist of digits possibly followed by a period and optional digits and optional exponent. Special symbols generally terminate the preceding symbol. Special symbols need not be surrounded by spaces and are usually only one character, but are occasionally formed by two consecutive characters.

To determine whether the next character is part of the current token, we have to read it. Unfortunately, if it is not, it may be the start of a new symbol. Consequently, we will use the approach of always reading one character ahead, and leaving that unprocessed *lookahead* character in a standard, global place.

Assume that we have a set called **letters** consisting of the letters of the alphabet and characters treated as letters, and that we have a set called **digits** consisting of the digits from 0 to 9. Also assume that the lookahead character is in **nextChar**. A giant **CASE** statement has already determined that the lookahead character is a letter.

```
REPEAT
    Write (nextChar);
    Read (nextChar);
UNTIL NOT (nextChar IN (letters + digits));
Writeln;
```

The repeat loop is used to handle the current character first since it has already been tested.

Handling numbers is trickier than words since their syntax is a slightly more complicated. A giant **CASE** statement has already determined that the lookahead character is a digit or a sign.

```
REPEAT
    Write (nextChar);
    Read (nextChar);
UNTIL NOT (nextChar IN digits);
IF nextChar = '.'
    THEN REPEAT
        Write (nextChar);
        Read (nextChar);
    UNTIL NOT (nextChar IN digits);
IF nextChar = 'E'
    THEN BEGIN
        Write (nextChar);
        Read (nextChar);
        IF nextChar IN ['+', '-']
            THEN BEGIN
                Write (nextChar);
                Read (nextChar);
                END (* sign *);
        IF nextChar IN digits
            THEN REPEAT
                Write (nextChar);
                Read (nextChar);
                UNTIL NOT (nextChar IN digits)
            ELSE Write ('*** bad syntax ***');
                (* There must be a digit after an E in a number *)
    END (* exponent *);
```

Symbols are easier to handle, but there are special cases. The compound symbols are (*, *), :=, .., <>, <=, and >=. We do not output comments since these are not considered part of the program instructions. Strings start and end with ' and may contain two consecutive single quotes, which denote a double quote; we will leave the double quote and output the entire string on one line with all the quotes.

```
CASE nextChar OF
    '{': BEGIN
        REPEAT
            Read (nextChar);
        UNTIL nextChar = '}';
        Read (nextChar);            (* do a lookahead *)
        END (* {...} *);
```

```
'(': BEGIN
    Read (nextChar);
    IF nextChar <> '*'
        THEN Writeln ('(')
        ELSE BEGIN
            Read (nextChar); (* finish (* token *)
            REPEAT
                WHILE nextChar <> '*' DO
                    Read (nextChar);
                (* just read a '*' *)
                Read (nextChar);
            UNTIL nextChar = ')';   (* ) after * *)
            Read (nextChar);  (* do a lookahead *)
        END (* comment *);
    END (* ( *);


':': BEGIN
    Write (nextChar);
    Read (nextChar);
    IF nextChar = '='        (* := *)
        THEN BEGIN
            Write (nextChar);
            Read (nextChar);
            END;
    Writeln;
    END (* : *);


'.': BEGIN
    Write (nextChar);
    Read (nextChar);
    IF nextChar = '.'       (* .. *)
        THEN BEGIN
            Write (nextChar);
            Read (nextChar);
            END;
    Writeln;
    END (* . *);


'<': BEGIN
    Write (nextChar);
    Read (nextChar);
    IF nextChar IN  ['=','>']        (* <= OR <> *)
        THEN BEGIN
            Write (nextChar);
            Read (nextChar);
            END;
    Writeln;
    END (* < *);
```

```
'>': BEGIN
     Write (nextChar);
     Read (nextChar);
     IF nextChar = '='         (* >= *)
         THEN BEGIN
               Write (nextChar);
               Read (nextChar);
               END;
     Writeln;
     END (* > *);


'*', '/', ';', '=', '[', ']', '∧':
     BEGIN
         Write (nextChar);
         Read (nextChar);
         Writeln;
     END (* other special character *);
```

We can now integrate these into a complete tokenizer.

```
PROGRAM Tokenizer (input, output);
(* reads a program and outputs the constituent tokens, one
   line at a time *)
   VAR nextChar: char;
       digits: SET OF '0'..'9';


   PROCEDURE GoodChar;
       (* this character is good: write it and read the next *)
   BEGIN
       Write (nextChar);
       Read (nextChar);
   END (* GoodChar *);


   PROCEDURE HandleLetter;
       (* first char of token is a letter *)
   BEGIN
       REPEAT
           GoodChar;
       UNTIL NOT (nextChar IN ['0'..'9',
           'A'..'I', 'J'..'R', 'S'..'Z']);
           (* this works in both ASCII and EBCDIC *)
           (* ['A'..'Z'] does not work in EBCDIC *)
       Writeln;
   END (* HandleLetter *);
```

```
PROCEDURE HandleNumber;
    (* first char of token is a digit or a sign *)
BEGIN
    REPEAT
        GoodChar;
    UNTIL NOT (nextChar IN digits);
    IF nextChar = '.'
        THEN REPEAT
            GoodChar;
        UNTIL NOT (nextChar IN digits);
    IF nextChar = 'E'
        THEN BEGIN
            GoodChar;
            IF nextChar IN ['+', '-']
                THEN GoodChar;
            IF nextChar IN digits
                THEN REPEAT
                    GoodChar;
                UNTIL NOT (nextChar IN digits)
                ELSE Write ('*** bad syntax ***');
                    (* There must be a digit after an E
                        in a number *)
        END (* exponent *);
END (* HandleNumber *);


PROCEDURE HandleOpenParen;
    (* open paren may be comment *)
BEGIN
    Read (nextChar);
    IF nextChar <> '*'
        THEN Writeln ('(')
        ELSE BEGIN
            Read (nextChar); (* finish (* token *)
            REPEAT
                WHILE nextChar <> '*' DO
                    Read (nextChar);
                (* just read a '*' *)
                Read (nextChar);
            UNTIL nextChar = ')';   (* ) after * *)
            Read (nextChar);  (* do a lookahead *)
        END (* comment *);
END (* HandleOpenParen *);


PROCEDURE HandleBraces;
    (* ignore comment in braces *)
BEGIN
    REPEAT
        Read (nextChar);
    UNTIL nextChar = '}';
    Read (nextChar);            (* do a lookahead *)
END (* HandleBraces *);
```

```
PROCEDURE HandleColon;
    (* colon may be followed by = *)
BEGIN
    GoodChar;
    IF nextChar = '='         (* := *)
        THEN BEGIN
            GoodChar;
            END;
    Writeln;
END (* HandleColon *);


PROCEDURE HandlePeriod;
    (* period may be followed by another *)
BEGIN
    GoodChar;
    IF nextChar = '.'         (* .. *)
        THEN BEGIN
            GoodChar;
            END;
    Writeln;
END (* HandlePeriod *);


PROCEDURE HandleLessThan;
    (* less than may be followed by = or > *)
BEGIN
    GoodChar;
    IF nextChar IN  ['=','>']       (* <= OR <> *)
        THEN BEGIN
            GoodChar;
            END;
    Writeln;
END (* < *);


PROCEDURE HandleGreaterThan;
    (* greater than may be followed by = *)
BEGIN
    GoodChar;
    IF nextChar = '='         (* >= *)
        THEN BEGIN
            GoodChar;
            END;
    Writeln;
END (* > *);


PROCEDURE HandleSpecialChar;
    (* one character symbol *)
BEGIN
    GoodChar;
    Writeln;
END (* HandleSpecialChar *);
```

```
    PROCEDURE HandleQuote;
        (* handle character string with pairs of quotes *)
        VAR done: boolean;
    BEGIN
        done := false;
        REPEAT
            GoodChar;
            IF nextChar = ''''
                THEN BEGIN
                        GoodChar;
                        IF nextChar <> ''''
                            THEN done := true;
                        END (* found one quote *);
        UNTIL done;
        Writeln;
    END (* HandleQuote *);

BEGIN
    digits := ['0'..'9'];
    Read (nextChar);
    REPEAT
        CASE nextChar OF
            ' ': Read (nextChar);        (* ignore spaces *)

            'A', 'B', 'C', 'D', 'E', 'F', 'G', 'H', 'I',
            'J', 'K', 'L', 'M', 'N', 'O', 'P', 'Q', 'R',
            'S', 'T', 'U', 'V', 'W', 'X', 'Y', 'Z':
                HandleLetter;

            '0', '1', '2', '3', '4', '5', '6', '7', '8', '9',
            '+', '-':
                HandleNumber;

            '(': HandleOpenParen;
            '{': HandleBraces;
            ':': HandleColon;
            '.': HandlePeriod;
            '<': HandleLessThan;
            '>': HandleGreaterThan;

            ',', '*', ')', '/', ';', '=', '[', ']', '^':
                HandleSpecialChar;

            '''': HandleQuote
        END (* CASE nextChar *);
    UNTIL Eof;
END (* Tokenizer *).
```

Chapter 17

Files

Until now we have only read from one file and written to one file. These files may have been disk files, but on interactive systems one or both files may have been the terminal. We now consider reading from and writing to multiple files. Interactive input-output is discussed in Appendix E, and will not be considered here.

Let us consider the reasons for reading from several files. We often want to read several different kinds of data. For example, if we are maintaining a mailing list, we will want one file with the old mailing list and another file that contains the changes to the mailing list. If we are writing a billing program, we will want one file containing information on each customer, one file describing the resources used by each customer, and another file containing the cost of each resource unit.

There are also reasons for writing to several files. We may want one file to contain a detailed report and another to contain only a summary report. It is often useful to have a separate error message listing rather than have simply a detailed report with error messages interspersed throughout. In this way, the errors can be found and corrected without scanning the entire report.

Using several input and output files is even more important when doing some interactive input-output. Then, we may want some information to come from or go to the terminal and the rest to use files.

17-1 EXAMPLE: JUNK MAIL

Many companies use computers and computerized mailing lists to print junk mail. Here is our chance to join that game too. We will write a program that prints personalized form letters. We need one input file with the mailing list, a second input file containing the text of the letter, one output file will consist of the letters, and an output file with the mailing list formatted for printing gummed labels.

In Chapter 13, we learned to manipulate strings. The mailing list file consists of an arbitrary number of entries, where each entry is six lines long. The first line contains the first part of the person's name, and the second line contain the last name. The third line lists the street address, the fourth line, the city; the fifth line, the state; and the sixth line, the zip code.

To personalize the form letter, we will sprinkle the person's name, street address, and city throughout the letter. We will need a way to specify the site of these insertions and the items to be inserted. We will read in the text of the form letter, and it should contain indications of the desired insertions. An easy way to indicate the insertion site is to use a seldom-used character. We will use the backslash (\). A number will follow the backslash to indicate which line of input is to be placed there.

17-2 SPECIFYING DIFFERENT FILES

We now need to know how to specify which file we want to read from and which file we want to write to. Thus far, we have used the files `input` and `output`, and these have appeared in the headers of most of our programs. We can also have other files, and we name them in the same way as identifiers. If we use `input` for the text of the form letter, we can use `list` for the mailing list. Similarly, if we use `output` for the letters, we can use `labels` for the gummed labels.

As for `input` and `output`, we will usually place the other files in the program header.* The files `input` and `output` have already been predeclared. However, other files must be declared.

```
VAR list: FILE OF char;
```

A file contains a particular type in the same manner that a set has a particular type of element and an array has a base type. Since our file contains characters, we will use `char`. A shorthand notation is to use the predeclared type `text` to indicate a file of characters.†

```
VAR list, labels: text;
```

The files `input` and `output` are predeclared to be of type `text`.

With any files of type `text`, we are able to use the `Read`, `Readln`, `Write`, and `Writeln` procedures, and the `Eof` and `Eoln` functions. These normally refer to the files `input` and `output`, but there is an easy way to specify that we want to use a different file. If the first parameter of one of these procedures is a file, the file operation specified is performed on that file.

---

* What it means to place the file identifier in the program header is implementation-specific. Refer to the manual for your implementation or ask your instructor for advice about how to specify other files.

† Actually, the type `text` refers to a `PACKED FILE OF char`. We will learn about `PACKED` in Chapter 21.

```
Read (list, ch);
Read (input, int);
Write (label, ch);
Writeln (label);
```

It is very easy to omit the file name when it is desired.

```
Read (ch);
Write (ch);
Write (label, ch);
```

Therefore, if we use multiple input or output files, we should *always* specify the file name, so that we can easily spot omissions since they will likely be wrong.

```
Read (input, ch);
Write (output, ch);
Write (label, ch);
```

17-3 JUNK MAIL, CONTINUED

Remember that we have two input files and two output files. The text of the form letter is in **input** and the mailing list is in **list**. The resulting letters go into **output** and the labels go into **labels**. We can describe the algorithm as follows.

Read text of form letter
WHILE NOT Eof(list) DO
    Read one entry from mailing list
    Write a filled-in form letter
    Write a mailing label

Reading the text of the form letter is done by repeatedly reading lines until end of file is reached.

WHILE NOT Eof(input) DO
    Read one line of form letter

The procedure **ReadString** from chapter 13 describes how to read an input line into a string.

Reading one entry from the mailing list involves reading the six lines from the mailing list file.

FOR line := 1 TO 6 DO
    Read one line of mailing list

Since reading one line from the form letter and one line from the mailing list are very similar operations, the procedure `ReadString` should be modified to take the file as an additional parameter and to read the data from that file.

Writing a mailing label consists of writing the six lines of the mailing label, but allowing `Writeln`s to appear only after lines 2, 3, and 6. Writing the filled-in form letter, however, is more challenging. Here we write the lines of the form letter a character at a time. Whenever we reach a backslach, we look at the following digit and print the appropriate line from the mailing label. We then continue with the rest of the line of the form letter. After each line of the form letter, we issue a `Writeln`.

```
FOR each line of the form letter
      FOR each character of the line
            IF it is not a backslash
                  THEN write that character
                  ELSE look at the next character
                       write the appropriate line of the mailing list
```

We can now proceed to writing the program.

```
PROGRAM JunkMail (input, output, list, labels);
(* prints junk mail:
    input: text of form letter,
         with backslashes indicating insertions
    output: filled-in form letters
    list: mailing list
    labels: mailing labels
*)
    CONST
        listLines = 6;        (* 6 lines per input entry *)
        maxTextLines = 50;    (* maximum lines in letter *)
        maxStrLength = 128;   (* maximum length of a line *)
        escapeChar = '\';     (* indicates insertion *)

    TYPE
        stringRange = 0..maxStrLength;   (* A string can be null *)
        string = RECORD
            length: stringRange;
            text: ARRAY [1..maxStrLength] OF char;
            END; (* string RECORD *)
        listRange = 1..listLines;

    VAR
        person: ARRAY [listRange] OF string;
        letter: ARRAY [1..maxTextLines] OF string;
        letterSize: 0..maxTextLines;   (* actual number of lines *)
        labels, list: text;

    PROCEDURE ReadString (VAR theString: string;
                          VAR theFile: text);
        (* reads a line from theFile *)
```

```
BEGIN (* body of ReadString *)
    theString.length := 0;
    WHILE (NOT Eoln(theFile)) AND
        (theString.length < maxStrLength) DO
        BEGIN
            theString.length := theString.length + 1;
            Read (theFile, theString.text [theString.length]);
        END (* WHILE NOT Eoln *);
    Readln(theFile);
END (* ReadString *);


PROCEDURE WriteString (VAR theString: string;
                       VAR theFile: text);
    (* writes a string to theFile *)
    VAR index: stringRange;
BEGIN
    FOR index := 1 TO theString.length DO
        Write (theFile, theString.text[index]);
END (* WriteString *);


PROCEDURE ReadLetter;
    (* reads from INPUT into LETTER *)
BEGIN
    WHILE NOT Eof(input) DO
        BEGIN
            letterSize := letterSize + 1;
            ReadString (letter[letterSize], input);
        END (* WHILE NOT Eof(input) *);
END (* ReadLetter *);


PROCEDURE ReadPerson;
    (* reads the information for a person on mailing list *)
    VAR line: listRange;
BEGIN
    FOR line := 1 TO listLines DO
        ReadString (person[line], list);
END (* ReadPerson *);


PROCEDURE WriteLabel;
    (* writes a mailing label *)
BEGIN
    WriteString (person[1], labels);
    WriteString (person[2], labels);
    Writeln (labels);
    WriteString (person[3], labels);
    Writeln (labels);
    WriteString (person[4], labels);
    WriteString (person[5], labels);
    WriteString (person[6], labels);
    Writeln (labels);
END (* WriteLabel *);
```

```
        PROCEDURE WriteLetter;
            (* writes a form letter for person *)
            VAR personLine: listRange;
                letterLine: 1..maxTextLines;
                col: stringRange;
        BEGIN
            FOR letterLine := 1 TO letterSize DO
                BEGIN
                    FOR col := 1 TO letter[letterline].length DO
                        IF letter[letterLine].text[col] <> escapeChar
                            THEN Write (output,
                                letter[letterLine].text[col])
                            ELSE BEGIN
                                personLine :=
                                    ORD(letter[letterLine].text[col+1])
                                    - ORD('O');
                                WriteString(person[personLine],
                                    output);
                                END (* slash in text *);
                    Writeln (output);
                END (* FOR each line in form letter *);
        END (* WriteLetter *);


BEGIN
    Reset(list);
    Rewrite(labels);
    ReadLetter;
    WHILE NOT Eof (list) DO
        BEGIN
            ReadPerson;
            WriteLetter;
            WriteLabel;
        END (* WHILE NOT Eof (list) *);
END (* JunkMail *).
```

Let us run this program on some test data. The following is a test letter:

```
Test letter
Name is \1 \2.
\3 starts the line
the city is \4
state and zip are \5\6
```

Notice that we have tested substitution at the beginning, middle, and end of the line. The addresses to be used are

```
Fred
Smith
123 Main Street
Anytown
WY
83104
Arthur
Keller
P.O. Box 6662
Stanford
CA
94305
```

The form letters produced are

```
Test letter
Name is Fred1 Smith2.
123 Main Street3 starts the line
the city is Anytown4
state and zip are WY5831046
Test letter
Name is Arthur1 Keller2.
P.O. Box 66623 starts the line
the city is Stanford4
state and zip are CA5943056
```

Notice that we still print the number following the backslash. The labels produced are

```
FredSmith
123 Main Street
AnytownWY83104
ArthurKeller
P.O. Box 6662
StanfordCA94305
```

We have to insert spaces between the fields of the labels.

In WriteLetter, we have to test if the previous character is a backslash. If so, we do not print the current character. Note that we must not do this test for the first character on the line; otherwise, we will have an array index out of bounds—the previous character would be 0. The corrected program follows:

```
PROGRAM JunkMail (input, output, list, labels);
(* prints junk mail:
   input: text of form letter,
        with backslashes indicating insertions
   output: filled-in form letters
   list: mailing list
   labels: mailing labels
*)
   CONST
        listLines = 6;        (* 6 lines per input entry *)
        maxTextLines = 50;    (* maximum lines in letter *)
        maxStrLength = 128;   (* maximum length of a line *)
        escapeChar = '\';     (* indicates insertion *)


   TYPE
        stringRange = 0..maxStrLength;   (* A string can be null *)
        string = RECORD
            length: stringRange;
            text: ARRAY [1..maxStrLength] OF char;
            END; (* string RECORD *)
        listRange = 1..listLines;


   VAR
        person: ARRAY [listRange] OF string;
        letter: ARRAY [1..maxTextLines] OF string;
        letterSize: 0..maxTextLines;   (* actual number of lines *)
        labels, list: text;


   PROCEDURE ReadString (VAR theString: string;
                         VAR theFile: text);
        (* reads a line from theFile *)
   BEGIN
        theString.length := 0;
        WHILE (NOT Eoln(theFile)) AND
            (theString.length < maxStrLength) DO
            BEGIN
                theString.length := theString.length + 1;
                Read (theFile, theString.text [theString.length]);
            END (* WHILE NOT Eoln *);
        Readln(theFile);
   END (* ReadString *);


   PROCEDURE WriteString (VAR theString: string;
                          VAR theFile: text);
        (* writes a string to theFile *)
        VAR index: stringRange;
   BEGIN
        FOR index := 1 TO theString.length DO
            Write (theFile, theString.text[index]);
   END (* WriteString *);
```

```
PROCEDURE ReadLetter;
    (* reads from INPUT into LETTER *)
BEGIN
    WHILE NOT Eof(input) DO
        BEGIN
            letterSize := letterSize + 1;
            ReadString (letter[letterSize], input);
        END (* WHILE NOT Eof(input) *);
END (* ReadLetter *);




PROCEDURE ReadPerson;
    (* reads the information for a person on mailing list *)
    VAR line: listRange;
BEGIN
    FOR line := 1 TO listLines DO
        ReadString (person[line], list);
END (* ReadPerson *);




PROCEDURE WriteLetter;
    (* writes a form letter for person *)
    VAR personLine: listRange;
        letterLine: 1..maxTextLines;
        col: stringRange;
BEGIN
    FOR letterLine := 1 TO letterSize DO
        BEGIN
            FOR col := 1 TO letter[letterline].length DO
                IF letter[letterLine].text[col] <> escapeChar
                    THEN IF col = 1
                        THEN Write (output,
                            letter[letterLine].text[col])
                        ELSE IF escapeChar =
                            letter[letterLine].text[col-1]
                            THEN (* null THEN: do nothing *)
                            ELSE Write (output,
                                letter[letterLine].text[col])
                    ELSE BEGIN
                        personLine :=
                            ORD(letter[letterLine].text[col+1])
                            - ORD('O');
                        WriteString(person[personLine],
                            output);
                        END (* slash in text *);
            Writeln (output);
        END (* FOR each line in form letter *);
END (* WriteLetter *);
```

```
    PROCEDURE WriteLabel;
        (* writes a mailing label *)
    BEGIN
        WriteString (person[1], labels);
        Write (labels, ' ');
        WriteString (person[2], labels);
        Writeln (labels);
        WriteString (person[3], labels);
        Writeln (labels);
        WriteString (person[4], labels);
        Write (labels, ', ');
        WriteString (person[5], labels);
        Write (labels, ' ');
        WriteString (person[6], labels);
        Writeln (labels);
    END (* WriteLabel *);


BEGIN
    Reset(list);
    Rewrite(labels);
    ReadLetter;
    WHILE NOT Eof (list) DO
        BEGIN
            ReadPerson;
            WriteLetter;
            WriteLabel;
        END (* WHILE NOT Eof (list) *);
END (* JunkMail *).
```

This time, we will use a longer form letter file for input.

```
\1 \2
\3
\4, \5  \6

Dear \1 \2:

Yes, it is that time of the term again.  It is your opportunity to
win that sporty, new Blimpmobile you've been hoping for.  Just
think about tooling around \4 with the whole \2
family.  And wouldn't your neighbors be envious when they see the
Blimpmobile parked in the driveway of \3.  Just
return this letter and you may be the lucky winner.

Of course there is no obligation, but now that we have your
attention, you should consider buying some of our fine products.
No home should be without our best-selling item, the Handy-Dandy
Slicer/Dicer.  It folds, it spindles, and it mutilates anything
```

found in the kitchen. Wouldn't this be a lovely birthday present
for Mrs. \2. Please check the box below telling
us whether you want the Handy-Dandy Slicer/Dicer sent to the
\2 home for a 15-day free trial offer.

                              Sincerely,

                              Bruce A. Davis
                              Housewares Clearing Center

We will use the same list of people for list.

Fred
Smith
123 Main Street
Anytown
WY
83104
Arthur
Keller
P.O. Box 6662
Stanford
CA
94305

Our form letters now are

Fred Smith
123 Main Street
Anytown, WY 83104

Dear Fred Smith:

Yes, it is that time of the term again. It is your opportunity to
win that sporty, new Blimpmobile you've been hoping for. Just
think about tooling around Anytown with the whole Smith
family. And wouldn't your neighbors be envious when they see the
Blimpmobile parked in the driveway of 123 Main Street. Just
return this letter and you may be the lucky winner.

Of course there is no obligation, but now that we have your
attention, you should consider buying some of our fine products.
No home should be without our best-selling item, the Handy-Dandy
Slicer/Dicer. It folds, it spindles, and it mutilates anything
found in the kitchen. Wouldn't this be a lovely birthday present
for Mrs. Smith. Please check the box below telling
us whether you want the Handy-Dandy Slicer/Dicer sent to the
Smith home for a 15-day free trial offer.

Sincerely,

Bruce A. Davis
Housewares Clearing Center

Arthur Keller
P.O. Box 6662
Stanford, CA 94305

Dear Arthur Keller:

Yes, it is that time of the term again. It is your opportunity to
win that sporty, new Blimpmobile you've been hoping for. Just
think about tooling around Stanford with the whole Keller
family. And wouldn't your neighbors be envious when they see the
Blimpmobile parked in the driveway of P.O. Box 6662. Just
return this letter and you may be the lucky winner.

Of course there is no obligation, but now that we have your
attention, you should consider buying some of our fine products.
No home should be without our best-selling item, the Handy-Dandy
Slicer/Dicer. It folds, it spindles, and it mutilates anything
found in the kitchen. Wouldn't this be a lovely birthday present
for Mrs. Keller. Please check the box below telling
us whether you want the Handy-Dandy Slicer/Dicer sent to the
Keller home for a 15-day free trial offer.

Sincerely,

Bruce A. Davis
Housewares Clearing Center

The file **labels** now contains these labels:

```
Fred Smith
123 Main Street
Anytown, WY  83104
Arthur Keller
P.O. Box 6662
Stanford, CA  94305
```

Many people find computer-generated form letters rather offensive. For example, the fictitious Bruce A. Davis does not know whether or not I am married. Furthermore, P.O. Box 6662 does not have a driveway!

Dynamic
Data Structures

We know how to read data from files, manipulate the data, and print the results. We can have several approaches for dealing with arbitrary amounts of data. In one method, we can process the data as we read it. This way we only need to allow room for the latest values and the running totals (or, for example, maxima and minima). In another method, we can store all data in one or more arrays.

The first method—storing only the latest values—is preferable, but cannot always be used. If multiple passes are made through the data, we must either read the data more than once or hold onto it. For example, when we calculated the standard deviation in Section 11-4, we made one pass through the data to obtain the mean (average) and another pass to find the standard deviation. To print out a list of numbers in reverse order, we need to read all of the numbers before printing any of them.

The second method—using arrays—does not always work either. If the data is too large to fit in memory, we can use the first method or we can resort to reading the input many times. When we declare an array, we must specify its size. We cannot make the array size depend on some input value. If a program has two potentially large arrays, we have to choose some maximum value for each of them and incorporate these restrictions into the program. Suppose that we are writing a program to print a report describing the status of college applicants. We may have one array for unprocessed applications and another array for processed applications. There will be either be many unprocessed applications and few processed ones, or few unprocessed applications and many processed ones, or some distribution in between. But our computer may be so small that we do not have room for both the maximum number of unprocessed applications and the maximum number of processed applications, even though it may be large enough to hold the actual combination.

In a third method, we can dynamically create records as desired to store the information. Unfortunately, dynamically created records are not as easy to use as ordinary arrays. We will soon learn how to use them effectively.

18-1 REVERSING A LIST

Suppose that we want to read a list of numbers and print them in reverse order. We do not know in advance how many numbers there are, and therefore we cannot use an array. We want a data structure that operates in a *last-in first-out* (LIFO) manner; that is, the last items entered into the data structure are the first ones to be removed. This is also known as a *stack* since new items are placed on top, and we removed items from the top.

There are two operations associated with stacks: push and pop. We *push* a new item onto the stack; we *pop* an old item from the stack. The sequence of pushes and pops is similar to the matching of BEGINs and ENDs in a program; an END matches the most recent BEGIN that has not yet been matched by an END. Another example is a stack of trays in a cafeteria. We push trays onto the stack, and pop them from it one at a time when we need one.

18-2 POINTERS

We know how to declare records. We will now learn how to declare dynamically allocated records.

```
TYPE
    rec = RECORD
        value1: integer;
        value2: integer;
    END (* rec *);

VAR
    oneRec: rec;          (* These are two records *)
    anotherRec: rec;      (* Both are type rec *)
    anyRec: ∧rec;         (* A placeholder for a rec *)
```

Notice that we have defined two records—**oneRec** and **anotherRec**, both of type **rec**. Both are ordinary records that we are already familiar with. However, **anyRec** is not a record like **oneRec**. The variable **anyRec** is a placeholder that may refer to records of type **rec**. This is indicated in the declaration by a caret (∧) followed by a record type name. Assuming the above declarations, we can say any of the following statements.

```
oneRec.value1 := 5;
anotherRec.value2 := oneRec.value1;
Write (anotherRec.value2);
oneRec := anotherRec;    (* assigns entire record *)
```

With the same declarations, each of the following are invalid.

```
value1 := 6;      (* which value1? *)
anyRec.value1;    (* anyRec is not a record *)
```

What can we do with **anyRec**? Since it is a placeholder, we can have it refer to records of type **rec**. For example, if we want to create a new record of type **rec** and have **anyRec** refer to that record, we can say

```
New (anyRec);
```

New is a built-in procedure that allocates a new record and makes its parameter refer to that record. The type of record created is based on the type of the parameter to **New**. The placeholder is technically called a *pointer*.

How do we specify the fields of this newly created record? To specify the fields of an ordinary record, we give the record name followed by a period and the field name. To specify the fields of a dynamically created record, we give the record name followed by a caret, a period, and the field name. Using the above declarations, these are valid statements.

```
New (anyRec);
oneRec.value1 := 3;
oneRec.value2 := 10;
anyRec∧.value1 := 7;
anyRec∧.value2 := oneRec.value2;
```

The caret here indicates that the preceding identifier is a pointer, and that we need to look at the record to which it refers. The period following the caret says that a field name follows.

We will use a graphic notation to illustrate the use of pointers. A box will represent a record. We may divide a box to represent the fields of a record. Inside a box, we may put the values of the various fields of its record. We sometimes label a box to indicate the record type or record name.

oneRec

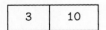

When we have a pointer referencing a record, we use an arrow between the pointer and the record.

anyRec

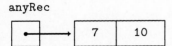

Pointers are similar to array indexes. The value of **anyRec** tells the record **rec** to which it refers. We can have several pointer variables, each pointing to its own record.

```
VAR
    anyRec1: ∧rec;        (* A placeholder for a rec *)
    anyRec2: ∧rec;        (* A placeholder for another rec *)

BEGIN
    New (anyRec1);
    New (anyRec2);
    anyRec1∧.value1 := 13;
    anyRec1∧.value2 := 14;
    anyRec2∧.value1 := anyRec1∧.value1 + 3;
    anyRec2∧.value2 := 18;
```

We now have two records: **anyRec1** points to one and **anyRec2** points to the other. These records are distinct and may be illustrated as follows.

anyRec1

anyRec2

We can have two pointers directed toward to the same record.

```
VAR
    anyRec1: ∧rec;        (* A placeholder for a rec *)
    anyRec2: ∧rec;        (* A placeholder for another rec *)

BEGIN
    New (anyRec1);
    anyRec2 := anyRec1;
    anyRec1∧.value1 := 1;
    anyRec1∧.value2 := 2;
```

This is illustrated as follows.

anyRec1

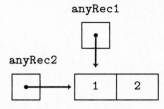

anyRec2

Notice that there is only one record, and both **anyRec1** and **anyRec2** point to it. If we change **anyRec1**∧.**value1**, we also change **anyRec2**∧.**value1**. This is called *aliasing*. We have more than one name for the same variable or record.

What is the value of a pointer before we made it point to a record? As for any other variable, a pointer cannot be expected to have any particular value before it is initialized. With arrays on most computers, PASCAL checks that the array index is within the bounds of the array. Pointer variables, however, are not defined to be constrained within a particular range. But there is a way to indicate that a pointer does not currently point to any record—the special value

NIL. If we try to reference the record to which a pointer with a value of NIL points, we will have an error that may be detected by PASCAL in the same way that an out of bounds array index is detected.

We can perform is another operation on pointer variables: we can test if two pointers have the same value.

```
IF anyRec1 <> anyRec2
    THEN Writeln ('different')
    ELSE Writeln ('same');
```

This example will print **same** if the two pointers refer to the same record, and **different** if they do not point to the same record. Note that if both pointers have the value NIL, they are equal.

There is a difference between two pointers that point to the same record and two pointers that point to two different records that have the same values. The following program fragment demonstrates this difference.

```
VAR rec1, rec2, rec3: ∧rec;        (* three records *)
BEGIN
    New (rec1);
    rec1∧.value1 := 17;
    rec1∧.value2 := 69;
    Writeln (rec1∧.value1, rec1∧.value2);
    rec2 := rec1;
    Writeln (rec2∧.value1, rec2∧.value2);
    New (rec3);
    rec3∧.value1 := rec1∧.value1;    } JUST getting
    rec3∧.value2 := rec1∧.value2;    } VALUE
    Writeln (rec3∧.value1, rec3.value2);
    IF rec1 = rec2
        THEN Writeln ('rec1 = rec2');
    IF rec1 <> rec3
        THEN Writeln ('rec1 <> rec3');
    IF rec2 <> rec3
        THEN Writeln ('rec2 <> rec3');
    rec1∧value1 := 0;
    Writeln (rec1∧.value1, rec1∧.value2);
    Writeln (rec2∧.value1, rec2∧.value2);
    Writeln (rec3∧.value1, rec3.value2);
```

```
        17          69
        17          69
        17          69
rec1 = rec2
rec1 <> rec3
rec2 <> rec3
         0          69
         0          69
        17          69
```

We notice that **rec1** and **rec2** point to the same record, but that this record is different than the record that **rec3** points to. This means that when we change **rec1**∧.**value1**, **rec2**∧.**value1** is also changed, but **rec3**∧.**value1** is not changed.

There is a shorthand notation for copying all the values from one record to another. We omit the period and the field name following it. For example, if **aRec** is declared to be type **rec**, then **aRec.value1** refers to a particular field in the **aRec** record, and simply **aRec** refers to the entire record. Consequently, **rec1**∧.**value1** refers to a particular field in the record pointed to by **rec1**, and **rec1**∧ refers to the entire record that **rec1** points to. To copy all the values from the record **rec1**∧ to the record **rec3**∧, we say

```
rec3∧ := rec1∧;          (* copy record *)
```

The previous statement indicates that we have two records with the same value. This statement differs from the following one, which indicates that we have a single record that 2 pointers both point to.

```
rec3 := rec1;            (* both point to the same record *)
```

The operation of following the pointer to the record it points to is called *dereferencing the pointer.*

The values of pointers are rather restricted. We have seen that we can obtain pointer values by using the procedure **New**. We have also seen that we can assign one pointer variable to another pointer variable, but only if they are of the same type. Two pointer variables are of the same type if they point to the same type of record. We cannot read or print the values of pointers. The only operations on pointers allowed creation of new records with the **New** procedure, assignment of the value of one pointer to another pointer of the same type, dereferencing of a pointer, and passing the pointer as a parameter to a procedure. Creation of new records is actually a special case of the last operation.

Dynamically allocated records come from an area of memory known as the *heap.* Ordinary variables are located in an area of memory called the *stack.* If there is not enough room for a data structure in memory, we will either obtain the message *stack overruns heap* or *heap overruns stack.* Every time that we allocate a new record, it is obtained from the heap. If there is not sufficient memory left, we will obtain the message that the heap overruns the stack. Every time that we call a procedure, the variables for that procedure and other control information are placed on the end of the stack (causing the stack to grow). If there is not sufficient memory for the stack frame (the variables for a procedure and the control information for that procedure), we will obtain the message that the stack overruns the heap.

What should we do if we get either of the two error messages *heap overruns stack* or *stack overruns heap*? There are two possible causes. There may be an infinite recursion loop. Does one of our procedures call itself? Does a procedure call another procedure that in turn calls the first one? If the answer to either question is affirmative, we may have an infinite recursion loop. (See Chapter 14 for information on this problem.) Are we allocating records using **New** inside a loop? If we are, we may have an infinite allocation loop. Note that either message may indicate a problem with the stack or the heap. The resultant message depends on when the problem was detected, and not on the nature of the problem.

18-3 LINKED LISTS

The power of pointers comes from the ability to have a pointer inside a dynamically allocated record. We can define a record to point to another record of the same type.

```
TYPE node = RECORD
    data : integer;
    next : ^node
    END (* node *);

VAR head : ^node;
    newNode: ^node;
```

We have a variable called **head** that points to the head of the list. That is, **head** points to a record of type **node**, which in turn points to another record of type **node**, and so forth. The last record in the list indicates that no record follows it by having a **NIL** pointer. This is illustrated as follows.

head

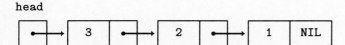

Let us now consider the process of pushing a new node onto the list. We first allocate the new node and place the new data (in this case, 4) in it.

newNode

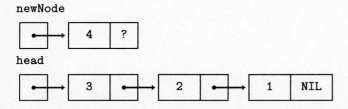

We then set the new node to point to the node at the head of the list.

newNode

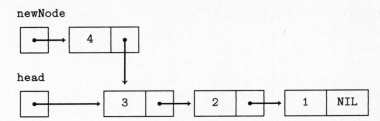

Lastly, we change the head of the list to point to the new node.

newNode

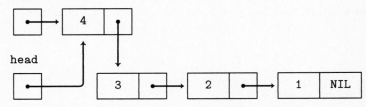

Redrawing the illustration makes it clear that we have placed the new node at the head of the list.

newNode

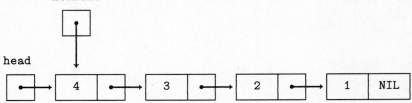

We can now proceed to writing the code for pushing a node onto a list.

```
New (newNode);
newNode∧.data := 4;          (* preliminary initialization *)
newNode∧.next := head;       (* the operations for push *)
head := newNode;
```

An *empty list* has a `NIL` pointer in the head. Let us see how the above code fragment works on empty lists. After executing the first two statements, we have the following situation:

newNode

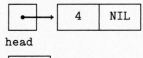

head

NIL

We then have the new node point to what **head** points to.

newNode

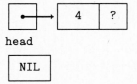

head

NIL

Next, we alter **head** to point to the new node.

newNode

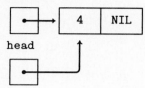

As we see, this process works well for empty lists.

Now that we understand the process of pushing a node onto the end of a list, we should learn how to pop a node off the end of a list. Since this is the inverse operation, the process is simply reversed.

topNode

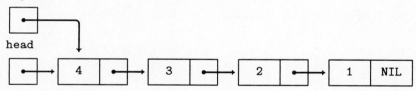

We first make **topNode** point to the first node in the list by assigning it the value **head**.

topNode

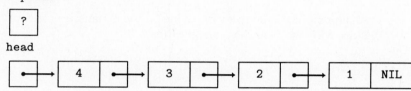

We then make **head** point to the node to which the first node also points.

topNode

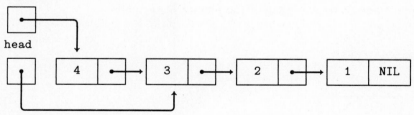

When redrawn, the structure appears as

topNode

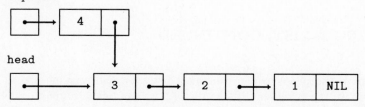

This is clearer if we put **NIL** in the node pointed to by **topNode**.

topNode

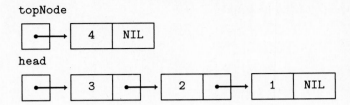

head

The code for the pop operation follows.

```
topNode := head;
head := topNode∧.next;
topNode∧.next := NIL;
```

Let us see what happens if there is only one node on the list and we attempt to remove it. We start with the following configuration.

topNode

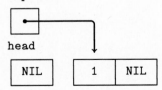

head

We first make **topNode** point to what **head** points to.

topNode

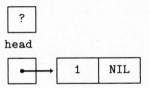

head

We then make **head** have the value of the pointer in the node.

topNode

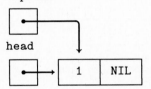

head

As we wanted, **head** now points to an empty list.

18-4 REVERSING A LIST, CONTINUED

We can now return to the problem of reversing a list. We will read numbers from the input until we reach the end of the file. As we read each number, we will push it onto the stack. Then, we will remove numbers from the stack until the stack is empty. As we remove each number, we will print it.

```
PROGRAM Reverse (input, output);
(* program to reverse a list of numbers using a stack *)
    TYPE nodePtr = ∧node;

        node = RECORD
            data : integer;
            next : nodePtr
        END (* node *);


    VAR head : nodePtr;      (* the head of the list *)
        aNode : nodePtr;     (* a node to push or pop *)
        value : integer;     (* value from input file *)


    PROCEDURE Push (VAR head : nodePtr; newNode : nodePtr);
    (* pushes newNode onto the beginning of list pointed to
       by head *)
    BEGIN
        newNode∧.next := head;
        head := newNode;
    END (* Push *);


    PROCEDURE Pop (VAR head : nodePtr; VAR topNode : nodePtr);
    (* pops first node off the beginning of list pointed to
       by head and returns it in topNode *)
    BEGIN
        topNode := head;
        head := topNode∧.next;
        topNode∧.next := NIL;
    END (* Pop *);


BEGIN
    head := NIL;            (* start with empty list *)

    WHILE NOT Eof DO    (* push input values onto stack *)
        BEGIN
            Readln (value);
            New (aNode);
            aNode∧.data := value;
            Push (head, aNode);
        END (* WHILE more input *);

    WHILE head <> NIL DO (* write stack to output *)
        BEGIN
            Pop (head, aNode);
            value := aNode∧.data;
            Writeln (value);
        END (* WHILE head list nonempty *);
END (* Reverse *).
```

Assume the input is

1
2
3
4

4
3
2
1

18-5 TRAVERSING A LIST

The program in the previous section printed out a stack by popping elements off it. This process destroyed the list. If we want to print the list twice, we must scan the list without destroying it. Visiting the nodes of a linked list is called *traversing* the list.

Suppose that we have the list shown in the following diagram.

head

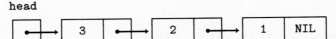

To traverse this list, we first set a pointer to the first node in the list.

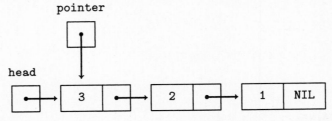

We then print the value in the node to which the pointer points. Next, we advance the pointer to the following node by the statement (which assumes the declarations from the previous two sections)

```
pointer := pointer∧.next;
```

The effect of this is illustrated in the following diagram.

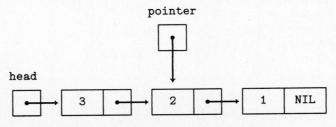

We repeatedly print the value of the current node and advance to the next node until we reach the end of the list. Let us look at that case.

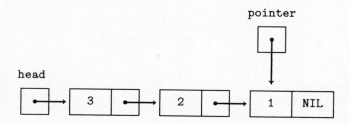

The value of **pointer**∧.**next** is **NIL**, which indicates the end of the list. The following diagram shows another advance of the pointer.

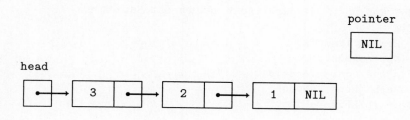

We can now proceed to writing the program that reads a list of numbers and prints it twice in reverse order.

```
PROGRAM Traverse (input, output);
(* program to reverse a list of numbers using a stack *)
   TYPE nodePtr = ∧node;

      node = RECORD
         data : integer;
         next : nodePtr
      END (* node *);


   VAR head : nodePtr;      (* the head of the list *)
      aNode : nodePtr;      (* a node to push or pop *)
      value : integer;      (* value from input file *)


   PROCEDURE Push (VAR head : nodePtr; newNode : nodePtr);
   (* pushes newNode onto the beginning of list pointed to
      by head *)
   BEGIN
      newNode∧.next := head;
      head := newNode;
   END (* Push *);
```

```
    PROCEDURE PrintList (head : nodePtr);
    (* prints the list headed by head *)
        VAR aNode : nodePtr;
    BEGIN
        aNode := head;          (* first node on list *)
        WHILE aNode <> NIL DO (* write list to output *)
            BEGIN
                value := aNode∧.data;
                Writeln (value);
                aNode := aNode∧.next
            END (* WHILE head list nonempty *);
    END (* PrintList *);


BEGIN
    head := NIL;            (* start with empty list *)

    WHILE NOT Eof DO     (* push input values onto stack *)
        BEGIN
            Readln (value);
            New (aNode);
            aNode∧.data := value;
            Push (head, aNode);
        END (* WHILE more input *);


    PrintList (head);
    PrintList (head);
END (* Traverse *).
```

Assume the input is

```
1
2
3
4
```

```
    4
    3
    2
    1
    4
    3
    2
    1
```

18-6 QUEUES

We have learned to print a long list in reverse order multiple times. The technique involves a stack that obeys a LIFO discipline. However, we may also want to print a long list multiple times in its original order. We will learn how to do that in this section.

With a stack, we insert and delete from the same end. With a queue, we insert onto one end and delete from the other. The elements are removed from a queue in the same order as they were inserted. Queues obey a *first-in first-out* or *FIFO* discipline. With a stack, we need only keep track of one end—the end we insert into or delete from. With a queue, we must keep track of both ends.

Let us consider the operations of deleting from and inserting into a queue. The **head** of a queue is the end from which we delete; the **tail** of a queue is the end into which we insert. An illustration of a queue follows.

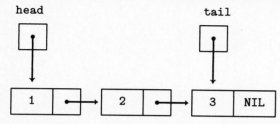

Deleting from a queue involves a similar process to deleting from a stack. We first make **topNode** point to the first node in the list by assigning it the value **head**.

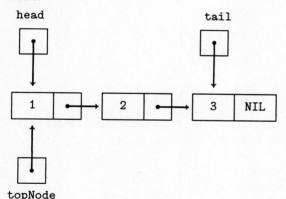

We then make **head** point to the node to which the first node also points.

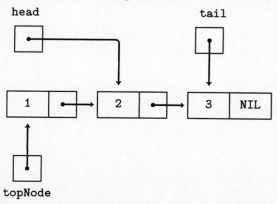

We then put **NIL** in the node pointed to by **topNode**.

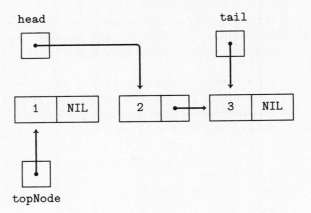

Redrawing this diagram results in the following.

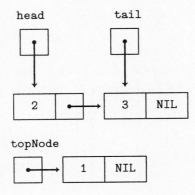

The insertion operation is different for queues than for stacks. Let us start with the situation illustrated by the following diagram.

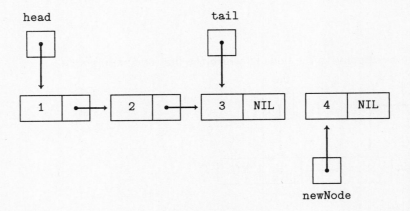

Note that we have set the new node to point to **NIL**. We set the tail node to point to the new node.

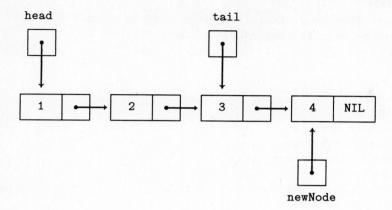

We then set **tail** to point to the new node.

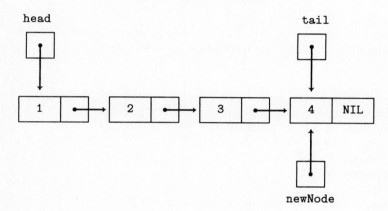

Problems arise when starting or ending with an empty queue. An empty queue has both its head and the tail set to **NIL**. Normally, insertion does not affect the head and deletion does not affect the tail. However, when an empty list is involved, the other end *is* affected. When inserting into an empty list, we want the desired state to be as illustrated below.

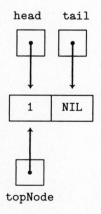

We can now proceed to writing the procedure for insertion.

```
PROCEDURE Insert (VAR head, tail : nodePtr; newNode : nodePtr);
(* inserts newNode onto the beginning of queue pointed to
   by head and tail *)
BEGIN
    newNode∧.next := NIL;
    IF tail = NIL
        THEN BEGIN
            head := newNode;
            tail := newNode;
            END (* was an empty list *)
        ELSE BEGIN
            tail∧.next := newNode;
            tail := newNode;
            END (* nonempty list *);
END (* Insert *);
```

When we delete from a queue that has only one node, we want both the head and tail to be NIL. The code for the deletion procedure follows.

```
PROCEDURE Delete (VAR head, tail: nodePtr; VAR topNode: nodePtr);
(* removes first node off the beginning of list pointed to
   by head and returns it in topNode *)
BEGIN
    topNode := head;
    head := topNode∧.next;
    IF head = NIL
        THEN tail := NIL (* was only one node *)
        ELSE topNode∧.next := NIL;
END (* Delete *);
```

We are now ready to modify the program Section 18-4 that reversed a list to print it in its original order. Also included is the procedure from Section 18-5 that traversed the list without destroying it.

```
PROGRAM Queue (input, output);
(* program to build a queue, print it nondestructively, and
   print it while deleting it *)
    TYPE nodePtr = ∧node;

        node = RECORD
            data : integer;
            next : nodePtr
        END (* node *);

    VAR head : nodePtr;     (* the head of the list *)
        tail : nodePtr;     (* the head of the list *)
        aNode : nodePtr;    (* a node to push or pop *)
        value : integer;    (* value from input file *)
```

```
PROCEDURE Insert (VAR head, tail: nodePtr; newNode: nodePtr);
(* inserts newNode at the tail of queue pointed to
   by head and tail *)
BEGIN
    newNode∧.next := NIL;
    IF tail = NIL
        THEN BEGIN
            head := newNode;
            tail := newNode;
            END (* was an empty list *)
        ELSE BEGIN
            tail∧.next := newNode;
            tail := newNode;
            END (* nonempty list *);
END (* Insert *);

PROCEDURE Delete (VAR head, tail: nodePtr;
                  VAR topNode: nodePtr);
(* removes first node off the beginning of list pointed to
   by head and returns it in topNode *)
BEGIN
    topNode := head;
    head := topNode∧.next;
    IF head = NIL
        THEN tail := NIL (* was only one node *)
        ELSE topNode∧.next := NIL;
END (* Delete *);

PROCEDURE PrintList (head : nodePtr);
(* prints the list headed by head *)
    VAR aNode : nodePtr;
BEGIN
    aNode := head;        (* first node on list *)
    WHILE aNode <> NIL DO (* write list to output *)
        BEGIN
            value := aNode∧.data;
            Writeln (value);
            aNode := aNode∧.next
        END (* WHILE head list nonempty *);
END (* PrintList *);

BEGIN
    head := NIL;          (* start with empty list *)
    tail := NIL;

    WHILE NOT Eof DO     (* push input values onto stack *)
        BEGIN
            Readln (value);
            New (aNode);
            aNode∧.data := value;
            Insert (head, tail, aNode);
        END (* WHILE more input *);
```

```
      PrintList (head);
      WHILE tail <> NIL DO (* write stack to output *)
          BEGIN
              Delete (head, tail, aNode);
              value := aNode∧.data;
              Writeln (value);
          END (* WHILE head list nonempty *);
END (* Queue *).
```

Assume the input is

```
1
2
3
4
```

```
             1
             2
             3
             4
             1
             2
             3
             4
```

More complex data structures, such as trees and doubly-linked lists, can be constructed with pointers, since we can have multiple pointers in each node. However, such data structures are beyond the scope of this book.

Procedures and Functions as Parameters

We can currently have only variables and expressions as parameters. We have **VAR** parameters, which have two-way communication and can only be variables. We have value parameters, which have one-way communication and can be variables or expressions. In this chapter, we will learn about other kinds of parameters.

19-1 PLOTTING GRAPHS

Suppose that we want to plot a graph. We have a function, such as $y = -x^2 + 3$, and we want to plot this function. Since functions such as this have one y value per x value, it makes sense to have y run horizontally—each column being a different y value—and to have x run vertically—each row being a different x value. We will have a loop that runs through the x values, and for each x value, we will calculate and plot the y value.

Since a terminal screen is smaller than a page of output, we will create a graph no larger than 80×24. If we place the origin in column 40, we can have negative values of y in columns 1 through 39 and positive values of y in columns 41 through 79. (For symmetry, we will have an equal number of positive and negative columns; this is not necessary.) We will allow 5 columns per unit. This means that the *y-scale factor* is 5 columns per unit. For the *x*-scale factor, we will use 3 rows per unit. This is because most output devices, such as terminals and printers, use character shapes that are approximately 3×5. For example, many printers print 10 characters per inch horizontally and 6 rows per inch vertically. The ratio of vertical to horizontal scale factors is called the *aspect ratio*, and in this case it is 3 to 5.

For each row and its corresponding x value, we will print a character, such as an asterisk, in the column corresponding to the desired y value. Given a value of x, we can easily calculate a value of y. The next step is to decide in which column to print the asterisk. If we multiply the y by 5—the y-scale factor—we will get a column offset. If we add 40 to this column offset, we will get the desired column. Let us try this for 0: multiplying by 5 gives 0, and adding 40 gives 40—the desired column. Let us try this also for -1: multiplying by 5 gives -5, adding 40 gives 35, and this also appears to be the correct column. Let us also try this for $+1$: multiplying by 5 gives $+5$, adding 40 gives 45, and the correctness of this value validates our formula.

Each row of the graph represents a different x value. If we want the origin in the center, we can have 11 rows before the y axis and 11 rows after. This means that the rows range from -11 to 11 for a total of 23 rows, which is less than a typical terminal screen size. Since there are 3 rows per inch, the graph will range from $x = -\frac{11}{3}$ to $x = +\frac{11}{3}$.

Let us now begin to describe the desired program.

FOR *each row of the graph*
    Print the row for the corresponding x value

To print the desired row, we convert the x value to a column number. How do we print the asterisk in the desired column? We can print the required number of spaces preceding the asterisk. That is, if we want to print an asterisk in column 27, we print 26 spaces followed by an asterisk. We can print 26 spaces using a field width specification.

Write (' ' : 26);

We can now proceed with describing how to print a row.

Compute the column number
Print the preceding spaces
Print the asterisk

Let us now convert this to PASCAL.

```
PROGRAM Graph (output);
(* Prints a graph of y = -x² + 3 *)
    CONST
        firstRow = -11;        (* first row number *)
        lastRow = 11;          (* last row number *)
        XScaleFactor = 3.0;    (* rows per unit *)
        YScaleFactor = 5.0;    (* columns per unit *)
        firstColumn = 1;       (* leftmost column *)
        lastColumn = 79;       (* rightmost column *)
        zeroColumn = 40;       (* column for y = 0 *)
```

```
VAR
    X: real;                    (* real value of x *)
    row: firstRow..lastRow; (* current row *)


PROCEDURE PrintRow (X: real);
    VAR Y: real;
        column: firstColumn..lastColumn;
                            (* column for asterisk *)
BEGIN
    Y := - (X * X) + 3.0;
    column := Round (zeroColumn + YScaleFactor * Y);
    Write (' ': column - 1);
    Writeln ('*');
END (* PrintRow *);


BEGIN
    FOR row := firstRow TO lastRow DO
        BEGIN
            X := row / XScaleFactor;
            PrintRow (X);
        END (* FOR row *);
END (* Graph *).
```

If we try to execute this, we may obtain an error message such as "Scalar out of range" before plotting any of the graph. The problem occurs on the first row of the graph. When **row** $= -11$, $x = -\frac{11}{3} = -3.666666$. The value of y is -10.444444, which corresponds to column -12. Unfortunately, columns go from 1 to 79. We need to insert a test so that we will only print an asterisk if the column is in range. The revised procedure **PrintRow** follows.

```
PROCEDURE PrintRow (X: real);
    VAR Y: real;
        column: integer;      (* column for asterisk *)
BEGIN
    Y := - (X * X) + 3.0;
    column := Round (zeroColumn + YScaleFactor * Y);
    IF (column >= firstColumn) AND (column <= lastColumn)
        THEN BEGIN
            Write (' ': column - 1);
            Writeln ('*');
            END (* column in range *)
        ELSE Writeln; (* No asterisk this row *)
END (* PrintRow *);
```

```
          *
               *
                    *
                      *
                        *
                         *
                          *
                           *
                            *
                           *
                          *
                         *
                        *
                      *
                    *
               *
          *
```

This curve has the expected parabolic shape.

Suppose we want to label this curve with x and y axes. Sometimes the asterisk will appear to the left of the x axis, and other times it will appear to the right. It is also possible that the asterisk will appear on the x axis when $y = 0$. We will use an array to represent the characters of a row. Then we can place characters for the axes and the asterisk in arbitrary order. Actually, since we would like an asterisk to appear instead of the symbol for an axis whenever they are in the same column, we will place the axes in the array first, and overlay them with an asterisk when necessary. Since the right edge of the parabola is in column 55, we will let the axis extend only to column 65. The revised `PrintRow` procedure follows.

```
PROCEDURE PrintRow (X: real);
    CONST epsilon = 0.001;   (* allow for rounding errors *)
    VAR Y: real;
        column: integer;     (* column for asterisk *)
        rowArray: ARRAY [firstColumn..lastColumn] OF char;
        spaceChar: char;     (* normal space character *)
        axisChar: char;      (* character for x axis *)

BEGIN
    IF Abs (X) >= epsilon
        THEN BEGIN
            spaceChar := ' ';
            axisChar := '|';
            END (* normal row *)
        ELSE BEGIN
            spaceChar := '-';
            axisChar := '+';
            END (* y axis row *);
```

```
      FOR column := firstColumn TO lastColumn DO
          rowArray [column] := spaceChar;
      rowArray [zeroColumn] := axisChar;

      Y := - (X * X) + 3.0;
      column := Round (zeroColumn + YScaleFactor * Y);
      IF (column >= firstColumn) AND (column <= lastColumn)
          THEN BEGIN
              rowArray [column] := '*';
              END (* column in range *);

      FOR column := firstColumn TO lastColumn DO
          Write (rowArray [column]);
      Writeln;
END (* PrintRow *);
```

19-2 PLOTTING GRAPHS, CONTINUED

Suppose that we want to plot multiple curves on the same graph. In the procedure PrintRow from the previous section, we would like to substitute different functions of x, each with a different character to appear on the graph. We should break the procedure PrintRow into the initialization of the row, the plotting of each curve, and the printing of the resultant row. Which curve we want to plot should be a parameter of the procedure that plots the curve. We could define a function to describe the desired curve:

```
FUNCTION F (X: real): real;
(* calculates the function to be printed *)
BEGIN
    F := - (X * X) + 3.0;
END (* F *);
```

Then we could use the following line in `PrintRow`.

```
Y := F (X);
```

Unfortunately, we still have only one such function defined. If we defined several functions, we would still be referring to only one of them. If the desired function were a parameter, we could then graph any function defined in the program. It *is* possible to pass a function as a parameter. To pass the function `F` as a parameter to the procedure `PlotFunction`, we can use the following declaration:

```
PROCEDURE PlotFunction (X: real;
    FUNCTION G (dummy: real): real;
    ch: char);
```

We notice that we have placed a declaration for the function as parameter `G` that is similar to the function header for the function `F`. The declaration of a formal parameter that is a function (such as `G`) should match the function header for all functions that will be passed as a corresponding actual parameter, except that the names of the parameters (such as **dummy**) specified in the formal parameter that is a function (such as `G`) may be chosen arbitrarily.

Let us write the program to plot functions $y = -x^2 + 3$ and $y = 0.5x^2 - 4$.

```
PROGRAM Graph (output);
(* Prints a graph of y = -x² + 3 and y = 0.5x² - 4 *)
    CONST
        epsilon = 0.001;          (* allow for rounding errors *)
        firstRow = -11;           (* first row number *)
        lastRow = 11;             (* last row number *)
        XScaleFactor = 3.0;       (* rows per unit *)
        YScaleFactor = 5.0;       (* columns per unit *)
        firstColumn = 1;          (* leftmost column *)
        lastColumn = 65;          (* rightmost column *)
        zeroColumn = 40;          (* column for y = 0 *)
    VAR
        X: real;                  (* real value of x *)
        row: firstRow..lastRow;   (* current row *)
        rowArray: ARRAY [firstColumn..lastColumn] OF char;
```

```
FUNCTION F1 (X: real): real;
(* calculates the function to be printed *)
BEGIN
    F1 := - (X * X) + 3.0;
END (* F1 *);




FUNCTION F2 (X: real): real;
(* calculates the function to be printed *)
BEGIN
    F2 := X * X / 2.0 - 4.0;
END (* F2 *);




PROCEDURE InitRow (X: real);
    (* initializes row with axes *)
    VAR column: firstColumn..lastColumn;
        spaceChar: char;    (* normal space character *)
        axisChar: char;     (* character for x axis *)

BEGIN
    IF Abs (X) >= epsilon
        THEN BEGIN
            spaceChar := ' ';
            axisChar := '|';
            END (* normal row *)
        ELSE BEGIN
            spaceChar := '-';
            axisChar := '+';
            END (* y axis row *);
    FOR column := firstColumn TO lastColumn DO
        rowArray [column] := spaceChar;
    rowArray [zeroColumn] := axisChar;
END (* InitRow *);




PROCEDURE PlotFunction (X: real;
    FUNCTION G (dummy: real): real;
    ch: char);
    (* marks rowArray with position of curve *)
    VAR Y: real;
        column: integer;    (* column for asterisk *)

BEGIN
    Y := G (X);
    column := Round (zeroColumn + YScaleFactor * Y);
    IF (column >= firstColumn) AND (column <= lastColumn)
        THEN BEGIN
            rowArray [column] := ch;
            END (* column in range *);
END (* PlotFunction *);
```

```
    PROCEDURE PrintRow;
        (* prints the row already set up *)
        VAR column: firstColumn..lastColumn;

    BEGIN
        FOR column := firstColumn TO lastColumn DO
            Write (rowArray [column]);
        Writeln;
    END (* PrintRow *);

BEGIN
    FOR row := firstRow TO lastRow DO
        BEGIN
            X := row / XScaleFactor;
            InitRow (X);
            PlotFunction (X, F1, '>');
            PlotFunction (X, F2, '<');
            PrintRow;
        END (* FOR row *);
END (* Graph *).
```

```
                                              |                      <
                                              |                  <
                  >                           | <
                       >                         <  |
                            >          <         |
                                 <        >       |
                            <                   |>
                      <                   |          >
                    <                     |              >
                  <                       |                >
                <                         |                 >
----------------<-------------------------+-------------->----------
                <                         |                 >
                  <                       |                >
                    <                     |              >
                      <                   |          >
                            <          >     |>
                         >          <         |
                    >                      <  |
                  >                           | <
                                              |        <
                                              |                  <
```

Note that functions as parameters is a current area that is being standardized in PASCAL. The description given corresponds to the current ANSI/ISO draft standard.* The earlier specification for PASCAL† did not list the parameter types for the formal parameters that are functions, but did list the result type. Thus, the header for procedure `PlotFunction` would be

```
PROCEDURE PlotFunction (X: real;
    FUNCTION G: real;
    ch: char);
```

Refer to your compiler reference manual or ask your instructor for details on your particular implementation.

Suppose that one of the curves we wanted to draw was the *sine* curve. We would like to pass the built-in function `Sin` as a parameter to the procedure `PlotFunction`. Unfortunately, some implementations do not allow built-in functions or procedures to be passed as parameters. Consequently, a simple function must be written which *can* be passed as a parameter.

```
FUNCTION MySin (X: real): real;
(* computes Sin (X) *)
BEGIN
    MySin := Sin (X);
END (* F2 *);
```

We can then pass this as a parameter.

```
PlotFunction (X, MySin, '!');
```

```
PlotFunction (X, Sin, '?');
```

19-3 ENCRYPTING TEXT

Suppose that we have a file containing on each line the code for the operation we want to perform on the words of that line. For example, some lines are to have the letters in each word reversed. Some other lines may be printed without any changes made. Still other lines will have each letter changed to its successor or to its predecessor. This is a simple form of encryption of text.

We will have a procedure that handles all words on a line. This procedure will take a parameter that is a procedure that manipulates the word in the appropriate manner.

Let us try to write the program. We will take advantage of the ideas from Chapter 13.

WHILE *there is an input line*
    Read the desired operation
    Perform this operation on the rest of the line

---

* *SIGPLAN Notices*, **15**, 4 (April 1980), ACM.

† Jensen and Wirth, *PASCAL User Manual and Report*, Springer-Verlag, New York, 1974.

We can now consider how to perform this operation on the rest of the line.

WHILE *there is more on this line*
    Read a character
   IF *it is a letter*
       THEN *Read the rest of the word*
            Perform the operation
            Write the changed word
       ELSE *Write the space or punctuation*

Let us write this procedure. The convention for declaring parameters that are procedures is similar to that for declaring parameters that are functions as described in the previous sections.

```
CONST maxWordLength = 20;
TYPE wordLength = 0..maxWordLength;
     word = RECORD
          length: wordLength;
          text: ARRAY [1..maxWordLength] OF char;
          END (* word *);

PROCEDURE ChangeLine (PROCEDURE AlterWord (VAR dummy: word));
     (* ChangeLine reads in words on a line and calls
        AlterWord on each word found *)
     VAR wd: word;
         wdln: wordLength;
         ch: char;

BEGIN
    WHILE NOT Eoln (input) DO
        BEGIN
            Read (ch);
            IF ch IN ['A'..'Z']
                THEN BEGIN
                    wdln := 0;
                    REPEAT
                        wdln := wdln + 1;
                        wd.text[wdln] := ch;
                        IF Eoln
                            THEN ch := ' '
                            ELSE Read (ch);
                    UNTIL NOT (ch IN ['A'..'Z']);
                    wd.length := wdln;
                    AlterWord (wd);
                    FOR wdln := 1 TO wd.length DO
                        Write (wd.text [wdln]);
                    END (* letter found *);
            Write (ch); (* Write trailing punctuation *)
        END (* WHILE more on line *);
END (* ChangeLine *);
```

Let us now write the procedures that manipulate words.

```
PROCEDURE Nothing (VAR w: word);
    (* This procedure does nothing *)
BEGIN
END (* Nothing *);

PROCEDURE Reverse (VAR w: word);
    (* Reverse reverses a word *)
    VAR index: wordLength;
        temp: char; (* for use in swapping chars *)

BEGIN
    FOR index := 1 TO w.length DIV 2 DO
        BEGIN
            (* Swap corresponding letters *)
            temp := w.text [index];
            w.text [index] := w.text [w.length - index + 1];
            w.text [w.length - index + 1] := temp;
        END (* FOR the first half of the word *);
END (* Reverse *);

PROCEDURE Increment (VAR w: word);
    (* Increment takes the successor of each letter in a word *)
    VAR index: wordLength;

BEGIN
    FOR index := 1 TO w.length DO
        BEGIN
            IF w.text [index] = 'Z'
                THEN w.text [index] := 'A'
                ELSE w.text [index] := Succ (w.text [index]);
        END (* FOR each letter in the word *);
END (* Increment *);

PROCEDURE Decrement (VAR w: word);
    (* Decrement takes the predecessor of each letter in a word *)
    VAR index: wordLength;

BEGIN
    FOR index := 1 TO w.length DO
        BEGIN
            IF w.text [index] = 'A'
                THEN w.text [index] := 'Z'
                ELSE w.text [index] := Pred (w.text [index]);
        END (* FOR each leter in the word *);
END (* Decrement *);
```

We can now proceed to putting this together into a complete program.

```
PROGRAM Encryption (input, output);
    (* Encrypts each line of text.  The first character in each
       line indicates the operation to be performed to the words
       on the line.   The operations are:
                N         do nothing
                R         reverse each word
                I         take successors (Increment)
                D         take predecessors (Decrement)
    *)



    CONST maxWordLength = 20;
    TYPE wordLength = 0..maxWordLength;
        word = RECORD
            length: wordLength;
            text: ARRAY [1..maxWordLength] OF char;
            END (* word *);
    VAR ch: char; (* which operation to perform *)



    PROCEDURE ChangeLine (PROCEDURE AlterWord (VAR dummy: word));
        (* ChangeLine reads in words on a line and calls
           AlterWord on each word found *)
        VAR wd: word;
            wdln: wordLength;
            ch: char;



    BEGIN
        WHILE NOT Eoln (input) DO
            BEGIN
                Read (ch);
                IF ch IN ['A'..'I', 'J'..'R', 'S'..'Z']
                    THEN BEGIN
                        wdln := 0;
                        REPEAT
                            wdln := wdln + 1;
                            wd.text[wdln] := ch;
                            IF Eoln
                                THEN ch := ' '
                                ELSE Read (ch);
                        UNTIL NOT (ch IN
                            ['A'..'I', 'J'..'R', 'S'..'Z']);
                        wd.length := wdln;
                        AlterWord (wd);
                        FOR wdln := 1 TO wd.length DO
                            Write (wd.text [wdln]);
                        END (* letter found *);
                Write (ch); (* Write trailing punctuation *)
            END (* WHILE more on line *);
    END (* ChangeLine *);
```

```
PROCEDURE Nothing (VAR w: word);
    (* This procedure does nothing *)
BEGIN
END (* Nothing *);


PROCEDURE Reverse (VAR w: word);
    (* Reverse reverses a word *)
    VAR index: wordLength;
        temp: char; (* for use in swapping chars *)


BEGIN
    FOR index := 1 TO w.length DIV 2 DO
        BEGIN
            (* Swap corresponding letters *)
            temp := w.text [index];
            w.text [index] := w.text [w.length - index + 1];
            w.text [w.length - index + 1] := temp;
        END (* FOR the first half of the word *);
END (* Reverse *);


PROCEDURE Increment (VAR w: word);
    (* Increment takes the successor of each letter
       in a word *)
    VAR index: wordLength;


BEGIN
    FOR index := 1 TO w.length DO
        BEGIN
            IF w.text [index] = 'Z'
                THEN w.text [index] := 'A'
                ELSE w.text [index] := Succ (w.text [index]);
        END (* FOR each letter in the word *);
END (* Increment *);


PROCEDURE Decrement (VAR w: word);
    (* Decrement takes the predecessor of each letter
       in a word *)
    VAR index: wordLength;


BEGIN
    FOR index := 1 TO w.length DO
        BEGIN
            IF w.text [index] = 'A'
                THEN w.text [index] := 'Z'
                ELSE w.text [index] := Pred (w.text [index]);
        END (* FOR each leter in the word *);
END (* Decrement *);
```

```
BEGIN
    WHILE NOT Eof (input) DO
        BEGIN
            Read (ch);
            CASE ch OF
                'N': BEGIN
                        Write('N');
                        ChangeLine (Nothing);
                    END (* Nothing *);

                'R': BEGIN
                        Write('R');
                        ChangeLine (Reverse);
                    END (* Reverse *);

                'I': BEGIN
                        Write('D');
                        ChangeLine (Increment);
                    END (* Increment *);

                'D': BEGIN
                        Write('I');
                        ChangeLine (Decrement);
                    END (* Decrement *);
                END (* CASE ch *);

            Readln;
            Writeln;
        END (* WHILE more input *);
END (* Encryption *).
```

Let us run this program on the following input.

```
NTHIS TEXT IS NOT SUPPOSED TO BE CHANGED.
RREVERSE THIS TEXT COMPLETELY
I TRY TO READ THIS!  INCREMENT THIS TEXT. ABCDEFWXYZ
D TRY TO READ THIS!  INCREMENT THIS TEXT. ABCDEFWXYZ
```

```
NTHIS TEXT IS NOT SUPPOSED TO BE CHANGED.
RESREVER SIHT TXET YLETELPMOC
D USZ UP SFBE UIJT!  JODSFNFOU UIJT UFYU. BCDEFGXYZA
I SQX SN QDZC SGHR!  HMBQDLDMS SGHR SDWS. ZABCDEVWXY
```

Notice that the first character of each line is now set so that the same program will decrypt the output.

GOTO Statement

The GOTO statement permits alteration of the standard flow of control for highly unusual conditions. It is not necessary to use GOTO statements, as the control structures we have already encountered are sufficient to express any program. However, in some limited cases, using a GOTO statement can improve the readability of a program.

Suppose that we have a file containing product numbers. We want to print a list of the product numbers and their quantities. The product numbers are arbitrarily assigned, but there is a limited number of items in our inventory.

We will want an array of records, where each record contains a product number and its quantity. Let us describe the algorithm.

Set size of array used
WHILE *there is more input*
    Read a product number
    Find corresponding slot
    IF *there is one*
        THEN *add one to the counter*
        ELSE *set a new counter to one*
FOR *each counter used*
    Print the product number and quantity

Let us expand "*find corresponding slot.*"

FOR *each array element in use*
    IF *it is the desired one*
        THEN *remember where it is*

But what if this is the first occurrence of the product number? We need some way of indicating that it was not found. Also, notice that once we have found the desired slot, we continue to search. We would like to exit out of the FOR loop where it says *remember where it is.* We can do this with a GOTO statement. We define a label number consisting of 1 to 4 digits. We place the label and a colon preceding the statement where we want execution to continue. We say GOTO followed by the label number is the statement that causes control to be transferred elsewhere. We also must declare the label.

With this knowledge, we can proceed to writing the program.

```
PROGRAM Frequencies (input, output);
    (* Find frequencies of product numbers *)
    LABEL 99;
    CONST maxItems = 50;
    TYPE range = 0..maxItems;
        counterRec = RECORD
            ID: integer;
            freq: range;
        END (* counterRec *);
    VAR counters: ARRAY [1..maxItems] OF counterRec;
        item: integer;
        index: range;
        top: range;      (* last slot in use *)

BEGIN
    top := 0;   (* no slots in array in use *)
    WHILE NOT Eof (input) DO
        BEGIN
            Readln (item);
            FOR index := 1 TO top DO
                BEGIN
                    IF counters[index].ID = item
                        THEN BEGIN
                            counters[index].freq :=
                                counters[index].freq + 1;
                            GOTO 99;
                        END (* slot found *);
                END (* FOR each slot *);
            (* not found *)
            top := top + 1;
            counters[top].ID := item;
            counters[top].freq := 1;
        99: (* counter found *)
        END (* WHILE more input *);
    FOR index := 1 TO top DO
        Writeln (counters[index].ID, counters[index].freq);
END (* Frequencies *).
```

Assume the following input.

```
5
7
5
7
4
3
7
2
1
9
9
1
3
```

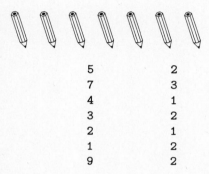

```
    5       2
    7       3
    4       1
    3       2
    2       1
    1       2
    9       2
```

There are several rules about using GOTO statements. When using a GOTO statement to exit from a FOR loop, it is necessary to save the index variable if it will be needed later. The value of an index variable is not valid outside of a FOR loop. Declaration of label values should precede all other declarations in the procedure in which the label appears. Labels may not appear inside loops nor inside IF statements. However, GOTO statements may appear inside loops or IF statements. Some implementations of PASCAL do not allow a GOTO to appear in a different procedure from its corresponding label.

Use the GOTO statement very rarely!

PACKED
Data Structures

In this chapter, we will learn about a feature that affects the efficiency of programs but does not affect the functionality of the language. In the process, we will learn how the computer actually stores complex data structures, such as arrays and records.

Computer memory is divided into units of allocation called *words*. Common word lengths are 32 or 36 *bits* (binary digits), but 16 or 60 bits are also used. Each datum may be allocated its own word for convenience in access. For example, even though only 7 or 8 bits are needed to represent a variable of type **char**, a full word is allocated. This does not represent much wasted space for ordinary variables, but a great deal of space can be wasted in large arrays and in records. It might be desirable to *pack* small components of records or elements of arrays so that fewer words may be used. While this saves memory for variables, it costs time to access as each component is packed or unpacked.

In PASCAL, we may declare a record or array to be **PACKED** by saying **PACKED ARRAY** or **PACKED RECORD**. This causes the elements of the array or the components of the record to be allocated part of words rather than an integral number of words. Where possible, use of subranges with **PACKED** will permit even greater savings, as it may take fewer bits to store a subrange than the complete range.

21-1 ADVANTAGES OF USING PACKED STRUCTURES

In Chapter 13, we covered the manipulation of strings. It was noted that the PASCAL features for manipulating strings were rather incomplete and often had to be augmented by routines written by us. Use of packed arrays of characters, however, permits additional functionality.

We noted that the **Write** statement permits the use of literal character strings. That is, we may place a constant character string in a **Write** statement and it will be printed. We cannot assign literal character strings to ordinary arrays of characters, but we can sometimes assign literal character strings to packed arrays of characters. The character string 'MUMBLE' is defined as

```
PACKED ARRAY [1..6] OF char
```

Thus, we can assign a literal character string to a packed array of characters of the same length. Note that the literal character string may not be shorter. However, the literal character string may contain blanks that pad it to the correct length.

Packed arrays of characters may also be printed directly by placing them in Write statements, as with literal character strings. The problem is that the entire character string is printed. It is not possible, however, to read directly into a packed array of characters.

Relational operators may be used to compare packed arrays of characters that are the same length. For example, we may say s1 < s2 if s1 and s2 are both declared as packed arrays of characters with the same lengths.

We have already considered the space saved by packing large arrays and records.

21-2 DISADVANTAGES OF USING PACKED STRUCTURES

There are also major disadvantages of using packed structures. No component of a packed structure may be passed as a parameter. This is because the called procedure or function expects the parameter to be allocated an integral number of words on a word boundary, and that is likely to be true for components of packed structures. In particular, this means that you cannot read a character directly into an element of a packed array of characters. This problem can be circumvented by using an assignment statement to copy the component out of the packed structure before passing it as a parameter. For a VAR parameter, we will also have to copy it from the parameter into the packed structure after calling the procedure.

```
Read (ch);
string [index] := ch;
```

Another disadvantage of using packed structures is that access is slower. This also involves more instructions for accessing components of packed structures, which in turn uses some more space. It probably does not pay to pack arrays or records with few components. It probably saves space to pack arrays or records with many components, provided that it does not add greatly to the complexity of the program.

21-3 PACK AND UNPACK

In some implementations of PASCAL, access to individual components of packed arrays may be costly. Two built-in procedures are provided to convert an array from packed to unpacked and vice versa.

Assume the following declarations.

```
VAR packedArray: PACKED ARRAY [low..high] OF t;
    unpackedArray: ARRAY [lbound..hbound] OF t;
    packedIndex: low..high;
    unpackedIndex: lbound..hbound;
```

Note that the cardinality of the range `lbound` to `hbound` must be larger than that of `low` to `high`.

```
CONST low = 5;
      high = 7;
      lbound = 5;
      hbound = 6;
```

```
CONST low = 3;
      high = 10;
      lbound = -36;
      hbound = -16;
```

Then, `Pack (unpackedArray, unpackedIndex, packedArray);` is equivalent to

```
FOR packedIndex := low TO high DO
    packedArray [packedIndex] :=
        unpackedArray [packedIndex - lbound + unpackedIndex];
```

   Also, `Unpack (packedArray, unpackedArray, unpackedIndex);` is equivalent to

```
FOR packedIndex := low TO high DO
    unpackedArray [packedIndex - lbound + unpackedIndex] :=
        packedArray [packedIndex];
```

Answers to Selected Exercises

Exercises for Section 2-1 Output

1. HI
    HOHI
    HO

2. ABCDEFGHI
    JKL
    MNOPQR

3. Aren't computers wonderful?Notice how we printed the quote!

4. Write ('''');

5. Write ('''Twas the night before Christmas');

Exercises for Section 2-5 Repetition: The FOR Statement

1. HI
    HI
    HI
    HI
    HI

2. HIHIHIHIHI

3. HI ARTHUR
    HI ARTHUR
    HI ARTHUR
    HI ARTHUR
    HI ARTHUR

4. HIHIHIHIHI AMY

5.  ```
    **********
    *        *
    *        *
    *        *
    *        *
    *        *
    *        *
    **********
    ```

Exercises for Section 2-6 Expressions

1.   7was for subtraction
        ABC   1   2   3DEF

2.   22
                52
                22

3.   5
                 0
                 3
                 4

4.   14
                14
                 4

5a. Write (6 * (2 + 3) DIV (4 + 5));   or
    Write (6 * ((2 + 3) DIV (4 + 5)));
 b. Write (42 DIV 7 * 5 * 5 + 6 * 3 + 4);   or
    Write ((42 DIV 7) * 5 * 5 + 6 * 3 + 4);

Exercises for Section 2-7 Iteration

1. It prints the first 10 squares.
    ```

2.
```
PROGRAM Cubes (output);
    VAR number: integer;     (* index variable *)

BEGIN
    FOR number := 1 TO 10 DO
        Writeln (number * number * number);
END (* Cubes *).
```

3a.
```
PROGRAM Series (output);
    VAR number: integer;

BEGIN
    FOR number := 1 TO 10 DO
        Writeln (5 * number - 2);
END (* Series *).
```

b. *Replace* Writeln *with:*
```
        Writeln (5 * number - 7);
```

c. *Replace* Writeln *with:*
```
        Writeln (53 - 5 * number);
```

Exercises for Section 2-8 Nesting Loops

1.
```
MUMBLE-MUMBLE-MUMBLE-MUMBLE
MUMBLE-MUMBLE-MUMBLE-MUMBLE
MUMBLE-MUMBLE-MUMBLE-MUMBLE
MUMBLE-MUMBLE-MUMBLE-MUMBLE
MUMBLE-MUMBLE-MUMBLE-MUMBLE
```

3.
```
PROGRAM SixRectangles (output);
    (* Written by Ethan Bradford *)

VAR rectangleIndex: integer;

PROCEDURE Write10Stars;
    (* Writes 10 stars in a row *)
        VAR col: integer;

BEGIN
    FOR col:= 1 TO 10 DO
        Write ('*');
END; (* Write10Stars *)

PROCEDURE WriteTwoRectangles;
    (* Writes two adjacent 5x10 rectangles *)

        VAR row: integer;
```

```
        BEGIN
            FOR row:= 1 TO 5 DO
                (* Write all the rows of the two rectangles *)
                BEGIN
                    Write10Stars;    (* row for the first rectangle *)
                    Write (' ');     (* separator *)
                    Write10Stars;    (* and next rectangle *)
                    Writeln;         (* to end the line *)
                END; (* FOR row *)
        END; (* WriteTwoRectangles *)
BEGIN (* Main procedure *)
    FOR rectangleIndex:= 1 TO 3 DO
        (* Write two rectangles three times. *)
        BEGIN
            WriteTwoRectangles; (* Write two of the rectangles. *)
            Writeln;            (* for a vertical separator *)
        END; (* FOR rectangleIndex *)
END (* SixRectangles *).
```

Exercises for Section 2-9 Nested Iteration

```
1.    1
      2
      2
      3 4
      3
      4 5 6
      4
      5 6 7 8
```

```
4.
PROGRAM TwoTriangles (output);
    (* Written by Ethan Bradford *)

    VAR col, triangle, row: integer;  (* Loop variables. *)

BEGIN
    FOR row:= 1 TO 10 DO
        (* Write out each row of the two diamonds. *)
        BEGIN
            FOR triangle := 1 TO 2 DO
                BEGIN
                    FOR col:= 1 TO (10 - row) DO
                        Write ('.');    (* Starting periods *)
                    FOR col:= 1 TO (2 * row - 1) DO
                        Write ('*');    (* Stars *)
                    FOR col:= 1 TO (10 - row) DO
                        Write ('.');    (* Trailing periods *)
                END (* FOR triangle *);
            Writeln; (* and end the line. *)
        END; (* FOR row *)
    END (* TwoTriangles *).
```

Exercises for Section 2-10 DOWNTO Clause

```
2.   1
     2    1
     3    2    1
     4    3    2    1
     5    4    3    2    1
```

Exercises for Section 3-3 Assignment Statement

```
1.   THE NUMBERS ARE          3          5

2.            96        96

3.            3         5         8        80       -10
              4         1         7        80       -10
```

Exercises for Section 3-5 Fibonacci Numbers

```
1.            39
```

Exercises for Section 4-1 Reading Input

2.   The program abnormally terminates with an error message. The error message may be cryptic, such as "input error in file input."

3.   The program fragment will print the following.

```
The value is        3
The value is now        8
        4        17        9
        5        36       10
        6         2       12
```

Notice that the last input value is not read. This does not cause an error.

Exercises for Section 4-2 Variable-Length Input

1.   A constant definition associates a permanent value with a name. Reading it from the input does not assign a permanent value, as we can subsequently assign another value to the variable, possibly by reading into it. We may want a value to be supplied as a constant or read from input depending on whether we want it to be changed from execution to execution.

Exercises for Section 4-3-1 Conditions

1. was the answer
2. foobazola

Exercises for Section 4-3-2 ELSE

1.   10   20   10

2. The variable c gets assigned the smaller of a and b. If a and b have the same value, b is used arbitrarily.

Exercises for Section 4-5 AND

1. IF (0 < a) AND (a < b)
        THEN c:= 0;

Exercises for Section 4-7 OR

1. IF (a < 4) OR (10 < a)
        THEN Write ('outside');

Exercises for Section 5-1 Type Boolean

1. A match is found in b and d only.
2. LOW since a + b is not less than 2 * a, and true AND false is false.

Exercises for Section 7-1 WHILE Statement

1. We add counter to sum for counter = 1, 3, 5, 7, 9, and 11. The output is:

        Some interesting numbers are: 13 and   69

2. Note that we do not test in between incrementing number and writing it. The output is:

            1   2   3   4   5   6

3. The output is:

        2 to the exponent 5 exceeds 17

4. Note that when we multiply **number** by 2 starting at 1, it will never equal 10. The output is:

```
1
2
4
8
16
32
```

and it will continue printing all powers of 2 forever.

5. The output is:

```
The travelers are at 19 and 22
The travelers are at 18 and 24
The travelers are at 17 and 26
The travelers are at 16 and 28
The final positions of the two travelers are 16 and 28
```

6. This program segment prints out *both* words. The important point is that once the WHILE loop decides to execute its body (if the boolean expression is **true**), it executes the *entire* body before it performs the test again. It does *not* continually monitor (when inside the loop) whether the test has become **false**.

7. It will loop forever.

Exercises for Section 7-2 Reasoning about Programs

1. Since **a** does not change, **r MOD a** is always **r**. The program does not terminate.

2. The correct solution is found in **b**, since **a** is not changed. The reader may wish to verify this simpler program. Does this algorithm terminate faster, slower, or the same as the original algorithm? That is, compare the number of iterations for the original and the revised algorithm.

Exercise for Section 7-4 REPEAT Statement

1. The following two are equivalent:

```
REPEAT
    code;
UNTIL condition;
```

and

```
code;
WHILE NOT (condition) DO
    BEGIN
        code;
    END (* NOT condition *);
```

Exercises for Section 8-2 Read and Readln

Several program segments are presented with input. The values of the variables *at the end of the fragment* are listed. The input and output are annotated to indicate where the input cursor is at the end of each **Read** or **Readln** instruction and where the output cursor is at the end of each **Write** or **Writeln** instruction. Declarations:

```
VAR
    r1, r2, r3: real;
    i, i1, i2, i3: integer;
    b1, b2, b3: boolean;
```

1. Fragment
```
Read (i1); (* 1 *)
Readln;  (* 2 *)
FOR i := 1 TO i1 DO
    Readln (i3);  (* 3 *)
```

Input
```
2  (1) 5  6  7  GEORGE
(2) 6  9
(3) 1
(3) 17  false
```

Variables

i1 = 2   i3 = 1

Output

i has no value since it was used as an iteration variable for a FOR loop

2. Fragment
```
Read (b1, i1, b2, i2);  (* 1 *)
Readln (r1); (* 2 *)
Read (i3);  (* 3 *)
Read (r2);  (* 4 *)
```

Input
```
false  6true
9 (1) 5.0E3   7
(2) 4 (3) false (4)
99
```

Variables

b1 = false   i1 = 6
b2 = true   i2 = 9
r1 = 5.0E3   i3 = 4

Output

A type error message

r2 has no value because false cannot be read into a real variable

3. Fragment
```
Read (i1, i2);  (* 1 *)
Readln (i3);  (* 2 *)
Read (r1);  (* 3 *)
Read (i1);  (* 4 *)
```

Input
```
1  5 (1) 9  5.0E3
(2) 5.0 (3) E3 (4)
17
```

Variables

i1 = 1   r1 = 5.0E0
i2 = 5   i3 = 9

Output

Type Error reading
E3 into i1

Notice the space between 5.0 and E3. So when we read in **r1**, we stop at the space. We then attempt to read in **i1** and find **E3** in the input.

4. **Fragment**
```
Read (i1);  (* 1 *)
Write (i1);  (* 2 *)
i2 := i1 * 7;
Write (i1, i2);  (* 3 *)
Read (i1);  (* 4 *)
Write (i1, i2);  (* 5 *)
Read (i3);  (* 6 *)
```

Input
```
5 (1) 7 (4) 9 (6)
```

Variables
```
i1 = 7
i2 = 35
i3 = 9
```

Output
```
5 (2) 5 35 (3) 7 35 (5)
```

Note that only the final value of i1 is listed here. Since each instruction is executed as a single step here, we compute i2 only once. After reading in another value for i1, we do not recompute the value of i2.

5. **Fragment**
```
Read (i1);  (* 1 *)
FOR i := 1 TO i1 DO
    IF i = 1
        THEN Read (r1)  (* 2 *)
    ELSE IF i = 2
        THEN Read (r2)  (* 3 *)
    ELSE IF i = 3
        THEN Read (r3)  (* 4 *)
    ELSE Writeln ('i = ', i, ' is too big');  (* 5 *)
    Write ('error');  (* 6 *)
```

Input
```
6 (1)

3.14159 (2)
1.7E1 (3) 690.0E-1 (4)
```

Variables
```
i1 = 6
r1 = 3.14159
r2 = 17.0
r3 = 69.0
i = 6
```

Output
```
       i =        4 is too big
   (5) i =        5 is too big
   (5) i =        6 is too big
   (5) error (6)
```

Exercises for Section 9-2-2 Programmer-Defined Functions

1. This function violates the rule that says the name of the function can be used as a variable within the function *only if it appears on the left-hand side of the assignment operator*. For this reason, we have been following the convention of using a "dummy" variable to hold the intermediate result and then assigning its value to the function at the end. The function should be rewritten as follows:

```
FUNCTION Factorial (n : integer) : integer;
    VAR factor, result: integer;
BEGIN
    result := 1;
    FOR factor := 2 TO n DO
        result := result * factor;
    Factorial := result;
END; (* Factorial *)
```

Exercises for Section 9-6 Summary: Value versus Reference Parameters

1. Since all the formal parameters of both `Sort` and `Swap` are `VAR` parameters, all changes made to the formal parameters are also made to the actual parameter variables in the calling statement. The output of this program is therefore:

25	50	90
1	2	6

2. If `third` is a value parameter rather than a `VAR` parameter in the procedure `Sort`, then the value of `z` in the main program is not changed. The output is:

25	50	50
1	2	1

Exercises for Section 9-7 Scope: Local and Global Variables

1. Since `q` and `a` are `VAR` parameters in the procedure `Mixup`, then whatever changes are made to them inside the procedure are also made to the corresponding actual parameter variables in the main program. This program outputs:

1	2	7	11		
4	2	-7	11	3	-2
4	2	7	11		
8	4	-10	11	4	-3
4	8	7	11		

Exercises for Section 11-1 Using Arrays

1.
```
FOR index := 1 TO 8 DO
    Read (listnum[index]);
```

Built-in Functions

This appendix describes the procedures and functions that are predeclared in PASCAL.

Arithmetic Functions

Abs (x)   computes the absolute value of **x**, which may be **integer** or **real**. The type of the result matches the type of parameter.

Arctan (x) computes the trigonometric arctangent of **x**. The parameter may be **integer** or **real**. The type of the result is always **real**.

Cos (x)   computes the trigonometric cosine of **x**. The parameter may be **integer** or **real**. The type of the result is always **real**.

Exp (x)   computes the inverse of the natural logarithm (base e) of **x**, that is, e^x. The parameter may be **integer** or **real**. The type of the result is always **real**.

Ln (x)   computes the natural logarithm (base e) of **x**. The parameter may be **integer** or **real**. The type of the result is always **real**.

Sin (x)   computes the trigonometric sine of **x**. The parameter may be **integer** or **real**. The type of the result is always **real**.

Sqr (x)   computes **x*x**. The parameter may be **integer** or **real**. The type of the result matches the type of parameter.

Sqrt (x)   computes the square root of **x**. The parameter may be **integer** or **real**. The type of the result is always **real**.

Boolean Functions

Eof (f)   determines whether the cursor of the file **f** is at the end of the file. The result is **true** if it is, otherwise **false**. If the parameter is omitted, the file **input** is assumed.

Eoln (f)   determines whether the cursor of the file **f** is at the end of a line. The result is **true** if it is, otherwise **false**. If the parameter is omitted, the file **input** is assumed.

Odd (x)   determines whether **x** is odd. The result is **true** if **x** is odd, otherwise **false**. The parameter must be an integer.

Transfer Functions

Chr (x)   returns the character whose ordinal number is **x**. The result is of type character. The parameter must be an integer.

Ord (c)   returns the ordinal number for the character **c**. The result is of type integer. The parameter must be a character.

The Ord and Chr functions are described in more detail in Section 10-3.

Round (x)   determines the closest integer to the real value **x**.

Trunc (x)   determines the greatest integer less than the real value **x**.

Examples of the use of Round and Trunc are in Section 5-4.

Other Standard Functions

Pred (x)   returns the value of the predecessor of **x**. The parameter and result are of the same scalar (other than **real**).

Succ (x)   returns the value of the successor of **x**. The parameter and result are of the same scalar (other than **real**).

The predecessor and successor functions are described in more detail in Section 10-3.

Data Transfer Procedures

The procedures Pack and Unpack are described in Chapter 21.

Dynamic Allocation Procedures

New (p)   allocates a new record and assigns to **p** its pointer reference.

New (p, *tags*) allocates a new record with the tag values as specified. The tag field values must be listed in the order of declaration. The new record may be of size sufficient only to store records of the specified variant tag values. Consequently, differing tag values should not be assigned to this record.

See Chapter 18 for additional details on use of dynamic data structures.

File Handling Procedures

Files other than text files are not covered in this book.

The procedures Read, Write, Readln, and Writeln are described in detail in Chapter 8.

Character Sets

Different computers use different character sets. The most common character set is ASCII (American Standard Code for Information Interchange). This character set is a 7-bit code. Of the 128 possibilities, 33 are reserved for "control" functions such as *carriage return* and *line feed*. Since fewer than a dozen of these are used for their intended purpose, many computers give additional meaning to some of these characters. For example, on some DEC computers, control-C is used for return to monitor level. The remaining 95 characters are used for the upper case (capital letters) and lower case alphabets and graphic characters such as $<$, $+$, $>$, and space. Each of these characters is assigned a numeric value for storage in a computer. This is the value obtained when you use the **Ord** function. (Computers understand only numbers directly, but they can be programmed to give interpretations to these numbers, such as characters.) The advantages of ASCII are that it is a standard, it is widely implemented, and the lower case alphabet and upper case alphabet are each contiguous.

	+0	+1	+2	+3	+4	+5	+6	+7
0	NUL	SOH	STX	ETX	EOT	ENQ	ACK	BEL
8	BS	HT	LF	VT	FF	CR	SO	SI
16	DLE	DC1	DC2	DC3	DC4	NAK	SYN	ETB
24	CAN	EM	SUB	ESC	FS	GS	RS	US
32		!	"	#	$	%	&	'
40	(	)	*	+	,	-	.	/
48	0	1	2	3	4	5	6	7
56	8	9	:	;	<	=	>	?
64	@	A	B	C	D	E	F	G
72	H	I	J	K	L	M	N	O
80	P	Q	R	S	T	U	V	W
88	X	Y	Z	[	\	]	∧	,
96	`	a	b	c	d	e	f	g
104	h	i	j	k	l	m	n	o
112	p	q	r	s	t	u	v	w
120	x	y	z	{	|	}	~	DEL

The ASCII character set

Another character set is EBCDIC (Extended Binary Coded Decimal Interchange Code). This is an 8-bit code based on 7-bit code BCDIC. It is used on large IBM computers and is related to the code used for the familiar Hollerith punched cards.* A disadvantage of EBCDIC is that there are extraneous infrequently used characters interspersed with the upper and lower case alphabets.

	+0	+1	+2	+3	+4	+5	+6	+7
64	space							
72			¢	.	<	(	+	
80	&							
88			!	$	*	)	;	¬
96	-	/						
104				,	%	,	>	?
112								
120		'	:	#	@	'	=	"
128		a	b	c	d	e	f	g
136	h	i						
144		j	k	l	m	n	o	p
152	q	r						
160		~	s	t	u	v	w	x
168	y	z						
176								
184								
192	{	A	B	C	D	E	F	G
200	H	I			hook		fork	
208	}	J	K	L	M	N	O	P
216	Q	R						
224	\		S	T	U	V	W	X
232	Y	Z			chair			
240	0	1	2	3	4	5	6	7
248	8	9							EO

The EBCDIC character set

Other character sets, such as the CDC Scientific Character set, also exist. That character set is a 6-bit code.

As described in Chapter 16, there may be a limitation on the size of a set. Since a set of characters may be implemented as a set of their ordinal values, it is possible that `Ord` will return a different value than that appearing in these tables. Therefore, `Chr` should only be used with values based on `Ord` and not with program constants.

---

* Herman Hollerith invented the punched card tabulating machine in the 1880s. These use the punched cards with the rectangular holes that we are warned to avoid folding, spindling, or mutilating. Hollerith's company, the Tabulating Machine Company, later became the International Business Machines Corporation through mergers. Hollerith cards are also called IBM cards because IBM computers are so prevalent and often use those punched cards.

Appendix D

P<small>ASCAL</small> Syntax

These diagrams of the syntax of the P<small>ASCAL</small> language are reprinted with permission from the *PASCAL User Manual and Report.** These diagrams were typeset by Jim Boyce based on a format by Michael Plass.

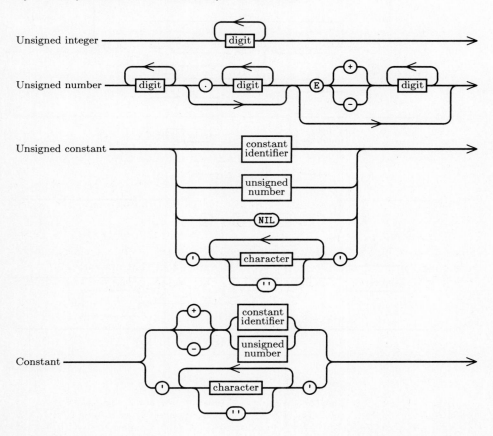

---

*   Kathleen Jensen and Niklaus Wirth, Springer Verlag, New York, Second Edition, 1974.

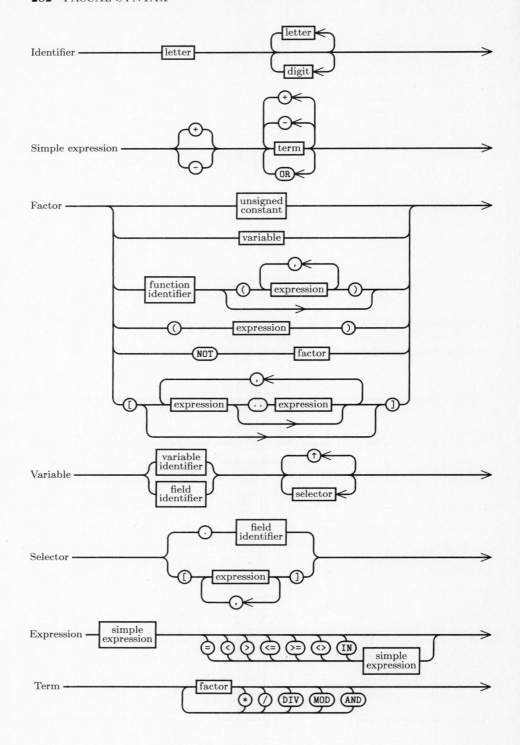

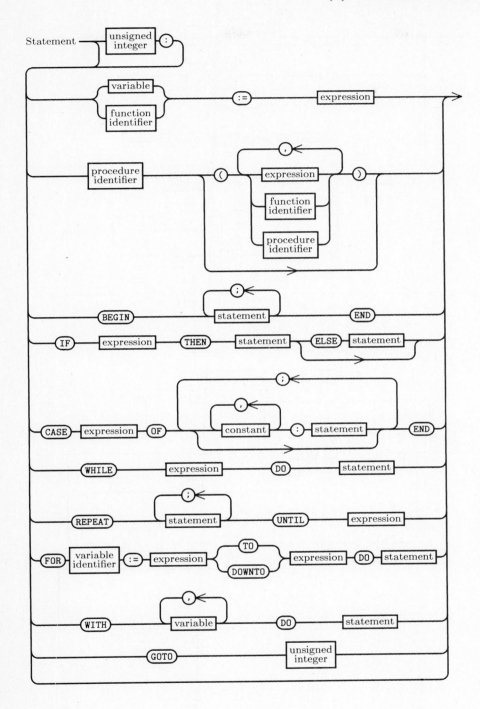

Type

Simple type

Field list

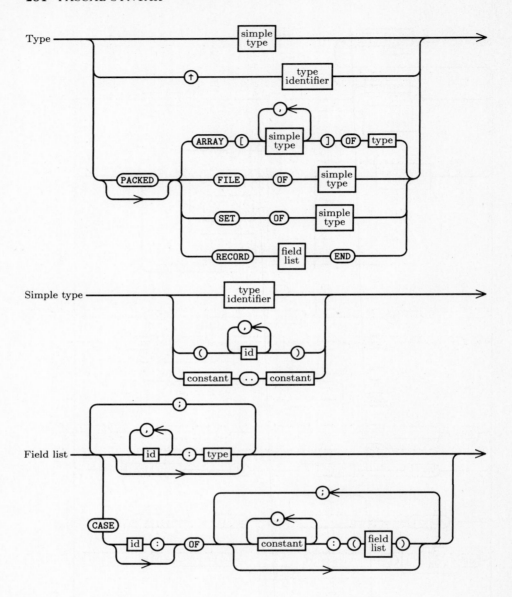

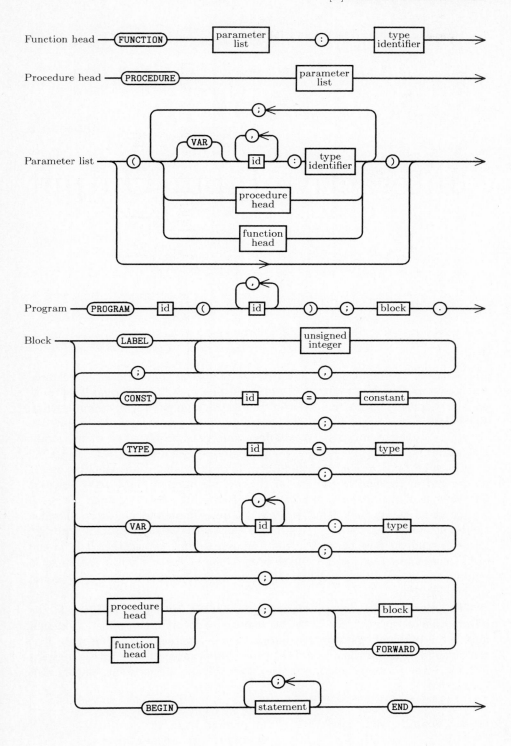

Interactive Input-Output

Using interactive input-output involves use of special conventions not required for noninteractive input-output.* We would like to write programs that work equally well using interactive input-output as using noninteractive input-output. Furthermore, we would like these programs to be portable to other PASCAL compilers and environments. We will first explore the problem and then examine a solution.

Consider the functions **Eof** and **Eoln**. In order to determine whether we are at the end of the line or the end of the file, we have to know what the next character is, if there is one. For example, after doing a **Readln**, **Eoln** is **true** if we are at an empty line. That is, PASCAL must know the character to which the input cursor is pointing. This means that when we do a **Readln**, PASCAL needs to read the next character from the user to find out whether it is an end of line character. In general, we have been doing a **Readln** when we are finished reading the values on current line. However, this request will cause us to go on to the next line.

The solution is to delay performing the **Readln** until we actually want the information on the next line. When we want to read from the terminal, we should inform the terminal operator that information is requested and what it is. This can be done with a **Write** or a **Writeln** to the appropriate file. Suppose we want to inquire the terminal operator's age. We will use the following sequence of statements.

```
Write('What is your age? ');   (* prompt user *)
Readln;                        (* read line separator *)
Read (age);                    (* read input *)
```

---

* See Bron and Dijkstra, "A Discipline for the Programming of Interactive I/O in PASCAL," *SIGPLAN Notices*, **14**, 12 (December 1979), 59–61.

A string written to the terminal to indicate that input is requested is called a *prompt*. Once we have written the prompt to the terminal, we can cause PASCAL to go to the next line. This is accomplished by the **Readln**. We are now ready to read the values on this line.

Note that we can consider lines to be terminated by end-of-line characters, or we can consider lines to be separated by them. Until now, we have always considered them to be line terminators. For interactive input-output, we will consider lines to be separated by end-of-line characters. In particular, this means that we are only to do a **Readln** when we are ready to go to the next line (that is, we have issued the prompt for that line). Furthermore, we will *not* use any variables in the **Readln** statement; we will say either

```
Readln;
```

or

```
Readln (fileIdentifier);
```

but not

```
Readln (fileIdentifier, variables);
```

In some interactive systems, input and output are buffered. This means that no input is sent to the program until the entire line, including the carriage return or enter key, is typed. This may permit the user to backspace away errors before they are read by the program. This is an implementation-dependent feature. Read the manual describing your system or ask your instructor to determine whether this feature exists on the system you are using.

Buffering of output is more of a problem. Some systems do not send anything to the terminal until a **Writeln** is issued. In this case, the prompt must end with a **Writeln** or the user will never get it before she has to type the next line. Other systems send the output to the terminal when there are *enough* characters waiting to be written. In this case, you will have to force the output to be sent to the terminal. For example, there may be a procedure called **Break** that will send the contents of the output buffer to the terminal.

```
Write('What is your age? ');    (* prompt user *)
Break (output);                 (* write buffer to terminal *)
Readln;                         (* read line separator *)
Read (age);                     (* read input *)
```

Some other systems do not buffer output to the terminal at all. In this case, we need not do anything special to get output to the terminal. Read the manual describing your system or ask your instructor to determine whether your system buffers output and how to force terminal output to occur.

When terminal or file output is buffered, it may affect debugging. For example, if you have not yet seen the output that a segment of the program produces, it does not necessarily mean that this segment of the program has not yet been reached. It is possible that this segment of the program *has* been reached, but that the output is sitting in a buffer waiting to be written to the terminal. To test this hypothesis, add `Writeln` or `Break` statements to the program, and see if this causes additional output to appear on the terminal or the same output to appear earlier. Debugging in an interactive environment will be discussed in more detail in Appendix F.

Interactive Debugging

Use of an interactive debugger can facilitate the process of debugging. However, there are some techniques that are applicable to the use of interactive debuggers. This appendix is dependent on understanding Appendix E.

An interactive debugger allows us to stop the execution of the program at a particular location or set of locations, and then query the values of particular variables. Some debuggers also permit single stepping of the program; in this mode, a single PASCAL statement is executed at a time. When a program is stopped at a breakpoint, some debuggers allow the user to change the value of particular variables.

How an interactive debugger is used depends on what the nature of the error is. Debugging an infinite loop involves determining the location of the loop. Debugging a run-time error, such as a divide-by-zero exception, entails determining the statement containing the error and examining the values of variables at strategic points of the program execution before the fatal execution of that statement. Debugging incorrect output also includes examining the values of variables at strategic points of the program execution to determine the cause of computing the incorrect value.

Infinite Loops

How do we debug a program that has an infinite loop? If the program is producing infinite output, then we have a statement—that which produces the output—that is inside the loop. On the other hand, suppose that the program loops without producing any output. We can interrupt the execution of the program using a system-dependent command. We then use another system-dependent command to enter the interactive debugger. For example, on DECsystem-10s and -20s, the interrupt command is control-C and the command to enter the debugger is DDT. The interactive debugger should state (or supply on demand) the statement currently being executed.

Now that we know the statement being executed, we can look at the program source to find out what the program is doing. Here is a good opportunity to request the values of variables controlling the loop. We can set breakpoints at strategic points of the loop. If there are several nested loops, we can set breakpoints at strategic points of each loop. We can then cause the program to proceed execution using an implementation-defined command. If the program loops for a long time without reaching another breakpoint, reissue the commands to enter the debugger; the breakpoint requests were either incorrectly entered or incorrectly chosen. When we reach another breakpoint, display the values of loop-controlling variables. Do these values vary from breakpoint to breakpoint as expected? Comparing the actual values with the expected values can shed light on the nature of the error.

Run-Time Errors

If a program has a run-time error, such as a divide-by-zero exception, running with a debugger may localize the error. For example, if the statement number where the error occurs is printed, we can compare that to a listing of the program to determine what variables may have incorrect values. In the debugger (or by `Write` statements), we can request the values of specific variables that may cause the error. Either a variable has a value that is incorrect, or the code does not handle a permissible set of values. If a value is incorrect, the cause may be obvious; otherwise, the next section has hints that may be useful in debugging this error. If the code does not handle values that are permissible, then we should rewrite the program to handle this case.

Incorrect Output

Finding the cause of incorrect output is rather like detective work. We have to track down the clues to find the source of the error.

The first step is to determine that there is an error by demonstrating that one or more values output by the program are erroneous. Knowing what the correct values should be facilitates debugging greatly. The next step is to identify locations in the program listing where critical values are computed that are used in the computation of the erroneous value. We then rerun the program specifying breakpoints to the debugger at these locations. When each breakpoint is encountered, values of interesting variables should be requested and checked against the expected values. Tracing continues until an incorrect value is encountered.

The process of localizing the cause of an error is an interactive process. Each time we determine more finely the location by placing the breakpoints closer together. Eventually, either we will trace the error to a single statement or combination of segments, or we will resort to single stepping the program and inquiring the values of variables set by each statement. Of course, single stepping a program can be time consuming, so it should only be done when the location of an error has been narrowed down to a small range of statements. For example, if we suspect that a loop contains an error, it is reasonable to put a breakpoint in the loop. Each time the program stops, we can request the values of desired variables. After a few times, we may be reassured that the loop does not have an error. Then we can set a breakpoint at the exit of the loop and remove the breakpoint from inside the loop.

Other Debugging Techniques

When we do not have an interactive debugger, the standard approach is to use appropriate `Write` statements sprinkled throughout the code. We can condition such `Write` statements upon a global constant, such as the `boolean` value `debugging`, or on some event that we do not expect to happen. For example, if a function does not expect an argument to be negative, it can test for a negative argument and print an appropriate error message. In the event that such an error message is produced, it can be debugged interactively by setting a breakpoint at the statement that produces the error message. Then we can use the approach of the previous section to track down the cause of the error.

Similarly, when a program is debugged, adding debugging code and writing exercising code can facilitate the process of debugging. For example, in a loop that is executed many times, if an error only arises after many iterations of the loop, the program can print a message after sufficient iterations of the loop have elapsed. An effective technique is for the program to request terminal input at that point so that execution of the program does not advance too far.

It is important to use a combination of appropriate tools in debugging. "If the only tool you have is a hammer, it is tempting to think of everything else as a nail." Furthermore, good programming practice, and writing programs and subprograms that check their input for validity, will make debugging considerably easier.

Appendix G

Glossary

Brief definitions are supplied in the glossary. For more detail, please look for the word or phrase in the index.

access   To refer to an item or its components.

actual parameter   A variable or expressions passed to a procedure or function in a call statement.

algorithm   An explicit step-by-step description of the solution to a problem. It must be unambiguous, precise, definite, and finite.

array   A structured type consisting of components of equal type accessed by an index.

array bounds   Limits of the permissible values of an array index.

assertion   A claim about the values of variables in a program. Also a statement that checks an assertion.

assignment   A statement that gives a variable a value.

base type   The type of values stored in an array. (See also index type.) Also the type of elements in a set. Not to be confused with index type.

batch   A mode of operation where requests are submitted to a computer and the program is then run, followed by results returned later without further interaction with the requestor.

bit   A binary digit. A bit can have the value 0 or 1.

body   The instructions associated with a procedure or function.

boundary condition   A condition that allows a loop to start or causes it to stop executing. An error in choosing the boundary condition is called a boundary error or a fencepost error.

bounds   The first and last values of a loop control variable when executing a loop. Also known as array bounds.

braces   The characters { and }. Also known as curly braces. Used as comment delimiters on some systems instead of (* and *).

brackets The characters [and]. Also any pair of symbols used to delimit what appears between them, such as BEGIN—END

bug An unwanted and unintended property of a program, or a difference between the specifications and behavior of a program. See also feature.

call To cause a procedure or function to execute.

code Instructions to a computer. Synonym: body.

collating sequence The ordering of characters in a character set. See Appendix C for details.

comment Explanatory material in a program not used by the computer and intended for people.

compatible See type compatibility.

compiler A program that translates a program to a form that the computer can directly execute.

component A part of a structured type: a field of a record, an element of an array or set, a character in a file.

compound statement A list of statements enclosed in BEGIN—END brackets.

constant An identifier with a value that cannot change.

control character A special, unprintable character in a character set used to control a printing device or communication link. For example, *carriage return* and *tab* are control characters.

control structure A statement that causes the exection sequence of instructions to be other than in the order in which they are listed. For example, looping constructs, such as FOR statements, are control structures.

crash A sudden failure. "I just lost all of my edits in that system crash."

data Values that a program computes with.

data structure The organization of data in a program. For example, arrays and linked lists are data structures.

debugging The process of removing bugs in a program. This operation often takes as much time as writing the program; its duration can be reduced by careful design and programming as well as good design and debugging tools.

declaration A description of the form of data or of the process to be followed by a procedure.

definition The process of deciding what a program is going to accomplish. A variable is undefined before it is given a value.

delimiter A mark that identifies the beginning or end of something. For example, (* and *) are comment delimiters.

digit A single character in a number other than punctuation. For example, in −1.23E7, the digits are 1, 2, 3, and 7.

disk A device for storing large amounts of data relatively inexpensively for extended periods of time.

documentation A description of what a program (or part) does, how it does it, or how to use it. Documentation is often written at different levels for different audiences. For example, users want to know what a program is used for, and program maintainers want to know how a program is organized.

down Not working. Also to deactivate, usually for repair work. Opposite of up.

dynamic   Varying while the program is running. For example, pointer structures involve dynamic memory allocation. Opposite of static.

efficiency   The consideration of how much resources a program uses. Space and time are scales for measuring efficiency.

elegant   Using good style.

element   A component of an array specified by an index value (or, for multi-dimensional arrays, a list of index values). Also a value contained in a set.

empty statement   A statement that does not cause any computation to be performed. It is caused by a semicolon following a statement prefix or preceding an end. For example, in a `WHILE` or `FOR` statement, if a semicolon immediately follows the `DO`, it is the empty statement which is repeated. A `WHILE` loop whose body is an empty statement will continue forever if the condition is initially true and never changes.

enumerated type   A type whose values are declared as an explicit list. For example, `TYPE colors = (red, blue, green);` declares the enumerated type `colors`.

evaluate   To compute the value of an expression.

exception   A run-time error detected by the hardware.

execute   To perform the stated sequence of instructions. Synonym: to run. See also invoke.

exit   To leave a section of code, such as a procedure. An exit condition is a criterion that will cause termination of a code fragment, such as the test in a `WHILE` loop.

expression   A collection of variables and function invocations together with operators that represent a value to be computed. Expressions are used as the right-hand side of an assignment statement, as actual parameters, and as the values in statements such as `FOR` loops.

feature   A documented bug. Also a well-known and beloved property.

fencepost error   The discrete equivalent of a boundary condition.

field   A component of a record.

file   A collection of computerized information external to a program. Files may be input or output of a program; they may represent the transcript of activity on a terminal or be physically on disk before or after the execution of a program.

fixed-length   Something that cannot vary in size, such as a string implemented by just an array of characters.

formal parameter   The specification of a parameter in a procedure or function heading.

fudge   To cause something to perform in an incomplete but marginally acceptable way.

function heading   The first part of a function declaration that lists the name of the function, the number and type of parameters, and the type of value returned by the function.

hack   A quick job that produces what is needed, but not elegantly, or the result of such a job.

hacker   A person who enjoys learning the details of programming systems and how to stretch their capabilities, as contrasted with most users who prefer to learn only the minimum necessary.

heap A collection of memory used for dynamic memory allocation (the procedure `New`).

hook An extraneous piece of software or hardware included in order to simplify later additions or debug options.

identifier A name used to refer to an object, such as a variable, procedure, or field of a record.

implementation Embodiment in programming language form. Features that are implementation-dependent may differ on different computers or on different compilers.

increment To increase the value of a variable, usually by a small constant. Most often this constant is 1. Decreasing the value is called *decrementing*.

indentation Spacing from the left margin. Indentation is used to illustrate the structure of the program.

index A value used to specify the desired component of an array. Also the control variable of a `FOR` loop.

index type The type of indexes allowed (for a particular dimension) in an array. Not to be confused with base type.

infinite loop A sequence of code that is executed without termination. Also the execution of such a sequence.

initialize To give a value for the first time. Variables that have not been initialized are said to be uninitialized or undefined.

input Values used by a program that do not appear in the program and are not computed by the program. Input can come from files, such as disk files or terminal operators.

integer A number without any fractional part (no decimal point). The integers consist of the negative whole numbers, zero, and the positive whole numbers.

interactive While-you-wait service. The computer is responding and collecting information from the requestor while it is operating. Opposite of batch.

invoke To cause the execution of something. Synonym: to call. Invocation refers to the act of causing something to be executed.

iteration To repeat something. The code being iterated may depend on which time it is being iterated.

justifying To adjust the allocation of words into lines such that all lines (except for the last) have the same length.

key A value used to access another variable. See also search.

keyword A reserved word used for a special purpose in PASCAL, such as `BEGIN`, `FOR`, and `WHILE`. Predeclared identifiers, such as `Read`, are not keywords. In this text, keywords are capitalized.

kludge A Rube Goldberg device in hardware or software. An obscure, fragile method for solving a problem. Often depends on an unintended side effect of some feature. Compare with hack.

label A number used to identify a location in the code for use with a `GOTO` statement.

level A number that represents the depth of nesting of procedures. Also the depth of nesting of other control structures.

lineprinter A glorified typewriter attached to a computer. Some lineprinters can print thousand of lines per minute, rather than a few characters per second. See also listing.

linked list   A dynamically allocated data structure that can grow and shrink over time.

listing   The output of a lineprinter.

literal   An unnamed constant in a program. This is a value that appears in an expression (not a variable).

local   Within the smallest enclosing procedure or function.

loop   A sequence of instructions and an enclosing construct that causes them to be executed repeatedly.

main procedure   The code surrounded by the outermost pair of BEGIN—END. Also the segment of code given control when a program is invoked. This contains the calls of the lower level procedures.

memory   Space in a computer for holding the program and its variables (in the stack and heap).

misfeature   An undesirable property of a program. Not as serious as a bug.

mnemonic   An abbreviation chosen for its potential as a memory aid.

modification   A change to a program or specification.

modular   Consisting of components (modules) that can be changed independently.

name   The string used to identify an object. Synonym: identifier.

nesting   Containing. We usually refer to nesting of like objects, such as procedures or FOR loops.

nil   The pointer value that specifies that it does not point to any record. Often used for ends of lists.

node   A record in a pointer structure.

object   A named component of a program, such as a procedure or a variable. Usually some action is possible, such as calling a procedure or assigning a value to a variable. Types are not usually considered objects, but variables are.

operand   A subexpression whose value is used by an operator.

operator   A keyword (possibly symbolic) of an expression that specifies some computation to be performed to one or two subexpressions.

order   A specification of the criterion for sequencing a list. See also sorting.

output   The results of running a program. The output is sent to a file which may be on disk or appear on a terminal as it is being produced.

parameter   A vehicle for explicit communication between a procedure or function and the point of invocation.

parameter list   A sequence of parameters passed to a procedure or function.

parse   To determine the syntactic structure of something.

pass   To use as a parameter.

patch   A temporary addition to a piece of code, usually as a quick-and-dirty remedy to an existing bug or misfeature. To install a patch.

pegboard   An object containing holes of various shapes and possibly pegs of matching shapes. Pegboards are used by analogy to describe a stack frame containing the variables and parameters declared by a procedure, function, or the main procedure.

permutation   A reordering of a sequence.

pointer   A variable (or its value) used to reference a record. It has a function similar to the index of an array.

pop   To remove an item from a linked list, such as a stack. Opposite of push.

precedence   The order in which operators are executed in an expression.

procedure   A named sequence of instructions that do not return a value using that name. Values may be passed to the procedure through parameters. Values may be returned from the procedure using **VAR** paraeters.

procedure body   The code associated with a procedure. This is the code that gets executed when the procedure is invoked.

procedure call   A statement that invokes a procedure.

procedure heading   The first part of a procedure declaration that lists the name of the procedure and the number and type of parameters.

program   An algorithm completely specified in a programming language.

program heading   The first part of a program that lists the name of the program and identifies the files used by the program.

prompt   A string printed by a program to indicate to the terminal operator that input is desired and may inform the user of the nature of the input requested.

push   To place a node into a linked list data structure, such as a stack. Opposite of pop.

queue   A data structure obeys a first-in, first-out discipline.

random   Unpredictable. A random series of numbers consists of numbers with no obvious properties.

readability   A measure of the ease of understanding something.

real   A numeric value that may have a fractional component.

real user   Someone paying "real" money to use the system, or using the system for an explicit purpose.

real world   In programming, those institutions at which programming may be used in the same sentence as FORTRAN and COBOL. Also anywhere outside a university.

record   A structured type which has components that may be of nonuniform types.

recursion   Self-reference, such as a procedure that calls itself. Two procedures that call each other is known as *mutual recursion*.

reference   To obtain the value of or store into. See also access. Also a parameter with two-way communication.

reserved word   A keyword given a special meaning in the PASCAL language.

result   The value or set of values returned by a procedure, function, or program. The value derived from interpreting an expression.

run-time   During execution of the program.

scalar type   One of `integer`, `boolean`, `char`, `integer`, an enumerated type, or a subrange of one of them.

scientific notation   A description of a number that uses a value between 1 and 10 (called the mantissa) multiplied by a power of 10 (called the exponent).

scope   The region in which a name is known because of the location of its declaration.

semantics   The meaning of something, as contrasted with syntax, which is exactly what is said.   An incorrect but properly phrased statement is a semantic error.

sentinel   A special value that follows the last value in a file.

set   A collection of values accessed by their name.

set type   The type of a variable capable of storing a set.

side effect   An effect of executing a procedure that is not apparent by looking at the parameters. For example, the `Read` procedure advances the file pointer as a side effect.

simple type   A scalar type, `real`, or pointer. Opposite of structured type.

sorting   The process of ordering a list according to some key.

stack   A data structure that obeys a last-in, first-out discipline.

statement   The unit of instruction in a program causing procedure execution. Most statements are surrounded by (or capable of being surrounded by) semicolons.

static   A property of a program that is independent of the execution state of the program; not varying while the program is running. Opposite of dynamic.

string   A sequence of characters. Literal strings (in programs) are enclosed in quotes.

structured type   A record, array, set, or file type. Opposite of simple type.

subprogram   A procedure or function. Also known as subroutine.

subrange   A range of values with a specially declared lower and upper range of values. See also *underlying type*.

subscript   An index value of an array.

syntax   Pertaining to the manner in which something is said. A statement that is malformed has a syntax error.

system dependent   Something that may vary from system to system.   See also implementation.

text   Sequences of characters, possibly broken into lines.   A program may be considered as instructions to a computer or may be considered as text consisting of lines of characters.

traversing   Visiting the notes of a pointer-based data structure.

type compatibility   A property of the declaration variables that affects use in assignment and expressions.   Variables and expressions must be compatible with each other. Values can only be assigned to compatible variables. Certain type incompatibilities are handled by type conversion.

type conversion   The reformulation of a value in another form, explicitly or implicitly.   For example, integer values are converted to real as needed to assign to real variables or to use in expressions with real values.

undeclared   Does not have a declaration whose scope contains this reference. (Contrast with undefined.)

undefined   Has not been given a value. Synonym: uninitialized. (Contrast with undeclared.)

underlying type   The scalar type corresponding to a particular subrange. The bounds of the subrange and all values in between are part of the subrange type and are also values of the underlying type. In particular, the bounds of the subrange must belong to the same scalar type, and that is the underlying type.

up   Operational. Opposite of down.

user   Someone who works with a program or system but does not understand its internals.

value parameter   A parameter with one-way communiation. Values are transmitted into the procedure through this parameter, but not out.

VAR parameter   A parameter with two-way communication. Values of the parameter are transmitted to the procedure, and changes are assigned to the actual parameter. Synonym: reference parameter.

variable-length   Something that can vary in size, such as a string implemented by a length variable and an array of characters.

word   The unit of memory in a computer. Common word sizes are 8, 16, 32, 36, or 60 bits.

Bibliography

This is a partial list of references for further reading.

Aho, Alfred V., John E. Hopcroft, and Jeffrey D. Ullman, *The Design and Analysis of Computer Programs*, Addison-Wesley, Reading, MA, 1974.

Deken, Joseph, *The Electronic Cottage*, William Morrow, New York, 1982.

Dijkstra, Edsger, *A Discipline of Programming*, Prentice-Hall, Englewood Cliffs, NJ, 1976.

Gardner, Martin, *aha! insight*, W. H. Freeman, San Francisco, 1978.

Jensen, Kathleen, and Niklaus Wirth, *PASCAL User Manual and Report*, Second Edition, Springer-Verlag, New York, 1974.

Kernighan, Brian, and P. J. Plauger, *The Elements of Programming Style*, McGraw-Hill, New York, 1978.

Kernighan, Brian W., and Dennis M. Ritchie, *The C Programming Language*, Prentice-Hall, Englewood Cliffs, NJ, 1978.

Kernighan, Brian W., and Dennis M. Ritchie, *Software Tools in Pascal*, Addison-Wesley, Reading, MA, 1981.

Knuth, Donald E., *Fundamental Algorithms*, *The Art of Computer Programming*, Volume 1, Second Edition, Addison-Wesley, Reading, MA, 1973.

McCorduck, Pamela, *Machines Who Think*, W. H. Freeman, San Francisco, 1979.

Papert, Seymour, *Mindstorms: Children, Computers, and Powerful Ideas*, Basic Books, New York, 1980.

Pattis, Richard E., *Karel the Robot: A Gentle Introduction to the Art of Programming*, Wiley, New York, 1981.

Tenenbaum, Aaron M., and Moshe J. Augenstein, *Data Structures Using Pascal*, Prentice-Hall, Englewood Cliffs, NJ, 1981.

Weinberg, Gerald M., *The Psychology of Computer Programming*, Van Nostrand, Reinhold, New York, 1971.

Weizenbaum, Joseph, *Computer Power and Human Reason*, W. H. Freeman, San Francisco, 1976.

Wirth, Niklaus, *Algorithms + Data Structures = Programs*, Prentice-Hall, Englewood Cliffs, NJ, 1976.

Index

Actual parameter, 108.
Algorithms, 3, 86.
Alias, 118.
Aliasing, 228.
Alphanumeric, 95.
Ambiguous ELSE, 49.
Analysis of algorithms, 183.
AND, 53, 59.
Arithmetic, 19, 64.
Arrays, 139.
ASCII, 279.
Aspect ratio, 245.
Assembly language, 6.
Assignment, 31.
Assignment statement, 32.
Base type, 143.
BEGIN, 16.
Binary search, 187.
Bishop moves, 54.
Bits, 263.
Body, 123.
boolean, 59, 62.
Boundary error, 38.
Bounds, 128, 141.
Bubble sort, 150, 188.
Cards, 6.
Carriage return, 10, 11.
CASE, 135.
Central Processing Unit, 5.
char, 62, 97.
Character, 62.
Character string, 10.

Characters, 97.
Chess, 51, 54.
Chr, 131.
COBOL, 9.
Code, 10, 13.
Code conversion, 147.
Colon convention, 94.
Comments, 12.
Comparand, 46.
Compiler, 6.
Compound symbols, 45.
Conditions, 45.
CONST, 38.
Constant, 38.
Contain, 123.
CPU, see Central processing unit.
Data, 150, 183.
Debugging, 2, 4, 69, 70, 71, 75, 231, _DATA Types p 62_
    289.
Debugging procedures, 76.
DEC, 14.
Declarations, 9, 13, 142.
    Order of, 14.
    Procedure, 13.
    Variable, 16.
Declaring Functions as Parameters,
    250.
Decrypt, 258.
Dictionary, 9.
Dietterich, Tom, 71.
Divide exception, 83.
DO, 15.

303